T0354721

GOD
IN
EVERY
Moment

Nothing is off Limits

Edie Bowman

WESTBOW
PRESS®
A DIVISION OF THOMAS NELSON
& ZONDERVAN

WestBow Press books may be ordered through booksellers or by contacting:

WestBow Press
A Division of Thomas Nelson & Zondervan
1663 Liberty Drive
Bloomington, IN 47403
www.westbowpress.com
844-714-3454

Because of the dynamic nature of the Internet, any web addresses or links contained in this book may have changed since publication and may no longer be valid. The views expressed in this work are solely those of the author and do not necessarily reflect the views of the publisher, and the publisher hereby disclaims any responsibility for them.

Any people depicted in stock imagery provided by Getty Images are models, and such images are being used for illustrative purposes only. Certain stock imagery © Getty Images.

Scripture taken from the King James Version of the Bible.

Scripture quotations marked (NLT) are taken from the Holy Bible, New Living Translation, copyright ©1996, 2004, 2015 by Tyndale House Foundation. Used by permission of Tyndale House Publishers, a Division of Tyndale House Ministries, Carol Stream, Illinois 60188. All rights reserved.

Scripture taken from the Amplified Bible, Copyright © 1954, 1958, 1962, 1964, 1965, 1987 by The Lockman Foundation. Used with permission.

Scripture quotations taken from the (NASB®) New American Standard Bible®, Copyright © 1960, 1971, 1977, 1995, 2020 by The Lockman Foundation. Used by permission. All rights reserved. www.lockman.org

ISBN: 978-1-6642-4030-8 (sc)
ISBN: 978-1-6642-4031-5 (hc)
ISBN: 978-1-6642-4029-2 (e)

Library of Congress Control Number: 2021914456

Print information available on the last page.

WestBow Press rev. date: 8/3/2021

Contents

Dedicated to my two PUSHERS
My husband Charles Bowman and My friend Joshua Pleasant

Joshua, you were the one who told me one day "Edie, you have so much to say, you have so much in you. You have more in you than just plays, you need to write a book!" You kept telling me this for years, but I didn't see it. You literally stalked me over and over again. You wouldn't give up on me. One day just to get you off of my back, I said "Ok, Joshua I will start it by the end of the month. That was January of 2019. I think I started on the 27th just to keep my word. It felt natural, I didn't want to stop! Thank you, Joshua for your continual support, phone calls, lunches, and coffee shop meetings to keeping me on track!

Charles, you have always been the one who supported my dreams, even when they were weird, you believed in me. During the process of writing this book I doubted myself, I cried, I talked your ears off with questions, etc., but you wouldn't allow me to pout. You remained strong the whole time. You'd tell me "If you believe that God put this in your heart to write, then do it, Edie!" When I often wanted to drag my feet on taking the next steps, out of fear, you'd sternly tell me to MOVE! That didn't feel good, but it was what I needed. Thank you, sweetheart for never letting me stay stagnant... you push me to keep moving.

Thank you, Lord for blessing me with two men of
God who see more than I do in me and hold me
accountable to be all that I can be in you.

Foreword

Personal tragedies or ordinary daily life occurrences often illicit a variety of human responses and those responses lead us to think where God was in those moments. I have witnessed my fair share of life-altering events while raising my three daughters. The moments when ear infections or unexplained sicknesses caused stubborn fevers and late-night emergency room visits. Moments when you are anxiously awaiting notifications on college admittance in the mail or final exam results to secure graduation requirements. I started my very own life in the N.I.C.U. for over a month because I came into this world three months premature. My parents faced difficult days as the countless doctors and nurses nurtured my frail body to a healthy state. Where exactly was God during those agonizing days? Where was God when my daughter careened in the front of a vehicle coming from the opposite direction? These are all very valid questions, and through each of these moments, I have found God.

Through most of these moments, my wife, Edie Bowman has walked alongside me seeking the presence of Almighty God. In the Book of Proverbs, we are instructed to seek God's counsel in everything, and through that counsel we will be given direction. That passage leads me to believe that God desires to be a part of every aspect of our lives. He wants to be a part of every moment. That means the pleasing, bad, happy, sad, traumatic, joyous, tearful, agonizing, silly, gut-wrenching, stressful, and triumphant moments. We often miss seeing God in every moment, or we misjudge and apply blame to God in unexplainable moments. My wife wrote *God in Every Moment* to offer a point of view from a mind that is constantly seeking and questioning God's participation in every moment. She shares these thoughts through poems, short stories, truthful life experiences, theatrical drama-filled pieces, and corky/ strange examples. She shares valuable insight on finding God in every moment. What should you do when your mind and thoughts don't shut off? How can you find God when your child is lying in an infant hospital bed paralyzed on one side of her body? How to find God when you are in jeopardy of losing your house to foreclosure. This memoir is like none other.

I wanted to write the foreword to this book because I have walked alongside this amazing woman, author, mother, and friend for 26 years. I have watched her find God in every moment of our lives. She has prayed for me through countless situations. Her heart is for all people. She knows how to communicate in a manner that speaks to every soul. *God in Every Moment* was written with you in mind. If you are a detailed-oriented person or a broad-picture kind of person, this memoir is for you. You will be taken on a journey, and yes, I will admit to thinking, man, some of the stories or visuals in this memoir are the workings of a beautiful mind. I am amazed at the inner workings of her mind. I believe God has gifted my wife to paint a picture for every moment.

Dr. Charles Bowman.

Introduction

Most of my life I've been told to stop thinking so much, and I've been asked, "Why do you have so many questions?!" My response was… "Because the questions are there floating around in my head, and the thoughts won't leave me alone!" Well, that's what I wanted to say…I actually said, "I don't know, I just want to understand what I don't understand…" and as far as the thoughts go… we all have them. They are just different for each person, but they are real, and they matter. I have also been told, many times, that I am weird—I know this, and now take it as a compliment (I didn't always feel this way). If being "weird" means that I am creative and choose to think outside of the box in ways that cause others to experience joy, entertainment, feel understood, inspired, and increase their understanding of God and others…then I gladly accept that description.

We are all fearfully and wonderfully made; we are complex and unique individuals. I used to try to hide my more eccentric, silly, crazy side from others, and just allow my creative, analytical, reasoning side to show. I now realize that all of these traits make up who I am and that they are all a part of being me. Creativity involves a synergy of thoughts, talents, life experiences, beliefs, feelings, teachings, etc. God is interested in the ALL of us—the whole of who we are. Since He created us spirit, soul, and body, He wants to be involved and redeem it all. EVERYTHING that matters to us, matters to God. I used to think that He only wanted to know the beautiful sides of us, but he wants to know the Ugly too. He wants to use them—redeem them.

This creative memoir is about finally embracing all that I am, trusting God to round off the ragged edges, and inspiring others to do so as well. We all have moments of sorrow, pain, fear, weakness, and confusion…we also have moments of joy, laughter, faith, strength, and restoration. There will always be good and evil and darkness and light in this world—these dichotomies will never end. My endeavor is to acknowledge the multifaceted experiences of life, and to express them in creative, redemptive ways. There is a plethora of emotions that we have moment by moment, and I know that some people may not be able to express them when they need to. Sometimes we just need someone to listen and understand us so that we can be free to open up, be honest in what we are going through, and heal. God is there and wants to be with us *in* Every Moment of life... but we have to acknowledge him, ask for his wisdom, and allow him to do life with us. He wants to be *with* us in the dark, the light, the joy, the pain, and the Funny/Crazy... Yep, I said it! He was there for me and He wants to be there for you.

IT ALL MATTERS...EVERYTHING
MATTERS...YOU MATTER!
HE'S GOD IN EVERY MOMENT.

You are so intimately aware of me, Lord. You read my heart like an open book, and you know all the words I'm about to speak before I even start a sentence! You know every step I will take before my journey even begins.

Psalms 139:3-4 (The Passion Translation)

Chapter One
God, Use My Overthinking Mind...

Let me start off by saying...if you knew how
many times I've changed the title/subtitle of this
book, you'd have me looked at professionally!

There's a phrase that I say just about every day "Well, here we go, Lord...it's me and you!" especially when I'm walking out the door or about to do something hard or uncomfortable. I say this because I realize that He is with me in Every Moment: wherever I go, whatever I do, say, think, etc. It's easy to forget that sometimes. We all tend to go about our daily activities without recognizing his presence with us. He knows us and wants to share life with us! He knows our personality and wants to use it to have a closer relationship with us, not to draw us away from him.

He knows that I have the tendency to be an overthinker... I take in a lot of things that are going on around me, and then dissect them, analyze them, mull them over...process them. This can be overwhelming at times—I seem to care too much about almost EVERYTHING! Looking back over my life, I've seen how he has used my mind in 'In Every Moment': leading me, teaching me, and giving me insight into various situations.

GOD has been with me in every fear, question, concern, uncertainty, hurt, and pain. He's been there in times of laughter, joy, and even in my crazy, silly, eccentric moments—which you'll see a lot of in this book! He has taught me how to put my thoughts into good use: to help others think through things, be a good listener, how to become a better playwright, life coach, and how to relate to people where they are.

So, if you think a lot like me...welcome to the club! You're engaging with someone who understands the constant spinning

1

wheels in your head: the questions, creativity, the vivid imagination, emotions, internal monologues, etc. NOTHING IS OFF LIMITS WITH GOD! He's there in the crazy, the silly, the serious, and in the sadness. He understands YOU and wants to be present with you "In Every Moment" of life. Now buckle up, hang on, and let's take this wild, creative ride together!

Behold, I Am Doing A New Thing in You!

Something that is uncomfortable...out of your box, out of your normal way of doing things—something that you haven't done before, but it's okay...it's ME working through you! I will use all of your gifts for my glory in new and strategic ways to help others emotionally and spiritually.

This is what the Lord spoke to me at the
ending of 2020, for 2021 and beyond.
This book is the beginning of My New Thing...

The Kiss

God caused the Sun and the Moon to Kiss...it produced droplets of Bronzed Gold that dripped down upon my dry skin entering into my flesh—nourishing it and filling my mind with vivid ideas. Then the droplets energized my arms and hands empowering my fingertips to Write. Write with Light as you're walking through the Darkness. Write the laughter and the pain, the crazy and the normal...I Am with you. Write It All...Everything! It All Matters.

UNDERSTANDING THE OVERTHINKER

I've been told that to overthink is a negative thing—it can be, if it's not tamed and used creatively and positively. I used to feel bad about this part of myself, for it has been untamed and has caused a lot of stress and indecision at times, but with the help of God, I'm able to use it to my advantage now. I still have moments in life that try to take me back to that place of unrest, but I refuse to stay there. I chose to use my imagination, creativity, the word of God, prayer, and the wisdom of others to help balance me. I realize that overthinking, or as I like to put it—"Thinking Deeply, A LOT" can have many benefits that helps others, as well as yourself.

Just the other day my daughter and I were shopping at the mall and I came across a T-shirt that seemed like it was there for me to see. I giggled and had a feeling of conformation as I read it. I held the shirt up so that she could read it also, and she instantly said, "Whoa, that's you, Mom!"

It read…

"Overthinking About Overthinking"

My mind instantly had a ton of thoughts like, *It looks too small, well maybe it's ok if it's a little snug, I can't try it on in the store because of Covid -19, if it doesn't fit I don't feel like bringing it back, why would they not allow you to try it on in the store but allow you to bring it back if you don't like it, that doesn't make sense…a person could try it on, tuck in the tab, wear it, and then bring it back with Lord knows what on it!…they'd be better off just letting them try it on in the store…*

I thought about it too long and ended up putting it back on the rack, proving that the shirt was right, but also helping me feel more comfortable about writing this book. Now I know that there are other people like me out there, and they're okay with sharing it on a T-shirt!

Better Than Gold...

I asked the Lord the other day exactly how I should go about writing, publishing, editing, and marketing this book—I needed to know EVERYTHING NOW! I asked, "Why won't you just tell me what to do, isn't it easier that way? Why all the mystery? Just tell me right now." (It made total sense to me...) Then, I heard a clear, short, soft answer in my spirit that— to be honest—gave me mixed emotions about it. I felt quite ambivalent about the answer because it still meant that I wouldn't have a step-by-step plan to follow to get to my desired destination. This is what I heard...

"You will know, as you go."

This is NOT what an Overthinker wants to hear!!!

BUT! I remembered...

"Your instructions are more valuable to me than millions in gold and silver."

(Psalms 119:72 NLT)

AN ODE TO KING DAVID

King David, you had the ability to say whatever was on your mind; you didn't care if it sounded crazy or not! You talked boldly, honorably, and honestly to your God in the middle of every situation you found yourself in. You had your faults...I mean you did have sex with another man's wife, got her pregnant and then had him killed to cover it up but... after you saw how it hurt God's heart you repented of that sin and humbly said, "Against you, and you only, have I sinned." And even after that...God still called you a man after His own heart.

You poured out your entire soul to the Lord with refreshing truthfulness—holding nothing back. You shared it all...you were vulnerable in every moment of your life! You danced before the Lord with all of your heart and you didn't care who saw you or what they thought of you. You danced for your King, not for man's approval. Your level of openness was uncanny—an exceptional trait that set you far apart from so many other leaders and made you a man of honor for generations.

You never shied away from asking a lot of questions—that makes you a man after my own heart! When you didn't understand something, you told God about it... you asked why, when, and how long. You knew that you could trust your God even in times of distress and uncertainty. You proved your continual dependence upon, and love for God through your words of praise and worship to him, so beautifully expressed in the Psalms.

The strength and ability you possessed in communicating your feelings and emotions to God without apology has encouraged me to keep writing, creating, and communicating with sincerity and genuineness—knowing that what concerns me, also concerns God. I will not be ashamed to be fully vulnerable with Him, always.

He's always listening to his children, intently...
Thank you, King David.

God In Every Moment

I woke up anxious today and I didn't know
why...so I quieted myself and listened.
The thoughts of what I had to do, what had
been done that I could not change,
who and what caused me hurt, and not knowing
how to remedy it all... it overwhelmed me.
Like a flood, these realities overpowered my heart
and caused my emotions to rule the moment,
so, I invited you in...into the torrential winds of my stormy mind,
and you came across the sea and rescued me.

Today, I felt the sunshine on my face, gracefully visiting
through the soft blue curtains above my bed.
In that moment I knew you were with me—I laid there
propped up by my pillows and thanked you.
Without warning, my soul began to sing
"Great is Thy Faithfulness..."
My eyes streamed with cascading tears of worship
and praise, for you were present—
just like you were yesterday in the darkness.

Today I laughed and I cried within 30 minutes
of each other, and it's okay...
Am I crazy? No... Just Human.

Tell Him all about it...He will listen.
He's God in Every Moment... Always available,
consistently there, faithfully present.

QUESTIONS...

When my father was in his final days in the hospital, he was unable to talk because of the damage from the tubes in his throat, so he had to mouth some words to me. Of course, this had to be frustrating to him, but it was extremely frustrating to me because I needed to know everything he was trying to say! We tried giving him a pencil, but he couldn't write it out. I had my husband and a nurse try to understand him, but they couldn't either. I began to cry as he grew more frustrated, and then a calm came over him...he didn't try anymore, he just looked at me with peace and love in his eyes. It was like he was saying, "It's okay...I'm not going to make it, but I'm alright." When I left the hospital that day, I kept rehearsing what he was trying to say, I needed to be sure. I prayed that God would tell me, I thought about it over and over...I tortured myself for years! Finally, one day...I rested with the truth that if God wanted me to know what he was trying to say, he had the ability to allow me to understand. He didn't, so I chose to Rest...

Everyone has questions—we may ask some questions out of confusion, concern, understanding, or just plain old curiosity. What is really frustrating is when our questions are not acknowledged or respected. Many of our questions will never get answered, and that can be very perplexing—leaving us yearning inside, but I have found that while my over-abundance of questions, answered and unanswered, can at times leave me unsure, they always lead me back to you, Lord. You will lead me to what it is I need to know, and what I don't know that I've tried to find out...well, that's when trust comes in.

Someday we will know fully...
(I Corinthians 13:12 AMP)

EDIE BOWMAN

Ridiculousness... (Not The TV Show!)

One day, at the spur of the moment, I was trying the credibility of my book out on my daughter—I wanted to make sure that it's actually a book where nothing's off limits. So, here's how it went down...

Me: Autumn, name something right now, anything... and I will see if I've talked about it in my book.

Autumn: Boogers!

Me: (laughing hysterically) Nope, ya got me on that one! (I guess it's in the book now though, huh?)

BOOGERS?... LOL! The youth of today, ya gotta love em'... or lock them in the basement!

This Is REALLY Sad... Don't Judge Me!

If I were Eve in the Garden of Eden, I don't think that a piece of fruit of any kind would tempt me enough to lose all the glorious comforts of such a beautiful dwelling, BUT...if I were offered a few slices of Thick Cut Hickory Bacon with the perfect amount of crispiness and flavorful fat...let's just say, I would've had my two slices of bread, lettuce, and tomatoes ready when that ole' serpent came, and I'd have second thoughts about telling Adam about it!

10 Things Overthinkers Should Do & Avoid Doing:

1. Thinking or talking so much about something causes confusion and anxiety: Pray about it, seek WISE counsel, then make a

decision, or wait until you feel peace to move, not perfection to move.

2. Don't wait for everything to be perfect before you move: The scripture tells us "Farmers who wait for perfect weather never plant. If they watch every cloud, they never harvest" (Ecclesiastes 11:4 NLT).

3. Don't ask too many people for their opinion: This will only confuse you and delay your decision—ask the Lord who to trust.

4. Stay in conversational communication with God all day: speaking with Him as a friend takes the pressure off—you don't have to be sackcloth and ashes!

5. As you think about what to do each day: **Psalms 3:5-7 will be your best friend!!!** "Trust in the Lord with all your heart; do not depend on your own understanding..." (KJV)

6. Take mental and emotional breaks often: Do something fun, creative, recreational, whatever you enjoy that puts your mind at ease.

7. Don't surround yourself with people that are just like you, regularly: It's okay to be around people like you sometimes, because overthinkers enjoy each other's company, and they can come up with awesome ideas and conversations... but to be around people like you too often can be draining!

8. Work on being honest with people even if it may hurt their feelings or may cause them to dislike you: Speaking truth, In Love, to people will keep you from saying things you didn't want to say, and keep you from doing things you didn't want to do in the first place.

9. Don't beat yourself if you thought about something over and over again...finally make a decision, and if you still mess up: Forgive Yourself! You Are Human!!!

10. Regularly place yourself around positive people who make good decisions quicker than you: You can learn from them how to take chances and trust yourself, and they can learn from you how to think things through a bit and make less mistakes—Win-Win!

Thank God for those who make fast decisions; we need you to get going… Thank God for those who take their time to process things; you help balance the quick… Thank God for dreamers; they keep you inspired and hopeful… Thank God for the doers; we need you to get things done… Thank God for the overseers; they keep you on task… And thank God for the Over Thinkers; they have carefully thought through all of your roles and have insight to share on them all!

<u>Just a Few Things Overthinkers
Can Be Good At…</u>

- We can be great people of prayer because we are concerned and can feel your pain. We are earnest in taking your concerns to God with great empathy.
- We MUST lean on the Lord continually for guidance. We know that we can't figure it out on our own or we'll go crazy. Therefore, we wait to hear from Him and then move.
- We tend to think things through before making decisions, weighing out the Pros and Cons—Especially the Cons. Focusing on the Cons isn't always a negative thing because they can prevent unnecessary harm, struggle, and mishaps—we have enough of those already!
- We take time to understand people well—their experiences, emotionally, spiritually, psychologically—in every way, because we want to really know them! Knowing takes understanding.
- We ask great questions! This can be seen as being nosey, but in most cases it's not. We truly want to get a clear understanding about whatever it is that is before us. Great questions can lead to great solutions!

- We are great listeners... Most of the time! Sometimes we can be so passionate about what we believe, after many hours of thinking about it, that we just KNOW we're right. **I didn't say we were perfect!**
- We are awesome planners—it may take us a while, though...we want EVERYTHING to be right. We are the kind of people you want to have when you want it done well, but it can be frustrating for you when we stress over minor details!
- We are good at seeing things ahead and are good at preparing for them. If you have an outdoor event on a day that has a forecast of 80 degrees and sunny, this person assumes that it *may rain*, so he or she has multiple umbrellas to share with others, plastic bags to put them in after the rain, and a change of clothes in case you get wet on this seemingly perfect, sunny day.
- We can be great business owners and partners—we are usually loyal, because we thought things over for a long time before we committed. We've studied you to make sure that you are honest, kind, orderly, patient, and hopefully make good decisions QUICKLY—Lord knows we need someone to balance us out!
- We can be very creative in doing what we feel passionate about. When there is something we like, be it art, ministry, teaching, writing, mentoring, etc., we tend to go at it with all of our heart. We feel a sense of freedom in our creativity when we are passionate about it, and when we are free to take the lead.
- We can be great mentors—we love to teach and give insight to others about what we have learned in life.
- We are good at seeing what's wrong or what can go wrong in almost any situation—this can come in handy for taking preventative measures.
- We are great problem solvers.
- We can be very detailed.

A New Beginning

I know that worrying does absolutely nothing
positive for me, so why do I continue to do it?!
For every moment of worry, I could be
trusting Your promises, Oh God...
I know this! So, why don't I DO IT?! I
have the ability, I'm intelligent...
Could it be that I've been doing this so long that I have to
learn another way of thinking, believing, and living?...
Perhaps I need to retrain my mind to respond
differently to negative situations...
Can I really replace fear with the truth and with the power of
scripture and begin to speak what I know, instead of what I see
and feel?! I think I can...I believe I can...You say I can...**I Shall**.

I will Trust in the Lord with ALL of my heart and lean
not to my own understanding. In ALL of my ways I will
acknowledge Him, and He will direct my paths.
(Proverbs 3:5-6 KJV Paraphrase)

AND NOW...
Being Human

Have you ever been talking to someone on your
cellphone while frantically looking for your cellphone?...
You're frantically rummaging around through things
around you like, "Now, where in the world did I put
that phone, I just had it!" (Uh...it's on your ear!)

Chapter Two
Know God & Love Thyself...

I used to base my value on how others treated me. If they didn't smile at me when I greeted them with a smile, I wondered why. If someone didn't like to be around me, or if they said something bad about me, I thought about it over and over again all day, and maybe the next few days. I used to think, *What is wrong with me? I'm a nice person, they'd see that if they only got to know me...* I found myself being a person who thought more about how I could make other people happy more than focusing on finding my own happiness in life. It took many years, many hurts, and disappointments to discover who I am.

I am a daughter of God. I am valuable and have worth because he says I have them. He proved it by dying on the cross for me while I was still in sin—even more...the scripture says that He was crucified before the very foundation of the world! That means I was in his mind and heart before my parents or their parents even met, before the world even began! He loved, still loves, and will always love me, and now I can love myself regardless of how others feel about me. If I never meet the expectations of others, it's okay...I'm still accepted by Him. I Am Enough!

<u>Wanted</u>

To God we are each one precious grain of sand
amongst all the grains of sand of all the beaches
combined in the whole entire world!
He knows YOUR name...He loves YOU personally...
uniquely...fully...unconditionally.
He loves you too much to leave you alone. He's
chasing after you...calling you to himself.
HE WANTS YOU!
LISTEN...

Best Friends

I long to be my own best friend—I practice every day,
telling myself to give me a break, relax, and forgive
myself—give myself a break from overthinking. I spend
time with me and encourage myself to be the best me that
God intended. And when I fall down...I not only pick
myself up and dust myself off, but I take myself out, go
see a movie, and I may even buy myself a new outfit.

Dare to be Loved

His bullies said he was weird
Her parents said she'd amount to nothing
His teachers said he was slow
Her boyfriend said she's not enough
His girlfriend said he was temporary
Her friends said she was average
God says YOU are Accepted.

KNOWING WHAT FEAR WOULD CONSTANTLY SAY
TO HER...SHE DID IT ANYWAY & EXCELLED

An Ode to The Arts

Sing, Play, Write, Sculpt, Direct, Act, Paint,
Dance, Draw, Compose... Create!
Just a few of the passions God has put within you...
Do them all—give them back to Him.
Use them for good. Present them to the world. We need them:
they heal us, inspire us, teach us, and excite us! Do them
with all of your heart, mind and soul. Don't worry about

perfection—be Excellent instead. Do it even if you're afraid! Leave it ALL here…the grave doesn't need it, we do!

Jesus, The Great Communicator

I am convinced that Jesus was, and still is a lover of theatre. Do you want to know why?... because he constantly spoke in parables! He wanted to make sure that whoever he was speaking to, understood what he was trying to portray to them. He knew the importance of giving people visuals and meeting them where they were—actually relating to their ways of life—what was familiar to them. He found a way to connect to them through story…we all have one, we all can appreciate and communicate through story! To fishermen he talked about being fishers of men. To farmers he talked about sowing seeds in different types of soil. To the woman at the well he talked about receiving water that would satisfy her soul and cause her to never thirst again.

He speaks to me in parables regularly…he speaks to me through day-to-day life situations. When I see a sunset, he's teaching me that there can be beauty found when moments in life are darkening. When I see a new-born baby, he's teaching me that he still is the giver and creator of life, and he values it. When the sun rises each morning, he's teaching me that there is purpose in me today—I'm here because he deemed it so. Each time someone shows me love, even in the smallest way, he's teaching me that he's loving me through the people around me. And every time I sit down to write a play, a skit, a poem, a teaching, a letter, etc., he is teaching and whispering to my heart, "This is who I created you to be…keep telling stories that lead others to me."

Live!

Laugh until your body loses strength even
if you're the only one amused.
Sing like Mahalia Jackson until it changes the atmosphere.
Run like Jessie Owens until you accomplish your dreams.
Play like a five-year-old in a plush green
yard full of toys on a sunny day.
Dance like the Nicholas Brothers on the stairs of life.
Preach like Dr. Martin Luther King until it
pierces the hearts of the hearers to change.
Cry until your soul is cleansed and healing comes.
And may those who see you living life to the
fullest be compelled to do the same.

*Instead of staying isolated in our loneliness, let's
take a risk and ask someone to be our friend.
What if they reject us?... In that case, try
again, and again...with someone else.
We're worth getting to know.*

Something I've Learned...

*It's not profitable to hold on to the past, but it sure
is beneficial to look back on it with fresh eyes of
wisdom, a changed mind, and a healed heart.*

KALEIDOSCOPE

Symmetrical, everchanging, mixed up and amazing,
a metamorphosis, of sorts, in the making.
But I control the twists and turns... don't I?
Shattered, mysterious, and frustratingly beautiful,
the colors evolve into something new.
Contrasting creations—telling all their
stories at one time...in one space.

A jumbled masterpiece that dares to be complete:
Stable...Fixed...Immovable...Astounding. I shall BE...

**With just the slightest motion of heart or hand,
it all begins to change again-- these
mirrors of life I see...**
**They're strategically making a work of
art, uniquely entitled...ME.**

I continue to hold myself to The Light,
in awe of all my complexities:
the beauty, the brokenness, the fear, the hope...
are all a part of the masterful design.

I am much more than meets the eye...
I AM... KALEIDOSCOPE

If I Don't Like What I'm Getting...

In many cases, not all... we teach people how to treat us...
We do it by giving our time to them when we know WE need it.
We do it by giving our last away to those we KNOW will waste it.
We do it by saying yes when we should say NO.

We teach them that we don't value ourselves each
time we allow them to hurt us again.
We teach them that we don't feel worthy by over-
thanking them for things they SHOULD do.
We teach them that we don't matter when they tell
us we don't, and we still take them back.
We teach them that we're not a priority when they
spend time with everyone else and NOT us.
Often times, we receive what we're putting out...
Teach them that you are special, worth respecting,
and loving, by believing it yourself.
GOD SAYS YOU'RE WORTHY... AND HE NEVER LIES!

Placing ME (YOU) In The Bible

Sometimes I'm like the **blind man**—I can't see your path in front of me because I'm blinded my own. What I want is always in front of me, distorting my vision. I cried out to you for help... and you reached out your hand and gave me spiritual sight! Now I can see clearly.

Sometimes I'm like the **woman at the well**—All people see when they look at me are the wrong things I've done. I soon began allowing their opinions to define me. One day you visited me and told me what you see...and now I know who I am! Your daughter.

Sometimes I'm like the **demoniac**—I'm controlled and possessed by desires that lead to isolation and death. You saw me from a distance, though I appeared out of reach... I screamed to be free from my bondage! You had mercy on me, cleared my mind, and set me free.

Sometimes I'm like the **leper**—filled with oozing sores and scars from the abuse of others. I'm looked upon with disdain—untouchable...damaged goods. I heard of your compassion and love, so I came to you. You looked at me with eyes of purity and acceptance. The scars began to heal.

Sometimes I'm like the **tax collector**—I've cheated and misused those who were close to me. I had no reason to be trusted again. I didn't look for you, but you presented yourself to me and invited me to follow you! You gave me another chance…and I'll never be the same.

Sometimes I'm like **Mary** the mother of Jesus—I've been broken by the violent death of a person I loved. The pain seems to become greater and greater. I'm full of bitterness and the need for justice. I'm still hurting inside, but you said vengeance is Mine! I'm leaning on and trusting in you to heal me and give me strength. You're doing it moment by moment.

Sometimes I'm like **Gideon**—in the midst of my fears and uncertainties, I still do what you tell me to do. Thank you, Lord for understanding my humanity and allowing me, like Gideon, to ask for signs to feel more comfortable with taking the next step. You are patient with me as I learn to follow and trust you.

Sometimes I'm like **Zacchaeus**—he climbed a tree to see Jesus, but once Jesus ate with him in his home… he began to KNOW Him. Regardless of my fears, inadequacies, hindrances, or struggles in life, I must do whatever it takes to SEE you Jesus—know you! I want to know you through relationship: your heart, your will, your ways…your love.

A Nugget of Advice…

BEING A PEOPLE-PLEASER IS EXHAUSTING! STOP NOW, BEFORE YOU'VE WASTED ALL OF YOUR ENERGY ON OTHERS AND REALIZE YOU DON'T HAVE ENOUGH LEFT TO DISCOVER WHO GOD CREATED YOU TO BE.

SHUT UP! NOW, SAY SOMETHING.

Sometimes our minds can go 100 miles an hour with doubts, fears, worries, and what ifs—these negative thoughts can overwhelm us and cause us to feel powerless. We have the power to counterattack those **Thoughts** with our **Words**! So, tell your thoughts to SHUT UP! Now, SAY SOMETHING—Tell those thoughts, "Since I have invited Jesus into my life, I know He loves me and wants the best for me. I am so important that He chose to die for me and there is nothing that we cannot handle together... NOTHING! So, fear...doubt...worry...what ifs...**SHUT UP!**"

The Tale of Two Thinkings...

The crowd gasped as he approached the stage of his Alma Mater dressed in his Doctoral attire. They had waited in great anticipation to hear the title of his next best-seller, and to glean something astounding from his words of wisdom and experience. His, by far, was not an easy road traveled; he overcame obstacles most could only imagine getting to this point. He beat the odds. He thought to himself, *I finally made it!* He looked down at his proud mother's smile, his father's stern eyes, trying to hold back the tears, and his admiring siblings. And just as he began to speak...the thought came. The thought that crippled him for many years. The thought that challenged his confidence time and time again, the thought that stole his peace and joy, and almost caused him to end it all a few years ago...
He thought, *No, not now... not at THIS moment!*
It spoke anyway.

You Are Still Not Enough...

The crowd silenced as he stood there awhile, staring off to the side as if the thought were visible to him. He was paralyzed by the thought but knew he had to press through it. He faked a coughing spell and cleared his throat, "Excuse me" he said, regaining his composure. *You are with me...You are with me...even in this moment,* He said to himself. "I have a thought that I'd like to share." His mother's look of concern began to subside. "Success or failure always begins with thoughts. It's up to you to decide which ones you will listen to and which ones you will ignore..."

An Ode to My Bible Favorites

Oh, how I desire to display the diplomacy and prudence of **Abagail** as her words and quick wit appeased the heart of King David and changed his mind to make a better choice, while also bringing herself into a higher status. To have the wisdom and courage of **Deborah** and be able to judge situations well and be a great leader in a time that was not favorable to women. May I show the discretion and dignity of **Esther** and know when and how to speak and to act with honor and respect on the behalf of others. I love how **Gideon**, like myself, felt safe enough in relationship with his Lord to ask him for signs to help diminish his fears. He remained faithful and obeyed the Lord even while afraid. I find myself weeping like **Jeremiah**, as I see the sins and transgressions of our families, communities, and our world. I weep, and pray, and warn, and prophesy, and yes, even demonstrate God's heart...and often, to no avail! And Oh, how I long to possess the strength and vulnerability of **David**... the way he maintained unrestrained openness and honesty with God and himself, acknowledged his failures and weaknesses, and was strong enough to know when to fight and when not to fight—that's strength...that's a relationship built on Trust.

Compelling Love

When I was with that person you told me not to be with
you still loved me.
When I ignored what I knew was the right thing to do
you still loved me.
When I went left after you told me to go right
you still loved me.
When I ended that life that you created in your image
you still loved me.
When I failed to listen for the 100th time
you STILL loved me...
But now I know
that the opulent love you have for me
will not allow you, to allow me... to remain the same.
Your love compels me to change.
This might sound crazy but, whenever I open my mouth to speak to my God, I
picture him with his hand to his ear leaning down from his throne in heaven
to listen attentively to what I have to say. I imagine him saying" Uh-Oh, my
daughter, Edie, is speaking..." And then He smiles with intense anticipation.
He Loves Me...and NOTHING can separate me from it!

EDIE BOWMAN

AND NOW…
Being Human

Have you ever noticed that on hot nights, we refuse to fully take the covers, but we allow one leg to hang out of the side of the bed? And, somehow, by that one leg getting a little air… it magically makes the whole body feel just right?

Chapter Three
In Dedication to Fathers

I'm noticing a disturbing paradigm shift in our society. It appears to me that men/fathers are being looked at with dishonor and disdain. Talk shows, "family" sitcoms, movies, comedians, and even some forms of social media, love to ridicule men and downplay their role in the family. Now, I will admit that some of it is because a lot of women have been forced into the role that some of these men/fathers should be fulfilling themselves.

I have often heard the saying, " Back in the day, fathers were the head of the family, and mothers stayed at home with the children, and children obeyed their parents..." Well, families have never been perfect, mothers and fathers have never been perfect, children have never been perfect, but I have to say, there was a significant difference " back in the day..." There was more respect for fathers as the head of the home: he worked, provided, disciplined, and brought a presence of respect and order in the home, and because of that, a lot of families did seem to be functioning better.

I know there are some exceptions to the rule, though...some families had fathers who brought home the bacon, so to speak, but on the weekends, these same fathers cheated, drank, and terrorized their wives and their children. So, having said that, having a father in the home in situations where abuse is involved is not healthy. I had a father who struggled with alcoholism, and our family was greatly wounded and divided because of that, even though he was an awesome provider. Through God's mercy and Grace, I was able to forgive him, love him, spend quality time with him, and lead my father to the Lord.

Bottom line... Families need JESUS. PERIOD. Families used to go to church together. Church was the foundation of the family, especially the African American family! The church community kept us grounded and reminded us of what God says a family should be. Fathers, get back to God, get back to church, and get back to your rightful place in the family. Be honest, trustworthy, faithful, loving, involved, hardworking, and strong. WE NEED YOU!!!!

Make Room

He wanted to be there, but something hindered him, again…
He said he'd call…I never heard the ring
I looked at the empty seat beside my
mother too many times to count
I waited by the door with a smile on my
face and an ache in my heart…
You were consistent with discipline but
scarce with time, so I became angry
You talked a lot and listened little, so I shut down…
My desire to make you proud grew stronger—you rarely noticed
So, I Stopped Trying Anything Anymore!!!
We became estranged
I started my own family
You showed up one day
You wanted me to let you in
I said NO!
I prayed about it…
I found out more about your past:
You were hurt, abandoned, abused
I began to understand…
God softened my heart
I let you in…
You let Me in…
We talked
We prayed
We healed
TOGETHER…

EDIE BOWMAN

"Daddy, I fell…"

A six-year-old was riding her bike. The pink and purple streamers at the ends of her handlebars were blowing in the wind. They made a soft flapping sound that subconsciously encouraged her to go on. "Look at me daddy…look at me!"

"I see you baby…keep going…keep peddling. You got it!" he said confidently, trying to mask his nerves that were trying to give him away. Suddenly, he could see her beginning to swerve. "Keep it up, baby…don't stop peddling, now don't stop!"

She turned around and looked at him. He could see the change in her eyes. "Keep looking forward, honey… don't look back, look ahead and keep peddling, don't stop!"

He slowly walked forward with undercover urgency, making sure not to allow her to see his growing alarm. He knew what was coming. She looked back at him and began to swerve more and more…She knew that he was getting closer for a reason, she felt it. "You got it baby, keep going…" he inched in even closer preparing himself.

"Daddy, I can't…I can't!"

"Yes, you can sweetie, slow down a little, keep looking ahead and keep the handle-bars right in front of you…you got this. I'm right behind you."

Tears were forming in her eyes, "Okay, daddy…I'll try…" She straightened up her back, gripped the bars tightly lining them up before her, bit her bottom lip and proceeded forward.

"That's it, baby! That's it! Keep her steady, now…"

From right peripheral view, she thought she saw something beside her, so she slightly turned her head to see what it was and just as quickly, she regained her focus. Her father was still behind her, "Remember, keep looking forward, sweetie…"

"Okay, daddy…"

There it was again…something light and pretty floating beside her. She had to know what it was. She took another quick glance to her left and was overtaken with glee. "Oh, daddy look, it's a butterfly!" She started to swerve all over the place.

"I see it baby, but don't look at it right now... baby, keep looking in front of you, keep the bars straight, honey!"

"Look! It's orange, black, AND yellow, daddy! Look!"

She drifted far left...

"Whoa, baby! Look out!!!"

Scre-e-e-e-ch!... Ker-PLUNK!

"DADDY!!!!" she cried with a guttural force, an unusually powerful force at her age.

Reaching down only seconds after her fall to swoop her up, "I'm right here, sweetie!"

"My knee...my knee! I hurt my knee!"

"I know sweetie, I got you...I'm right here" he said as he carried her in his right arm and rolling the bike beside him.

He carried her over to a grassy section just a few feet away covered with yellow dandelions. "Here we go sweetheart..." placing her gently on the grass, allowing the bike to naturally fall. He reached into his pocket and pulled out a Kleenex he had crumpled up inside of it.

"Oh daddy, it's bleeding!"

"I see honey" he said dabbing her knee as lightly as the butterfly that flew past her, causing her great fall. "There...there...feel better?"

"A little ..."

The red speckled Kleenex was mixed with tiny particles of debris.

As he blew on her knee, he braised the Kleenex back and forth across it removing every particle with tender care.

She lovingly looked at her father, staring at him with curious confusion. "Daddy, I fell...Why did I fall, daddy?" Her eyes were the color of newly made pennies, as they glowed in the warmth of the sun afternoon sun. Her eyelashes almost touched his face as he held her close.

"Well, honey..." pausing calmly to carefully study his words before allowing them to touch her ears—He knew this was a teachable moment. Suddenly, He had an unwelcomed flashback of his father yanking him off of the ground when he was seven, just a year older than his daughter.

He came to himself again…

"Daddy…did you hear me? Why did I fall?" Her tears were drying up now, they left behind trails like airplane smoke in the blue sky on her chubby cheeks.

"Well, baby…"

"Get up boy! I showed you three times now, how to steer this bike! What more I gotta do?! Are you dumb or somethin'?! Must have gotten that from your mother!"

He felt a tugging on his sleeve. "Daddy, you listening to me?"

"Yes… yes sweetheart I am, I'm listening to you. Sometimes we fall when we're learning new things, it's a part of being human. We all fall sometimes…"

"But I was doing so good until I saw that butterfly. Did that butterfly make me fall?"

"Well, it didn't make you fall…you just happened to notice something that you liked, and then you decided to switch your focus to the butterfly and off of your bike riding, that's all."

"It was so pretty, daddy…It had my favorite color in it!"

"Yeah, I know sweetie" he said while picking her up and slowly walking towards home.

Looking down at her knee, "Look, it stopped bleeding, daddy."

"It sure did! Did it stop hurting?"

"Yes! It just itches a little…"

"Okay, well, we'll go home and clean it all up and put a band aid on it, okay?"

Grabbing his neck and kissing him on the cheek, "Okay, daddy, can I try again tomorrow?"

"Yes, WE can… I'll be right there with you."

She nestled her face in his chest and listened to his heartbeat, he caressed her hair as he carried her down the long road. She looked at her bike in his right hand and knew she'd conquer it tomorrow.

A Funny Thing My Daddy Used To Do...

My daddy, Eddie West, was a singer, a lover of music, and quite the entertainer. He loved to entertain whoever was around him. He'd sing, for you, make you laugh, pick on you, cook for you, lay cards with you, and sometimes cuss you out and put you out of the house (That's another story for another time)! LOL!

He also enjoyed watching other singers perform. Sometimes, when another person was singing, the music would get so good to him that he'd stand up, dramatically walk a few steps forward towards the person/group, look at them like he wanted to fight them and say, "Got Dog it!!! Ooo...Wee! Boy, you gone make me...!" he'd say while looking crazed (Now, I don't know what their singin' was going to make him do...slap them, maybe? I don't know). Then, he would laugh, look around a bit, and keep yelling and looking intensely at the person until they were done! Sometimes he would just stand there with that cool stance he had—with his legs apart and his head swung to the side, and just listen with a grin on his face as happy as can be! If he was watching them on the TV he'd do the same thing as if they could hear him, it was quite the sight to see.

My father wasn't a Christian, but he believed in God, respected the people of God, and loved to listen to preachers, especially T.D. Jakes! One of his favorite genres was gospel music... he loved gospel the music and sang it often! One of his favorite songs was "Christian Automobile." He used to have my sisters and I sing that song with him. One of the lines of that song goes, "Prayer is the driver's license... Faith is the steering wheel...just like an automobile..."

Those were good times that I will always cherish!

Can you imagine the day that he came to my church! I knew that he would thoroughly enjoy the music...but what was he going to do?! He stood in the front row while I sang on the worship team—he was proud to see any of his children singing. Not only was he proud of me, but my pastor is a professional singer, so let's just put it this way...my dad was Extremely impressed and showed it that day. To Daddy, singing was medicine—it was life!

Who's Yo Daddy?...

Did you know that you can chose your Father? Spiritually that is...
We all have the choice of two. They both want
us and have a strong desire to have us
All to Themselves...
One will Love us, while the other one will Hate us!
They both want us to live with them for Eternity—
One in Darkness, the other in the Light.
It's Our Decision.
So...Who's Yo Daddy?
It's up to You.

father/Father

I thought you were like my father, so I didn't trust you
I felt unprotected and unsure.
I thought you were unpredictable: I never
knew what mood you'd be in
I became anxious and insecure in all my relationships.
I thought you'd leave me like he did
or that you'd stay and still be absent.
I thought I wasn't enough and that caused you to ignore me
If I were enough wouldn't that have made you love me,
provide for me... stay?
I thought you were like my father, so I stayed away from you
convinced that you were just like him
that you would treat me just like him
But you didn't...you are different.
You welcomed me into yourself—prepared a place for me
accepted me as your own...you said you've been waiting for me.
You said you'd never leave me, even in the dark times...
You are there.
I am yours and you are mine, FOREVER!

Reconciliation...

For those who are trying, don't give up!
Keep showing up, be there...
Endure the pain that you may have caused—
pray and God will give you instruction.
Allow Him to heal you as you initiate healing
with your sons and daughters.
Don't give up...they see your effort—though
they may not acknowledge it, yet.
Respect their mother(s), even if she doesn't
deserve it—they see that too...
They see you more than they hear you—
may your actions speak loudly.
Do what is right, though what is wrong feels
much better and is much easier.
Money helps a lot, but time and attention develops relationship.
When you can't do something, explain why,
and don't allow guilt to eat at you.
Don't allow guilt from the past drive you
to value the things you give them
more than the love and discipline they need from you.
Let them see that you are determined to be in
their lives, and nothing will stop you.
Don't give up!

A Note to Mothers

Mothers who are hurting and wounded by
these fathers who ARE trying...
Allow the Lord to help you heal and forgive, and don't hinder
your children from having a father in their lives—they are
needed in their lives, and they will make a positive difference.
If they are not abusive to you, or hurting your children in some
way, PLEASE, don't allow bitterness to rob your children of
this privilege...You will have to answer to God for that.

EDIE BOWMAN

I watched The Temptations movie today and I thought of you, Daddy. When David began to sing, it reminded me of how talented you were, and what a show-off you were, too! I guess every group has its David Ruffin, huh?

<u>For Those Who Stayed</u>

I'm thankful for all the fathers who never left—who hung in there, who fought through the struggles, who married the mother of their children. The fathers who worked like a dog to put food on the table and clothes on the backs of their wives and children... Thank You! For the fathers who argued and disagreed with their wives, but still stayed and worked it out. For the fathers who messed up sometimes and made many mistakes, but apologized and kept loving. For the fathers who said, "No" to those women who wanted to wreck their homes through infidelity. For the fathers who hugged and kissed their wives in front of the children as they danced in the kitchen to "We're in This Love Together" by Al Jarreau. For the fathers who worked over-time to get that extra special thing we all wanted. For the fathers who have no problem holding the house down when Mom's at work or just too tired—he knows who he is. For putting your family first and doing what you promised to do in your vows.
I see you...We need you... Thank you.

A Call to Fathers

Fathers, we need you...we need your Strength
and Faithfulness in God, and in the home.
We need your Love and Gentleness towards your wives
and children, this makes families strong. We need to
see your Vulnerability just as much as we need your
Protection and Provision, for this makes you human...
Therefore, approachable and influential to those around
you. We need you to be Present, not just there... but,
engaged in our lives, daily. When you stand firm in these
attributes and in Godly Character, we ALL are strong—
in our homes, communities, nations, and the world.

EDIE BOWMAN

AND NOW…

<u>Being Human</u>

I just ran upstairs really fast with an intentional
purpose raging in my veins to achieve…
When I reached my destination, I stood there with my hands
on my hips, out of breath, staring into the abyss, and scratching
my head saying, "Now what did I come up here for, again...?"

Chapter Four
Crazy Silly Things

Often times we think that God is only present or interested in us the most when we are praying to him, reading the bible, or doing something "spiritual." Well, If God is in us...actually living in us as a result of asking him to come into our hearts and lives...if he promised to be with us always...then, isn't he there in our crazy, weird, silly moments too? I mean, he doesn't turn his face away from us in shame when we do something funny! As a playwright, I use all of my creative abilities. I have written serious plays about fatherlessness, like *Kingdom*. I have also written plays just to make you laugh hysterically, like "Good Like Medicine" which was an evening full of skits that were ridiculous! God gave me this kind of mind for a reason, and I've found it!

Those who REALLY know me, know that I have an extremely quirky, crazy, ridiculously comedic side that only they have seen. I've actually been warned by my mother, husband, and children, NOT to allow others to see that side! Well...since I believe that God is with us in EVERY moment in life, I can feel free to share these moments with him just as much as I share the serious ones. God has, evidently, created us to laugh or we wouldn't all do it, or have the need and desire to do it. It wouldn't feel so good to laugh if it wasn't necessary and embedded in us to do it! Now...I do realize, as you will see in this book, that some have quite different ranges of what they deem funny. I have, let's say... "A Beautifully Crazy Mind." That's what I choose to believe and I'm sticking with it!!!

Into The Light Productions
Mableanne JohnsTon

W E I R D?...

Is it weird that I talk to squirrels through my window, and they seem to understand?

Is it strange that the trees seem to whisper things to me as they sway in the wind, and they feel heard?

Can it be that dogs can really talk, but choose to bark instead?

Is it okay that I have thoughts so weird that I keep them inside my head?

Is it peculiar that I take soulful songs and hip-hop songs and R and B songs and turn them into opera songs, just because it feels wonderfully humorous coming out of my vocal cords and into my body, and then out into the atmosphere?

Is it not okay that I have two oversized teddy bears on my bed named Billiam and Billfred, and that we laugh, cry, cuddle, and share our feelings? But sometimes they get a little rowdy and I have to settle them down. Billiam...he usually responds to everything with the love of God, but Billfred... he's the ornery one—the big baby, we're working on him. I must admit, my husband, on occasion, makes me kick them out of the bed. I think he's jealous of our relationship, Lol! By the way...he bought both of them, sooo....

EDIE BOWMAN

Talking to yourself and then answering is not so weird… as long as you give yourself the right advice, right?

Why is it that the songs, "The Gambler" by Kenny Rogers, "What You Won't Do for Love" by Bobby Caldwell, or "We're in this Love Together" by Al Jarreau, often come to my mind when I go to the bathroom? And of course, being me…I'm compelled to sing them with all of my might so that anyone in the house can hear me. The funny thing is… sometimes my family joins in on the other side of the bathroom door, go figure.

A True Story of Alliteration

(Seriously…I really had a great fall at the skating rink!)
Falling Fast she Finally Found her Footing
but Struggled to Simply Stand again.
She Still Seemed to Sustain Some Strength, at
least enough to Find a Fresh new Feeling of
Fearless Freedom to Start Skating Strongly once more.

Strangely Pleasing Annoyances?...

Isn't it a strangely unsettling experience to be laughing
at the same time you're feeling irritated?...
--To be tickled by someone while you're upset about something
that just happened by the hands of that same person that is
tickling you…you're laughing, but you want to punch them!
--To be laughing with a person who verbally and physically
is picking with you, and at the same time you're wanting
them to stop because it's starting to aggravate you…
but you're still laughing because it's funny!!!
--To be removing a splinter from your finger
and it is feeling good in the process—
"It Hurts So Good!"

--To be scratching a mosquito bite that keeps
itching and experiencing the heat and agitation the
scratching is producing at the same time.
(Okay…the last two just might be exclusive
to my weird experiences)

<u>Lord, Help Me with These Ghetto Squirrels!</u>

(How can something so cute be so relentlessly disturbing?)

Sooo…we have to redo our deck this year, not only because it's weather worn, but because of these Ghetto Squirrels out here in Deez Streets! They scratched up the wood something fierce, and they even leave their nut shells all over the place. One day I went outside, and they had left a chicken bone and a piece of hamburger on the banister, so yeah…they raid our trash cans too! I actually believe that it's only one Ghetto Squirrel causing all of the havoc, or maybe two… I never see more than that. You know…it could be a Bonnie & Clyde situation—I often see a couple fighting on top of the garage roof, or maybe it's more of an Ike and Tina Turner thing. But I'm pretty sure it's the same squirrel that daily goes up to the top of our roof and stores his nuts, or the bodies of other squirrels… He probably stares down at us like he's the Don Corleone of the Squirrel Mafia. He probably stands on his tiny hind legs, raises up one of his smuggled nuts in the air, looks out over the hood and says, "Yo! I rule this block, and one day I will own all the trees and nuts on this whole block, son!" (Okay, that was more like the hood mixed with a little mafia, but you know what I mean). These squirrels be trippin 'round here!

Heads Up!

I asked my husband the other day, "What if all we were made of were heads?... No arms or legs, or torsos—just heads?" You can imagine his look of wonder and confusion! I went on to say, "I wonder what kind of world we'd create for ourselves. We'd bounce or roll around from place to place, I guess. Where would we go, and what would the places look like? How would we reproduce?..." (I don't want to think about that too long, Lol!) "Congratulations! You have a bouncing baby head... girl!" Another thing...what would we compare each other to? I'm sure we'd find something...we always do. Would it be on how large or small our heads are? "His head is very large and contains quite a substantial frontal lobe...He's a Genius! He Shall Lead Us ALL!!!" (lead us in what?... I'm not sure). The smaller your head was the weaker you would be perceived. "There couldn't possibly be enough knowledge in there...He's an Ignoramus!!! He shall be a worker head!" (what kind of work do heads do...I'm still not sure)

You know... there could be a sport's club called The Ultimate Head Bangers League (U.H.B.L). The game would comprise of the Smartest, Largest, Most Powerful heads in the world. They would compete by seeing who could knock the other head out in the least amount of time while answering highly intellectual questions between each round. It's kind of like Boxing meets Jeopardy...except without arms or legs! What would be their prize?... I don't know, perhaps a hat made of Gold (how was the hat made?... Again, I don't know).

Well, this has been a wonderful stretch of the imagination, friends. Thanks for going on the journey with me.

Actually...now that I think about it...The Veggie Tales have already achieved this crazy world of just heads, DUH?!... Except, they can do everything without arms and legs, so... It Is Possible.

Try This...

If you need a laugh or just a quick pick me up, try this...
The next few sentences that you say, say them like the counting
vampire on *Sesame Street*. You know...pronounce words that
start with the letter *w* instead, with the letter *v* sound and roll
your *r*'s. Make sure that you speak with excitement, great
volume, guttural energy, fast paced, and end each sentence
with "AH! AH! AHHH!..." kind of like you're laughing. Oh...
and if it has a number in the sentence...Even Better!
For example: I Vant to Go to the store to get Vone Apple! Vone!...
Not Two, Not Three, but Vone Apple! AH! AH! AHHH!...
Vould you like to come Vith Me?! AH! AH! AHHH!...

Hey!... Everybody Does it!

One day I was feeling rather silly (Let's face it, that's
a lot of the time!) and I asked my husband...
"What if, whenever we passed gas, it not only smelled
badly, but a purple cloud filled the air around us also?
Wouldn't it be hard to get through meetings, conversations,
dinners—serious moments? And..." I continued, "what if
it always made a funny sound and was really loud?"
He didn't care to continue the conversation any further after that!
(It would be pretty hard to act like you didn't do it either,
wouldn't it? You'd have a gaseous cloud around you!) LOL!

Sooo...Where do These "Experts" Come From?!

I'm convinced that "The Experts" are empowered
by the devil to drive us all mad!!!
One day "they" say that coffee, chocolate, dairy,
and certain fish are good for you, and then 6 months

later, "they" say that they may cause memory loss, shortness of breath, and the loss of limbs!
So now you have to carry a recent medical review in your pocket with you to the grocery store and choose the lesser of two evils. "Let's see...do I get the ice cream and snicker bar and risk losing a limb, or should I just eat the fish, have a cup of coffee, and end up forgetting about what I ate all together as I gasp for air?"

One Day This Word Will Be in The Dictionary

Timonergy: the use of time, money, and energy together over a specific period of time.
Example: while trying to get her new business off to a good start, Sally has used a lot of timonergy in the last 6 months.

I'm Psycho!

(I let Charles make up this title, so enjoy! Perhaps...)

Okay, so my husband is not a fan of cremation. He has made it clear that he does not prefer it, but if it gave me comfort to bury him instead, he wouldn't fight me on it (*after all he is dead, right?*). The other day while driving home from church, we got into a discussion about this issue again, and he mentioned his reason for not thinking that cremation was the best option after one dies. He stressed that if not having enough money wasn't the reason for going that route, then it made more sense to save the money that you'd used for a burial and just use cremation. (*While I know this sounds a bit morbid, just stick with me...a better moment is coming*).

As we continued to go back and forth sharing our views, I had a thought... (*are you ready for this?*). I asked him, "Well would it be so bad if I just had them cut off your pinky finger, you know...to get just enough to have necklaces made for me and our three girls to wear in remembrance of you?"

His response was "Edie, stop! That's crazy! You are not going to cut off my pinky finger, burn it up and then bury the rest of my body, no!" (*I think it necessary to tell you that he did say this with extreme laughter!*).

I responded by saying, "What's the big deal? It gives me more peace to know that if I wanted to visit your grave, I could, rather than having an urn on the mantle that I have a chance of breaking" (*those who know me know that this is a huge possibility*).

"Stop!" He said, "I don't even want to discuss this anymore... this is dumb!"

We laughed so much during this discussion, despite how morbidly ridiculous it was.

<u>Mixed Nuts</u>

Man... I'm tired of being trapped up in here with all you Jokers; I'm a peanut! You find ME everywhere—weddings, parties, bars, restaurants, etc. I'm the world's most favorite nut, look it up! I don't belong here, mixed between all of you...am I right my fellow Peanuts?! Am I right?!
The fellow peanuts: Yeah!
Radical Peanut: It's time for us to rise up and take our place!
The fellow peanuts: Rise Up!
Radical Peanut: We are better than this! We are...
CRUNCH!!!

SO, IF A PERSON WERE TO TAKE A FEW SICK DAYS
OFF OF WORK...DOES IT COUNT IF WHAT IS ACTUALLY
MAKING HIM OR HER SICK, IS THE WORK ITSELF?
JUST KIDDIN'... OR AM I?

I Wonder What Jesus Would be Like if he Was on Earth Today?...

Would he wear the latest Nike shoes and the popular clothes of today or would he have his own line called the "J-Look"?

Would he hang out at my house, chill on the couch eatin' Hot Cheetos, and laugh at my craziness?!

Would he speak in the latest lingo, saying stuff like "Maaan that hat is Dope, Yo!"

Would he sing old school songs with me and my friends and dance the two step and the Monorail?

Would Jesus go to the mall, and while there, cast a demon out of someone right in the food court?

Would he grow up in Da Hood and get all of the gang bangers saved and start his own gang called the "D-12" Gang? Doin Life fo da Kingdom!

Would Jesus eat collard greens, cornbread, and Mac 'n' Cheese at the cookout or bring his own quinoa casserole?

Would he play the dozens and crack on yo momma?! Would he be like "Yo momma soo ugly..." Nah, I can't see that one.

Would Jesus stop the rain and make it exactly 70 degrees for 3 days so that he and his disciples could have fun at Disney World? That would be soo cool!

Would Jesus wear a mohawk, and keep his beard crispy at the neighborhood barber shop? And would he take over the conversation and shut all the crazy talk down that goes on in there?!

A Simple Request

I just got done talking my husband's ears off for a while, right? So, I gave him a brief break. Then, I noticed him going up the stairs, so I followed him... (he was going to the bathroom). He went in, shut the door, and locked it quickly. I asked him another question, and he said...

"I just want to poop in peace and not answer any questions!"

Just A Few More Things About These Squirrels

Why won't they get out of the way when we're driving down the street?... Have you had those conversations in the car too? "Get out of the way little squirrel...come on...I don't want to hit you...hurry up..." I think they hold secret meetings on how they can annoy us and make us love them simultaneously. The best weapon they have is using their cuteness to deter you while they use your property. Here's how it goes down: a couple of them will do something adorable in front of you in the back yard, and while you're gawking at them... their three cousins are tearing up your flowerpots on the porch to hide their nuts in!... GENIUS!

AND NOW...

Being Human

Now, all babies are beautiful because they come from God and are created in his image, but... have you ever seen a not so, let's say...attractive, baby? (Be honest, you know you have...) What do you do? What do you say? Do you lie?... Of course not! You just avoid all the usual words like cute, pretty, handsome, adorable, etc. You say things like "Aww...look at him" or, "she's such a blessing" or, "he's soo beautiful" (this is a safe word) or, "she's soo cuddly" or, "Aww...such a sweetie pie" or, "hello there... look at you..." or, "He's soo sweet" or, "she's soo precious" or just keep saying, "Hey, you...." (Don't judge me, you know you've been there, you know...)

Chapter Five
Beauty & Pain

How I wish that there was only beauty in the world...but that will never happen until Heaven comes down to earth or until we, individually, get to heaven. Until that happens, beauty will always be shared with pain. We can experience the beauty of a new-born child, and at the same time, grieve if we find out that child is ill. We mourn the hardships that child will face in life. We can bask in the beauty of nature around us today, and by tomorrow some king of natural disaster can destroy that beauty we just delighted in.

I remember when I was in high school, one of my favorite teachers was a home economics teacher. She was one of the sweetest, patient, caring teachers that I ever encountered. She had a way of making each one of us feel like you were her child. I remember the day that I heard the news...she died of cancer. I was devastated! I had prayed for her, cried out to the Lord for her, asked others to pray for her...I really believed that she would make it. I was even trying to figure out a way to get to the hospital in Cleveland, Ohio to pray for her myself! Why?... She made soo many feel loved and accepted at that school. Why did she have to go out like that?... Because beauty & pain exists together...I hate it, but it's inevitable.

This is not a chapter to depress us, sadden us, or steal our joy, but to address the truth that there is another side of beauty and laughter—pain and suffering. They are real, we all have, or will have them at some point in our lives. The good news is... God is with us through it all. He doesn't want us to hide from our moments of pain, but to talk to him in the midst of them: allow Him to carry us, hold us, direct us, and guard our hearts from bitterness and anger. He promises to be there with us...even if it hurts so much that we can hardly feel anything else but the pain. He's there even if we don't understand...

Why does Revelation 21:4 say, "And God shall wipe away all tears from their eyes..."? (KJV) Because He KNEW that we'd have many of them, on this side of Heaven.

Sunrise at Sunset

He sat upon the sandy beach at sunrise gliding his fingers through the warm, moist comfort that cuddled him. Although it was a frequented place that brought an assortment of emotion...in that moment the only one was anger. And although he knew that the world was his to take, to do with it as he pleased... he remembered...it. The flood inside overtook his will, forcing its way through the rocky, jagged, dark places.

EDIE BOWMAN

The water that was once cleansing and healing became foreign and strange, and now the possibility to take in the resplendency the skies were offering him, was deadened by...that. Instead, he looked upward and screamed at its presentation, for in the face of present beauty was adjacent pain. "Why?!!!!!!" he said, as he squeezed the sand in his fists feeling more frustration as it poured from his firm grip, failing to allow him to hold on to it!

You see... he has everything that a man
could ever desire, and more...
except her...Oh God...
Except her...
Weeping may endure for the night, but joy
will come in the morning...Hold on.

The CRAZY Thing About Tears

There's something about tears...something that puzzles me.

I've shed gazillions in my 48 years here—my body should be in constant dehydration.

Sometimes I don't even know why—they just flooooow without warning.

"You just feel too deeply," some have said.

"You think waaaay to much!" others say—not in a positive way...

I look at a blue and white sky and think, "How amazing is that? It's soo big!" While searching for words, my description sounds painfully elementary, as I'm aware of my deficient ability to adequately express its vast complexity. So I just cry.

And then, as I'm basking in the wonderment of it all, I'm suddenly heisted of that moment: overcome by the dismal realities of this world's Present-ness...I began to cry, again.

My salty sweet tears of stupendous tranquility have morphed into a strange flavor of what has been and what may come, and the taste is unsettling.

The breathtaking sunset of amber and soft tones of purple and pink are tainted by sudden hues of distorted memories felt... and I cry?

A constant battle to unmarry the mixture of the bitter and the sweet remain unsuccessful, for life and death, good and evil, happiness and sadness comes... intertwined like salvation at a funeral.

I sat on the shore watching the ocean's grand performance: a standing ovation, an unending encore. The air was welcoming, and the sun had just made its entrance to the left of me, seeming to reaffirm my place there. Taking in the applause of the waves, the gentleness of the breeze. The family to my right was playing soft music, which complemented the scene, and all the glory surrounding me. I felt blessed to have such a moment. My eyes soon adverted to my youngest child who accompanied me so early this particular morning at sunrise. I proudly grieve as she walks to the edge of the ocean, taking pictures. I remember that she'd be leaving soon to go to college, and guess what?... These tears choose to invade once more, deciding to interpret for me—the Morris Code of my thoughts. Right in the midst of serenity I experienced heartache—strange, isn't it?... These unruly, untimely droplets of what is.

It was around 11:30am today when I received the call from my sobbing mother. The fear gripped me instantly, for only sorrow brings this sound from her soul. My beautiful, 14-year-old niece had been shot!

WHAT?!...

Just moments before my husband and I were planning a day together—nothing big, just being together...

"Let's do a movie and go to lunch, maybe go to Starbucks and talk?"

EDIE BOWMAN

So long, beautiful moment in time . . .**Did you know you'd soon be brutally destroyed?!**

How could this be?!

She was only a baby! It was not long ago that we all helped put up the tree at Mom's house. We took pictures and laughed, talked while listening to Christmas music, ate snacks together... then, we hugged and kissed each other goodbye. Wasn't it just a moment ago when you were in the back seat of my red Lumina asking me questions about Jesus and God, with that innocent, breath-taking smile on your face, and those big, beautiful brown eyes?

Please! Don't let this be true, Not You...

"She died, mommy?" I asked, reluctantly.

"Yes, she died, baby."

"But she was just a little girl! Why would someone do this to her?!" I cried.

. . . Someday God shall wipe every tear from their eyes, and sin and death will be no more—those enemies of all.

But until then...

We Continue to Cry...

For Justice to dominate our land,
for Truth to rule our minds,
for Righteousness to persist in our hearts,
for Peace to possess our souls,
and for God's Love to drive our actions.
—In Remembrance of my beautiful niece, Lil' Sylvia Lokia McGee

The Hope of Heaven

I woke up this morning with you on my mind…and while the pain was not as great, my heart still feels the void and longs for complete justice. I keep your obituary in one of my favorite books beside my bed so that I can see your smile before I go to sleep. The Truth that gives me solace is knowing that God is merciful, loving, and full of justice: He knows everything and will weigh it all out perfectly, He makes no mistakes, and He will repay. And though we won't see it here, you are in a place where you can't even remember what you suffered. Sorrow and fear are foreign to you—you have a joy that we will never experience. You are Free…pure and holy, just like your Father…you do not have the ability to feel pain. He has wiped ALL tears from your eyes. You cannot come back to us, but we can come to you…that's all you hope for now… that we will come to you.

Illumination

The sky looks confused today…
One side gray, blue, and dark, and haunting…
the other side, even darker.
The sun was diligent to break through from behind.
Desiring to bring balance and an emerging hope, it persisted,
wrapping arms around the clouds like a lighted lantern.
Giving its perspective… it had much to say.
Bringing hope in the moment like a Rembrandt painting,
a perfect mixture of light and darkness on a live canvas.
How unsettling and serene this view above me looms.
An awkward beauty—An elegant sharing of
the same space—An understanding…

EDIE BOWMAN

The Longest Ride

Stop world—listen! Don't you know what's happening today?

You don't?... Then why don't you? Is the cause of the quake not strong enough to affect your plans?

It may be a tremor to you—therefore, no pause to recognize my despair

Didn't you sense the change in the atmosphere?

Yes, the sun's still shining, but it's cold and dark, and bitter inside.

Haven't you felt the same? The hallowed chest echoing the beat of a heart once secure,

now...carved open like a Jack-o-lantern on Halloween; empty... gutted with a drawn on face and a flickering candle.

The Longest Ride I've ever taken—around the corner, down the street—five to ten minutes away...

A ride I wished would take all day, as long as it prolonged the final say...

Goodbye?...

No... not that! Not goodbye—

It's way too soon for him—it always is...

I refuse to no longer hear the way you called me your baby— the way you'd always say, "be careful" before I'd leave your presence.

While on the ride, I remember how you'd often say how proud you were of me, and how beautiful I was to you...I was your baby girl...

I look down and see my body, my legs, my feet...I'm awake, I know...though numb all over.

Someone's holding my hand.

Am I really here...now...today?

My eyes glance out of the window...

I think, *Hey you over there—gaily passing by, carefree, sauntering, enjoying life—I envy you at this moment.* I know that I shouldn't, but I do.

Don't just watch the long dark figure passing by…it's not a free show, I'm in here!

I'm in this luxury car of death—don't let it deceive…

It's heading to a place where dreaded words are spoken, words I wish could mean something else…

"Ashes to Ashes, Dust to Dust."

Do you care?!

Sun…Stop shining!

Traffic…Halt!

Laughter… Cease! At least… for a moment?

Please?...

"Life must go on." I know the saying, but must it…go on?...

You're not here…it can't go on—I don't want it to…not if, "Life" means carrying on as usual.

I'll miss your arms around me telling me it'll be ok, seeing your smile, smelling your cologne.

Who will look at me the way you did? As only you could…

All these thoughts fill my head as we approach the final destination.

I'll never feel that specialness again—that feeling only you could give…

They'll try so hard to tell me words meant to comfort—

Those comfortless words of comfort—words…then more words…

Words that never will suffice.

I look back towards the spot—the place where you are laid.

I stare until I see the last glimpse of the corner of your beautifully colored box…

With one final rose in view, I stretch my neck further than it should stretch trying desperately to hang on to the image—the box… the rose…

I can no longer see the skinny tree I chose to mark your grave as I look through the rearview window, of this all too familiar car…

This Wretched… Silent… Dreaded car.

Times' Ambivalent Opus

I hear YOU!
Stop Haunting, Taunting—Remaining...
Menacing dance of Love, Hate—Life and Death
A fixed marriage tied to my wrist!
RELENTLESS HOVERING—
as a once barren mother over her only child
Pulsing breath on my neck set to rhythmic tone
Syncopated laughter in my ear...Dripping water's melody
Song of the fly—Maddening REPETITION!!!!!! STOP!
Keeping me on task.
Bringing to mind what matters, and that which can wait.
Making it clear what needs to be done...is Now.
Putting in perspective All Things.
Steady...Dependable...Reliable.

UNRELIABLE! CAPRICIUOS!

Familiar key composed to mock
Remind me No More... I know Your Tune
Deafening Persistence   Sound of Perfection   Constant Enemy

OMNIPRESENT...Friend.

Sorrow's Contender

I have to laugh, please don't stop me—it's
vital...or why would I have the urge?
Why were we created to feel rumblings in our
bellies and release strange sounds out of our
mouths, only to feel energized afterwards?
Could it be that we'd need this ability to
balance what life would bring?

I have to laugh, please don't stop me—it helps
keep me sane in a world that seems insane.
It trains me to appreciate the beauty of the weeping
willow as I sit underneath its shadow.
It grounds me when life is shaken, and my
heart is confused in its direction.
Laughter fights off the hounds of worry and the
vampires of hope that come to destroy my peace.
God gave me this gift to supplement my body
and bring joy to the lives of others.
I have to laugh, please don't stop me—it heals,
it refreshes…it's existential to the soul…
Contend for it and Win!

SCIATICA

An aggravating, gnawing, aching, pain
like something is eating my bones, muscles and sinews
from the hip to the tips of my toes.
Torment!
Fiery waves of Tingling numbness—
how can they All exist at once
as if they're trying to get their equal time?
Violators!
How did you get here?
Who told you to invade my space, enter my body,
my world…unexpectantly?
Couldn't you warn me, allow me time to prepare?
I woke up and you were there.
I pampered you for months, giving you Chiropractic care,
gradually you seemed to leave.
Taking your appetite with you—you pretended to loosen your grip
allowing me to live pain free again.

A

B

R

U

P

T

L

Y

returning, when just the day before you almost closed the door…
You demanded your way in again, swiftly bringing back your stuff!
Almost at a level 4 now, you exacerbate me!
Burning throbbing and drawing my attention.
I started at a level 7! You're expensive! You've
cost me time, money and energy
"Timonergy"—a word I created for times like these,
it fits you so well…Robbing me of what should be
daily niceties and mundane commitments.
I long for them now.
But you won't win!
I'll keep walking, pressing through the pain, reclaiming
my routine, ignoring your displeasure.
You will not debilitate me! I control you
now, you diminish as I live.
In the nucleus of enjoying beautiful things, I won't think of you
(I know that you can't stand that, you feed off my attention)
instead, I'll fully embrace God's healing and look up and you'll be

GONe.

I Laugh just as much as I Cry...
while this balance is good, I believe that my
moments of laughter, will at the end of it
all... have greatly exceeded my tears.

AND NOW...

Being Human

Have you ever been on a walk with someone and were
constantly complaining about your knees, or feet, your
back, legs, ankles, etc., and then out of nowhere a tiny
chihuahua came running across its yard barking and running
towards you? Man...you surprised yourself! You didn't
know how fast you could get those knees a movin'!

Chapter Six
Faith & Hope In God

Hope is to have a happy expectation that things will get better, that something good is going to happen. Faith is to be fully persuaded about something that you believe—you believe it so strongly... it's as if you already have it. They both are a gift to have from God. These two things are something that we need to hang on to, never let them go! Life can challenge these two friends of ours—it can be a struggle to stay connected to them at times. We have to choose to walk in faith and choose to have hope in the goodness of God, in all situations, at all times, and in every moment...in all things.

I remember when I was around sixteen years old, I went through a period of loneliness in my life. The sister who I was closet in age with, and the closet to, graduated high school and left home, and I felt a huge emptiness in my heart. I had friends at school and friends at church, but I still felt alone. I had people around me who treated me well and cared about me that were my age, but God was calling me closer to him—deeper in Him. This kind of relationship with Him caused me to separate from some friends and family, and it was very difficult and lonely.

The next few years were full of tears, sorrow, much prayer, reading God's word, and going to church. I grew the most during these years, and God gave me older women to hang with. I learned soo much from these ladies: they told me their stories of pain and triumph. I listened to them, watched their lives, and became stable through their example. I know that I dodged a lot of wrong relationships in my life because of them. I was picked at in high school for being a virgin and not dating, but I didn't care...I had to do what HE told me to do! I didn't have to go through what I saw many other young ladies go through because I held on to the words of my Lord, my mother, and these older women.

Thank you, Sis. Peggy Danzy, Sis. Vera Roberson, and Sis. Jan Burr for being there for me and spending a lot of time with me in my teens and early twenties. I also want to thank Sis. Carole Clark and Sis. Viola James—two women who talked to me, taught me, spoke into my life throughout the years and led by example, their faith and hope in God.

The Great Director

Lead me, guide me, be that Light in darkness—
navigate my course, "Oh Sailor of my heart..."
Like a star in the night's sky, give hope in The Moment.
Orchestrate the seasons of life, show me which way I should go.
Detour my steps when my feet get confused, and
change the scenes not staged for me.

EDIE BOWMAN

TRUST

What this Coronavirus has rehearsed within me is the fact
that I need you, Oh God... in Every Moment of life.
When my day is going well, and if it suddenly
takes a turn for the worst, you are there poised
and ready knowing that I'll need your help.
I'm also awakened to the fact that my job is NOT my
provision, for it is gone now...you have been and will
always be my Provision. I TRUST IN YOU ALONE!
Our leaders can only do so much: we can't depend on
them for long...they are fallible. You are constant.
And as cliché as it may be we ARE all connected—
susceptible to disease, but united in finding a cure.
If the blood of a cured person could possibly
heal an infected person, would the color of their
skin or their social status matter?... NO.
We are an interdependent... and once we
finally let go of our prejudices,
(A slight paraphrase to Dr. Seuss) ... "Oh, the Places We'll Go!"

Lessons I've Learned from Bees

So, we kept getting bees (yellow jackets to be exact) in our living room window. This was causing a lot of unrest in our home, especially since I and my daughters are the ones in the living room the most during the day. I was getting so sick of killing them for hours, constantly looking at that window, and thinking every small dark spot on the wall was a bee! I prayed out loud to the Lord, "Now you said no plague shall come nigh my dwelling, and this feels like one, you have called me to peace, and this is stealing it, please help us. Destroy them with in the walls and cause them to stop coming in, Lord."

I went outside to sweep the porch a short time after that prayer. As I was sweeping, I accidently bumped the wooden railing on the porch. When I did that, a few bees swarmed around me. After I regained my composure...I stepped back to see where they were headed. They were going in and out a small hole in the corner of our porch that was very close to out window in the living room. *Ah-Ha!!! Ya little peace stealers!!!! I gotcha now!* I ran downstairs to my husband's office to tell him. He came back with a spray that foams up and hardens after it fills the area you spray it into.

After filling the hole up, I was still watching them closely to make sure that they couldn't get back in... an hour later, I was finally convinced. *Phew! It's finally over*, we thought, but a couple days later they showed up again! My daughter Tatiana and I acted, and sounded like maniacs as we screamed, sprayed and swatted bees. We were so loud that Charles came up from his office looking at us like we were crazy, and we were just that, CRAZY!!! I went back outside and studied the situation a little closer. I stayed there until a bee showed up and I saw where it was going. There were still a few tiny holes on the porch, and they were going in one by one.

Charles filled in those holes, and he thought it was over, but I was not convinced. We forgot that the ones already inside the wall had to get out! I knew they'd still end up in that room. Where were they coming from to get to the window from inside of the house? I began to investigate near the window and ask many questions of my husband. He realized that he had two choices: keep hearing my questions and watching my investigations, or join me! He joined me! He moved around a few things on the mantle, dismantled a few things, and found a couple holes he drilled through the mantle to wire cable through, near the window. He covered those up and all is well...I think!

I learned, by watching those bees, that they are relentless! They would not give up, even after hours and days of finding their home closed up—they kept coming back!

I learned that they are innovative: they found new ways to get what they wanted: they kept searching for other places and ways to find a dwelling.

I learned that when we ask God for something, he can do it right away, but oftentimes, it seems… he works with you to get it done. I asked for him to destroy the bees, well he did through the use of our minds, hands, and ingenuity.

I learned not to give up when what I desire, need or want (that's according to His will) doesn't work out smoothly like I wish it would. Keep moving, keep searching, and keep believing!

And Now…The Stinkbug Miracle!

Not only did we have the plague of bees, but we had an even larger plague of stink bugs! They were these black bugs, that looked like lightning bugs, but with red stripes and a red sack of some sort of blood-like sack underneath them (I knew every inch of these creatures because I studied them. A swarm of them was on our house, particularly on the back of the house. *But why?…* I thought to myself.) One day, I was standing in my dining room with great fear as I watched them crawling around the window and on the walls and ceiling. I was a killing machine, little did I know that killing them produced some kind of odor that caused many others to come, MAN!!!! It looked like a bloody massacre, and as I smashed them all, they left red stains everywhere!

I began to wonder…what was it about the back side of the house that they liked? Is it the sun? do they like heat? Do they like windows for some reason?… I went on a massive Google search, and guess what?!.. They love the sun! this was why they mostly came in the dining room window and the bathroom window—that's where the sun was the strongest. Like usually I prayed my "LORD DESTROY THEM ALL!!!" prayer. It didn't happen right away—I had to kill them quick and hard like I was Jason Bourne in *The Bourne Identity!* (you should know by now how much I love movies, right?!)

One day I was praying fervently… "Lord, you have to do something, I can't take this anymore! We don't have the money to get an exterminator right now and I feel like I'm in the days of Moses and the plagues!" There were so many bugs that the back side of our house, in this one area was black with these bugs. A couple of days later a heavy rain came in the evening, it was a *very* heavy rain. The next morning when I left out of the door, I looked over to see the bugs, and they were gone! There were just a few here and there, and just a few I had to kill around the house. It was over just like that! That was a miracle! Just for me!!!

What did I learn? I learned that answered prayers come in all sorts of ways and not to judge the ways that they come. Actually, I'm still learning that! It's about Trusting.

The Day You Hear My Voice...

Salvation is like a beautifully decorated box with wrapping
made of twenty-four karat gold, given to a poor man. It
contains all kinds of the finest jewels, and a check written
out from a multibillionaire for 2.5 million dollars, and
then the POOR MAN saying... "No, I'm just not ready to
receive it right now, maybe later, I still have time..."
Whoa!!! If he'd only known that his time would be up soon!

Ruah

God breathed and we speak
God breathed and we sing
He breathed so we dance
He breathed so we write
God breathed...so we create,
we laugh, we cry, and we love...
God breathed into us the breath of life, and so we Live.
Live Fully....

Endeavor

"To use all the gifts that God has given me...All of them...is one of my greatest goals in life. That they may change minds and hearts to look towards Him for the answers in life, that's my endeavor."

A Heart 2 HEART Prayer

(David had them often...)

In Psalms 13:1-3,5 (NLT) David poured his heart out to the Lord and asked intense questions of him. He said, "O Lord, how long will you forget me? Forever? How long will you look the other way? How long must I struggle with anguish in my soul, with sorrow in my heart every day? How long will my enemy have the upper hand? Turn and answer me, O Lord my God! Restore the sparkle in my eyes, or I will die. But I trust in your unfailing love. I will rejoice because you have rescued me."

I'm learning that honesty in prayer is essential to a closer relationship with God. Many times, our prayers are full of questions, thanks, praise, and trust, all at once. Hear my honest prayer O, God...

Lord, I don't know what in the world I'm doing right now...I'm confused, and I don't know what step to take next. I'm hurting so bad inside; it feels like I'm going to die...sometimes I want to...I can't share that with anyone, though...Can I? I don't always feel close to you, I don't feel you at all many times. I'm afraid of the future, because I see more bad things than good around me...Please help me! I feel like I can't go on sometimes.

My thoughts are continually daunted and full of fear. Lord, I need you so much…you are my light in this darkness. Rescue me, bring me out of this state of helplessness and set me free! I want to feel your presence and know that you hear me. You said that if I call upon your name that you hear me! Please, give me a sign that you are near. Answer me now, Lord…I need you now, Oh God! I don't think that I can make it this way much longer…you promised to be my help, so I trust your word…I believe.

The Sun came up AGAIN today…promising
another chance. Later, The Moon provided
Light in Darkness promising a tomorrow.
Great Is Thy Faithfulness!

EDIE BOWMAN

An Ode to Psalms 1

And I shall be like a Tree...
May I be planted by the river and bring life to all around me
That my leaves would bring, beauty,
refreshing, and shelter to the weary
That I may produce much fruit and flourish to supply for others
May my branches protect the weak and gather those who are alone
May my roots be that of wisdom and Truth to give direction
May my trunk stand firm as a beacon of strength and wisdom
That I would never wither or decay but thrive always
And that I may prosper in all that I do.

Praying in the Spirit

This is too much for me, Lord...I can't even form words to pray—I can barely breathe...the pain is indescribable...I'm so full of emotions...My heart is heavy and confused. Holy Spirit, please pray through me, you know exactly what to tell the Father on my behalf—

All I can do is groan...

Deluge

**I want to be soaked by a Deluge of your Love,
and Never Ever know what it feels like to be
dry again—whatever life may bring.**

The POWER of Starvation

Because I have a dramatic mind, love movies, musicals and plays, I have made up a helpful theatrical game in my mind to help me resist saying negative things. Whenever I'm tempted to speak the bad things I see, think, or feel—no matter how real they are... I picture that green, man-eating plant in the musical *"The Little Shop of Horrors,"* with its enormous, soulful voice, and I remember how it grew when it was given the blood of humans. The plant started off with just a couple of drops, but soon it needed more and more, and as a result it got bigger and bigger, eventually eating everyone.

Let me be clear... (Lol! I sounded like Bernie Sanders) I'm not talking about not expressing my emotions and speaking truth about what's happening in my life, or not sharing my feelings with someone—that's normal! I'm talking about saying and believing that things will not get better—constantly saying negative things and never speaking faith!

This is my theatrical game: I picture that plant eating my negative words and getting more fulfilled...bigger...more powerful... stronger...and saying, like in the musical, "Feed Me! Feed me! Feed Me!!!" In my imagination, I see it becoming eviler and demanding— wanting me to keep feeding it and eventually becoming its slave. Everything within me rejects that! I see it as one of my greatest enemies and I must starve it by praise, worship, and speaking God's word in faith! Soon, the picture in my mind will be a weak, shriveled, brown Punk of a plant, that now speaks with a faint whisper instead of a thunderous shout!

Eventually, all it can do is mouth the words, "Feed me...feed me...Please feed me..."

Yes...I Invited God into this Moment too! It's what I do...

You Know What?...

Lord, I want to be in a place with you where if you said…
"My daughter, I want you to go sit down on the curb dressed
in a black onesie, a black baby's bonnet, and a black bottle
in your mouth, while shaking a black rattle in your hand,
and if someone stops and asks you, "Why you are doing
such a crazy thing like this?!" you must say to them…
"Because this represents your 'human wisdom' and YOUR truth,
in comparison to
'God's wisdom' and THE TRUTH, and it will
lead to eternal death unless you turn to Him in
repentance and seek a relationship with Him."
I want to be able to say, "Father, Thy Will Be Done…"
then, immediately search Amazon for Black colored
baby items, LOL!!! (it would have to be God to find
a black rattle and bonnet wouldn't it? …)
(Hey! Don't count this out as too bizarre…remember God
had the prophet Ezekiel lay on his right side for forty days
signifying one day for each year of Judah's sin. God loves
dramatic demonstration; it's found throughout the Bible!)
I know…it's a little extreme, but you get the
point. Crazier things have been done.

FAITH WITHOUT WORKS IS DEAD… DO WHAT GOD SAYS!

She said she loves to dance. "I dream of being on stage one day, dancing before thousands," but she stayed in her room in front of the mirror twirling…twirling…twirling…never leaving her imagination.

He said he wanted to be the fire chief in his local community, "I love to help people, even at the risk of my own life. I feel close to God when I serve." He worked hard every day to get his body in shape, but never walked down the street to take the test.

Everyone told her that when she sang, they felt uplifted and inspired, but one person said, "You sound mediocre, and will never make it in the business. I sing better than you, and I didn't even make it," so she stopped singing for others, except to a few family and friends.

When she speaks, people listen…they laugh, they think, they imagine, they learn. "You should write a book" they said. She thought about it but listened too long to fear and became immobilized—her writings stayed in her computer and on pieces of paper scattered around her house.

He and his son were excellent at landscaping, better than anyone in the city… "We should own our own business, dad."

"Well son, my pops couldn't make it in this business, and he was good too, what makes us think we can do it?"

He not only dashed his own dreams, but also the dreams and confidence of his son.

Her mother and father said she was beautiful, so did many others…most of all, her God said she was. She felt it and carried herself gracefully with that knowledge—she was confident in her beauty. "I'm trying out for that modeling agency next month," she told herself. He told her she was ugly…she believed it and felt ugly—she stayed home.

He loved to read God's word, study it, teach it, memorize it, and preach it! He longed to explain and demonstrate the love of God to everyone he met and felt the call to pastor. "All preachers are hypocrites…all they want is your money," his family said. He stayed around their negative talk, lost his fire, and let doubt creep in his heart. His family lost their souls, and so did many others he was called to save from Hell.

They believed that they'd make it—they'd beat the odds together… "You know you'd be the first marriage to make it on both sides of the family, don't you? Don't be surprised if it doesn't work out…" he said. They worked hard, doing all they could think of to make their marriage strong for over five years, but they believed what they heard from that person on their wedding day…so when times got rough, they stopped fighting…

What I Learned by Watching the Game Show *Press Your Luck*

My husband and I were watching *Press Your Luck* tonight, and there was a young man man on there who had won over $120, 000, a cruise, and a few other things. When he was asked if he wanted to keep going and press his luck, I angrily yelled at the TV saying "No! Don't be greedy, just take what you have and be happy, don't risk it all!" Well, he decided to keep going and ended up getting a Whammy! Don't you hate those Whammies?... They make you laugh and make you want to kill them at the same time! We were so excited and nervous: I was fussing at him, cheering for him, and pulling my hair...my husband was cheering like he was at a football game.

The young man quickly got up to over $120, 000 but he also kept getting free spins, which heightens your chances of getting another Whammy! It was very intense. His mother and his fiancé were off to the side—huddled up, and frantically screaming and jumping. He worked his way up to over $200,000, two 'his & her' Teslas, and another spin. The audience, and us...were going crazy now, saying with all our hearts, "Don't get a Whammy! Don't get a Whammy!" He hit the button, yelled "Stop!" and...NO WHAMMY!!! He totaled $310,000 and that wasn't all...if the two Tesla's he won added up to $190, 000 equaling the total of $500, 000 ... the rules say that they'd have to give him another $500,000—equaling One Million Dollars! We rooted for him like he was our own family member! Well...it came a little over $17, 000 short, but he, his fiancée, and his mother didn't care! He walked away with a Mercedes, which he gave to his mother, a cruise, two Tesla cars, a year's supply of socks, and a lot of other wonderful things! He pressed his luck and came out better than before!

After I calmed down, I thought about something...If you never take a chance, then you will stay where you are and always wonder what if? Yes, in the beginning he won a lot, but each person has to ask themselves "Is that all that I want?" If the answer is yes, then perhaps that's ok for some. But, if the answer is "no, that's not enough, I want more!" Then, go for it! At first, I saw it as him being greedy, but actually... he was probably thinking about his future: his wedding, helping his mother, his fiancé, being financially stable, the children they may have. I don't know for sure, but I do know that he made the right decision...if he would've listened to me (hollering at the TV!), he would've stayed with good, but not better.

You may be a person like me –one who does not like to take risks, but I'm learning that they are necessary sometimes. Choosing to love someone is a risk, working a job is a risk, starting your own company is a risk, having children is a risk, investing is a risk, sharing your gifts with the world is a risk. People may not like what you're doing—they will always have opinions, but PRESS through anyway! Having a goal, a plan, a strategy, savings, people to encourage you, etc., is great, but sometimes you may find ourselves at a crossroad where we have to make a quick decision at that moment, like the man on the show. When it comes to that point you have to ask those questions "What do I want? Do I want more, Am I happy where I am?" (I'm talking to myself also right now). It's up to you...you may even lose something the first or second time, but to get something different you have to take risks! And, Yes! This is definitely a time when you cannot Overthink It!!!

AND NOW...

<u>Being Human</u>

Have you ever been in such deep thought that you were
staring off into the distance with a strange look on your
face, and then someone said "Hey, whatcha thinkin' about?"
and you were too embarrassed to say," Oh, I was thinking
about me flying in the sky with pink elephants and dancing
on colorful clouds that taste like banana and strawberry!"
No, you can't say that... so you just say, "Oh nothing, I was
just thinkin'..." (Yeah! About somethin' CRAZY! Lol!)

Chapter Seven
The Art of Being Me...
(and those who have to suffer because of it)

Me: I don't know if I'm supposed to write this book, people may think I'm crazy, silly, weird, and unstable...

God: You ARE crazy, silly, weird, and unstable sometimes...but you trust me to guide you through each moment. Write the book anyway!

<u>Being Me</u>

I was sitting across from my daughter the other day watching
a movie, and for some reason...I jumped up (startling her)
and started doing a ridiculously crazy, STUPID dance,
and ended it with some kind of silly outburst (this happens
often...). I don't even remember what I said, and there's
a big chance they were not understandable words.
She said, "Mom, you act like a black, female Jim Carrey..."
I said, "WOW! What a compliment!"

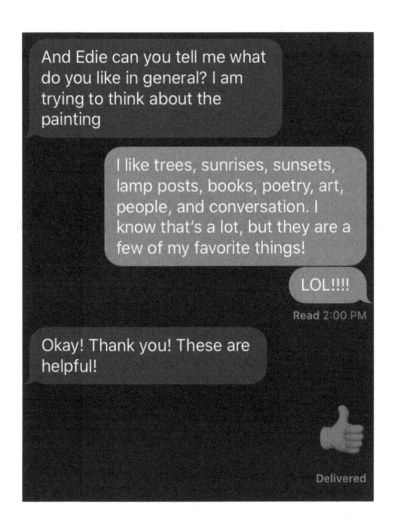

These Are a Few of my Favorite Things

I was once asked by an art student to send her a
text informing her of a few things about myself that
would better help her create a painting for me.
The text read: "I like trees, sunrises, sunsets, lamp posts,
books, poetry, art, people, and conversation." Now how
she'd make that into a painting...I don't know!

Mommy Dearest's Worst Nightmare!

Soo...I LOVINGLY tortured my girls when they
were young... I was a severe prankster.
And, since I may need protection when I'm older, and I need
witnesses...here are a few things one of my daughters said she'd
do to me when I get really old (because she's too afraid to do it
now, knowing that I'm still young enough to get her back, LOL!).

HER:
- KEEP MY PAMPER ON ALL DAY!
(Just go ahead and kill me...)
- PUSH ME DOWN THE STAIRS IN MY WHEELCHAIR
- PUSH ME IN MY WHEELCHAIR REALLY
FAST, AND THEN LET ME GO!

ME:
*"LORD JESUS, PLEASE...ALLOW ME TO LIVE A
LONG, WEALTHY, HEALTHY, MOBILE LIFE, AND
PROTECT ME FROM MY OFFSPRING!"*

The Art of Botheration

(Please don't turn me in to the authorities...it was all in fun!)

He just looked a little too pleasant lying beside her on the bed, and
she had to do something about it. Looking at him, she felt the warm,
tingly sensations of humor bubbling up inside of her, from the tips of
her toes to the center of her cranium cap. It felt like the un-numbing
of a leg after it has been sat on for a while, except without the painful
aftermath. Tiny little needles stabbing the top of her head in the most
delightful way. She stares at him for a while, trying to override the
whisper of her intellectual self. It's drowned out once again as the
right side of the brain is screaming...

Do it, do it! It'll be so funny and bring such pleasure to us!

The "us" is all of the billions of cells in her body, multiplying and being enthused with life-giving power as she awaits the joys to come. They tell her what to do and what to say at any given moment.

What shall we do? Look at him, so cute and comfortably watching television after a hard day's work. He deserves to rest...leave him alone!

Shut up Lefty, let Righty speak, now!

I started to talk to him and could quickly see by the shortness of his answers and frustrated look, that he was not in the mood for conversation. I proceeded forward. I began asking questions about the crime show he was watching.

"Why did he do that? Why did she look at him that way? Why would they say that?"

"I don't know, I just started watching the show," he said, with a slight touch of frustration—trying hard not to hurt my feelings.

It didn't matter to me if he did, there already were too many endorphins scattering around inside of my entire being. Crazily they buzzed about inside my veins as my plans began to unfold. Like a mathematician with chalk in hand busily working magic on the board, or a painter holding the brush in anticipation of the design. My victim is my canvas.

"Can you just watch the show? You know just as much as I do at this point. If you just watch, you might find out the answers to your questions, Dear," he said sarcastically.

"Okay," I said, but they were overpowering now.

What could I do? Should I press on and run the risk of being annoying or aggravate him further?... Of course!

As I turned away for a moment to face the TV, I'm sure he thought, "Great, maybe she'll leave me alone now."

Nope!

I slowly turned towards him again—his eyes looking even more intense as he relaxed himself more into the comfort of the king sized, heavily pillowed bed, confident that he'd enjoy the rest of the show in quietness. In a low conversational tone, I spoke...

"Oh, yeah...I think that's a good idea, maybe we can do that tomorrow."

Looking at me strangely, "What did you say?"

"Oh, nothing," I said.

He continued to watch the show.

"It's up to you though...I'll have to ask my husband first," she said to his Ear.

"What? You did say something... what are you talking about? That's annoying!"

"Oh, don't worry about it, I'm not talking to you."

"What?! Stop playin, you're making me miss my show!"

"Watch it then, I'm not even talking to you."

He angrily turned his back to watching the TV.

I know that I am walking on thin ice. I look intently at his ear, focusing on it like it's a human being: a separate entity of its own, attached to the side of his head. I speak again...

"Really?! You think so? I'm gonna have to think about it..."

"Okay, stop!"

"Stop what? I told you, I'm not talking to you, so stop being rude and interrupting our conversation. It has nothing to do with you!"

They are totally out of control now, they have taken over, I am completely overtaken. There's no stopping me: I'm committed!

"Would you please, stop! You play too much!"

"You just watch your show and let me and EAR talk!"

"Ear?... What are you doing? That's weird Edie! What do you mean, ear?"

I snuggled in closer to EAR, whispering to him—this separate entity who had nothing to do with Charles at all.

"Ear...I'm talking to him, not you."

I lovingly touched Ear, and said to him, "You are so perfectly shaped and such a good listener, I appreciate that."

Pausing the TV show and beginning to laugh, Charles tried nudging me away from his ear.

"Edie, Stop picking! Stop acting crazy! What's wrong with you?!"

I continued… "Don't pay him any attention, Ear, he doesn't understand our relationship."

Laughing hysterically now, Charles surrendered and looked at his annoying, crazy, insane wife, filled with the "Art of Botheration," smiles at her and says, "You are so annoying! Why can't you just stop?! You know…you could have a PhD in Pickology, if it were a study."

I, tingling with exuberance and laughter, said goodnight to Ear, kissed her husband, and said…

"You give me such joy allowing me to lovingly torture you all of the time, Charles. Thank you for letting me be me." Oh, and we finished the TV show together. I was relieved now. I got it all out of my system.

The very next day, I looked at him and asked him a question, and while not even looking at me, he responded by saying, "No!" to the question.

"I'm not talking to you," I said. He immediately covered the ear that was facing me and started shaking his head back and forth in fear, begging me with his eyes, to not start this up again. I acquiesced, for now…

Just a Little too Far… Ya think?!

When Tatiana was around six years old, I got into an intensive game of hide and seek with her. "Ready or not here I come, Mommy." She sounded so cute with her sweet, soft voice. I giggled as I peeked through the cracked closet door, making sure that I could still hear her. *Plat, Plat, Plat, Plat, Plat,* was the consistency of her short, little feet across the hard wood floors. The running seemed to never stop. She was very persistent trying not to give up. Soon the pursuit dwindled. "Mommy, where are you?

I continued to giggle more and more, being careful that she wouldn't hear me.

"Mommy…I can't find you." Her voice lost a little something now, but I continued to laugh.

"Mommy…"

Yeah, it had definitely changed from the happy little child who was joyously on a journey to find her mommy who she thought was only hiding from her for a moment. That was her first mistake! Never, never assume when it comes to my art. Now don't get me wrong, I was a good mom. I taught my girls their ABC's, their numbers, their house address, telephone number, and how to spell their names at an early age. I'd soon find out another thing I'd forgotten that I taught them.

"Mommy, I can't find you…"

I could hear the pitter patter of happy feet slowing down now, and strategically planning out their next steps. To the other closet they anxiously went, hoping to find me. Then, to the bathroom, and the bedroom again…nothing. Oh, I forgot to mention, she did open the door and stare into the closet that I was in, but I hid myself underneath a pile of clothes, making sure that she wouldn't find me. As she closed the door, my laughter lightened up a bit, but it was still there sitting right in the middle of my gut, egging me on! There it was again! One side of me saying, "Okay, Edie that's enough, she's getting scared now, come out of the closet." But, the other side of me, the side that likes to hold on to the laughter for as long as possible, waited too late. All of a sudden, I noticed that she wasn't walking around anymore. *Boop, boop, boop…* I heard this familiar rhythm before. No! She couldn't have, she didn't do that did she?! Tatiana! Where are you, what are you doing?!

It's funny how the tables have turned, isn't it?

Where are you, Tatiana? I threw all of the clothes off of me and started down the hallway trying to find HER now! There she was hunched over in the middle of the kitchen floor with the phone in her short, stubby hands. I was a good mommy, I taught my children that if they're ever scared, and can't find mommy or daddy, and if mommy or daddy are hurt and need help, or if they need help, call 9-1-1. Needless to say, I'm not proud of this, but it was hilarious at the time, well…up until the *boop, boop, boop* sound, anyway.

"Why did you call 9-1-1 Tatiana?!"

Duh... I knew why.

"Cuz I couldn't find you, mommy, and I was scared."

I quickly got on the phone, but it was too late! The officers showed up quickly. While I was explaining myself to the officers, Charles was just pulling up from work. What a mess I'd gotten myself into, and all for the joy of laughter. But it wasn't MY fault, it was theirs, you know...those bloated cells inside of me I told you about—controlling me with their wicked need to feed off of others for their own fulfillment until they themselves become full, remember? Like ticks on a fat dog who gladly lays around all day, they sumptuously feed.

The officers were very understanding; they laughed it off and told me to be more careful next time, but I had to explain to my child that her mommy went too far and that she should have come out of hiding a little sooner. Trying to explain to your baby, that her mother was acting like a big baby, and laughing at her pain, was pretty humbling, and embarrassing. Of course, she instantly forgave me, like most children do, especially Tatiana. She was very forgiving, and still is as I sit across the table from her in Starbucks laughing with her about that awesome (for me), terrifying (for her) day. Much to my surprise, Charles took it well also. He did another one of those shaking of the head things, and looked at me strangely, saying "What is wrong with you?"

"I don't know...I was playing hide and seek, and it was funny hearing her run around looking for me and listening to her little feet and her cute voice, and I just took too long to come out, I guess." I sounded like a child trying to explain to her parent why she was caught with her hand in the cookie jar! Listening to myself explain, I realized that my actions didn't justify the means, but I'm sad to say that I have done even worse after that (Oh, my...I'm giggling inside as I write this), shame on me! Within minutes, Tatiana was back to her happy, smiling self, embracing me with a hug, with those short munchy arms of unconditional love. Her father, on the other hand, was still looking at me like a creature from another planet for the rest of the day, BUT...I tell you the truth with accepting love in his

EDIE BOWMAN

eyes. He was probably thinking, "Who did I marry? I need to get this woman out of the house!"

"Hee-Hee-Hee" (By the way...that's my sneaky laugh in case you didn't understand).

When the Word "Surprise" Gives you Pause

One day Tatiana, Autumn, and I were getting ready to leave the salon where I worked. Before, we walked out of the door, in the corner on the floor, I saw a large, interesting looking, dead bug. I later found out that the bug was a locust, and that they only come around every seven years. I, being the weird person that I am, quickly picked it up by its wing, only because it was dead, though... and began to study it. The wings were quite colorful, and its body was round and crunchy from death. I tried to show the girls, but of course, they screamed, "No, Mommy, No!" I decided that I wanted to take this amazing little discovery of mine home to further explore its wonder. The girls...not so much. I energetically ripped off a couple of paper towels and ever-so gently placed the locust in the middle of the paper towel, leaving plenty of space around it, not to damage its structure. I carried the creature with great care, pinching the paper towel at the top making sure that it would not open. We walked down that long road called Fulton, lined with beautiful green trees and a mild zephyr that made us feel at ease. On our walk, I shared with the girls my plans that had suddenly arrived in my bothered mind.

"Hey girls," I said devilishly. "Why don't I put this under Jazzmin's (my oldest daughter who was a teenager) pillow and tell her that I have something for her when she gets home from school?" Seeing the humor in it, they laughed with me as we got closer to home. Now, mind you, if it were one of them that I was going to do that to, they would've been totally against such an evil act of love. We unlocked the door to our home with such anticipation of the secret we were holding within ourselves waiting to be unleashed upon our sweet, loving sister/daughter.

"*Hee-Hee-Hee.*"

It was almost time for her to get home, so I drilled the girls for one final time on how to act "normal" when she got here.

"Don't, giggle or start smiling when she gets in the house, that will give it away!"

After all, this was serious business to me, the plan had to reach its full climax, or I would have failed.

We heard the keys in the door. "Hey Jazzmin!"

"Hey!"

"How was your day at school?"

"It was okay, I have a lot of homework, though," she said, while kissing and hugging the girls. She's six years older than Tatiana, and 9 years older than Autumn, and they treated her like a big sister, but often like a second mom.

"Oh, well I may have something to cheer you up a bit. I have a surprise for you."

Because she was used to my double-minded, two-fold trickery she had her apprehensions. You see…although my left and right side of the brain are in constant hostility, they know both the logic and artistry of every bothersome act. They analyze and create at the same time: creating and expressing comical moments with those I love, knowing that one day they will nostalgically be called to our remembrance. At the same time, the brain is using the ability to logically and strategically plan out each step, contemplating the responses of each individual or group before-hand, in order to perfect every detail to bring about the best results.

"A surprise…Edie, what do you mean a surprise, what did you do?"

"Jazzmin, it's a surprise, I'm not going to tell you what it is, that'll spoil it. It's something you'll like, I promise."

I cautiously eyed Tatiana and Autumn with a gentle grimace to ensure that they did not respond facially to what I had just said.

"Girls, what did she do? What is the surprise?"

Trying not to give it away, Tatiana turned away, not to reveal her smiley face. I don't think Autumn, said much at all. She usually mimicked whatever Tatiana said and did.

Tatiana, very unconvincingly said, "You'll like it Jazzmin!" I'm sure this was parroted by Autumn.

"Jazzmin, whenever you want to see it, just go upstairs and it's up there waiting for you on the bed."

"Edie, No! What is it?"

"Jazzmin, I'm not going to tell you anything else, it's a surprise, just go look, I got it for you!"

"I'm not going up there."

"You gotta go see it Jazzmin, you'll like it," Tatiana said.

"You'll like it Jazzmin," echoed Autumn.

Shame on me for involving her little sisters as culprits. *"Hee-Hee-Hee"* seriously though…shame (*not really*).

"Jazzmin, you have to go up there for bed eventually… it's okay, it's a gift. If you don't like it, you don't have to keep it."

A few hours later after dinner, and after actively avoiding her room, she finally went to her room.

"I'm going to my room, Edie!"

The girls and I (I…being a 30 something year old woman with an eight-year-old on one side, and a 5-and-a-half-year-old on the other) gathered together in a huddle in the living room, bubbling over with quiet laughter at what was to come.

"Okay, let me know if you like it.""

It was about 30 seconds of silence for what seemed like an eternity as she looked around her room. Then she anxiously reported again,

"I don't see anything…what is it, Edie. I'm telling daddy!"

What she should've known by now was that her father, had given up. He'd long ago come to the truth that what he thought about my "gift" really didn't matter at all…they were ALL mine now! *"HeeHeeHee…"* You get the point, I'm lovingly wicked!

Suddenly, it happened, the moment I'd been waiting for, well… the little ones too, but they were just pieces in my twisted game.

"What is that?!" She said hysterically, "Edie!!!... Edie!!! What is it?! Why would you do that?!"

She ran down the stairs, red faced and looking at me with

awfulness and unbelief. Well…kind of, for she knew me all too well. She found the three of us, her family, enjoying every minute.

"I can't believe you'd do that; you know I hate bugs! Tatiana and Autumn, you knew, too?!

"Yes" (giggles).

We were a united front.

Jazzmin's shock subsided and turned into laughter.

"I can't believe you guys…"

We all couldn't wait for Charles to get home to tell him the joyous tragedy.

I'm sure you can imagine by now, that he shook his head, looked at me in disbelief, and total belief, and said once again, "What is wrong with you, ya nut? Why are you torturing our kids?" Then, like the loving, trusting man that he is towards me, he rested…or should I say relented or succumbed, to the art of botheration. Fourteen years later, this story comes up when were all together, and there is nothing but smiles, laughs, and a little fear. I guess I should mention that if I ever say the words, "I have a surprise for you," my children don't rejoice, Oh No…they stand afar off and take a moment to think deeply, first—very deeply.

Impulsive Demonstrations of Relief

(Yeah, that's a better sounding way to describe my…shall we say, "artwork?")

One day, Autumn and I were in the living room watching a movie. She was in her dad's recliner, and I was directly across from her on the couch. The movie must have been sad, heart wrenching, or just did not have the outcome that I thought it should have had. Perhaps, someone died of cancer when I thought that they'd survive. Maybe, an abusive boyfriend got away with murder. Or…possibly, it was about a man who secretly loved a girl since kindergarten, he sees her 30 years later and finally gathers up the courage to tell her when he sees her from afar at a local diner, the one he visits every Tuesday. Suddenly, he gets hit by a Mac truck as he's crossing the street to tell her.

Honestly, I don't know what the movie was about, but I did not like the outcome, so I jumped up off of the couch to my feet with a loud growl and chilling scream, grabbed the pillow that I was laying on, and began to beat it, and holler at it, and scream at it, and stomp it on the ground, and bite it, and kick it across the room, and pull on it to rip it apart, and stomp it again, and tell it how much I hated it, and loathe it, and despise the pillow, and how much I wish that I could destroy it.

"Ugh!" "You mess up EVERYTHING!" I screamed.

And In a state of total confusion and surprise, Autumn asked, "Mom, what are you doing?! I'm recording you; someone needs to know how crazy you are!"

Breathing heavily, and with a contorted face that looked the part of a mass murderer sadistically enjoying her display of wrath, I replied, "This pillow is the Devil and Sin all bundled up in one, and I'm beating them up, UGH!" I threw Sin and the Devil on the couch and continued to pummel them like John in the John Wick movie: Part 3!

I continued until the powerful feeling seething through my entire body subsided. I ended up on the floor on my hands and knees panting like a thirsty dog who had just finished the fight of his life and won. Autumn...my poor...poor... Autumn, she stared at me for a moment, reminded me that I was recorded, and continued the evening like nothing ever happened. Me...I sat back down on the couch, still in the moment, and continued to slowly decrease my fierce breathing until the feeling passed. The pillow? It was across the room, crumpled and murdered.

Fortunately, I have these random bouts of creative energy that bring freedom and relief on a regular basis, sometimes whether others are around or not...now that even frightens me...even me. I see God in these Moments too, because we still talk about them today, and we Laugh!

Hollerin' at the TV!

Have you ever found yourself talking to the TV? I find myself doing this regularly. I actually have had full-fledged conversations with the TV! Well...I guess in order to really have a conversation there has to be another party listening and responding to you, so...what am I doing then? Why am I not giving any thought to my intellectual side?... I know they can't hear me, and yet I still talk to the people on the screen. I give the people on the screen advice, instructions, I get frustrated with them... I even get angry with them. Oh, and don't let it be the singing competition, *The Voice* because I have all kinds of critiques to give them! I'm like, "Oh No... you picked the wrong song...you should've picked a song that showed your range a little more...It's too boring, you need some high notes in there, this is your shot, why did you pick that song?!"

My husband is usually beside me saying, "Would you just be quiet and watch the show?! You don't have to critique everything Edie, just enjoy it!" It was so hard for me to just sit back and enjoy it!

When *American Idol* first came out, I used to get angry and fuss at the judges saying, "Why are you letting America judge?! You're the experts! The people of America don't know what they're doing, they'll pick a person because they're cute, and best singer/entertainer will lose because he/she is a little chubby! That's not right! You guys are the ones who should be making these decisions, especially at the end!" I'd yell.

If I'm watching a thriller (that's the closest I get to a scary movie), I get so upset with characters that fall all of the time, I say things like, "Are you falling again, Becky?! Yaw'l should just leave her, she's getting on my nerves!" or, "Here we go again...does anyone EVER have a decent car that starts whenever you turn on the ignition in one of these movies?...See this is the kind of stuff that makes me mad?!" Now, of course I know that these kinds of movies wouldn't be good if they had no conflict: people falling, cars not starting, the overly inquisitive guy or gal who just has to go back in the dark haunted house to see if they heard a noise... but come on people!!! All of the time?! I guess I could never write a scary movie because it would be over in ten minutes. It would go something like this...

A group of six friends find themselves on a dark road, they call 911, because out of 6 people someone's phone has got to work, Right?!...While they wait, they see a man with a chain saw, Jim Bob takes out his gun and shoots him. Susan is cold so she wants to leave the car and find shelter in an old, abandoned mansion on the hill. The rest of her friends let Susan go BY HERSELF... to the mansion. As she's on her way she sees a little girl in a dirty white sheet-like dress staring at her. Susan decides to run back to the car with her friends, and she DOES NOT FALL! They all welcome her back with open arms and assures her that they would not have left her, except Gary... Gary tells her, "If you do something dumb like that again, I will leave you up there and fight everyone who disagrees with me, you big Dummy!" (he'd do it too, because he's a big dude and he can care less what you think!) Suddenly, they see the little girl appear in front of their car. Susan says, "Hey guys that's the little girl I saw up the hill!" James pulls out his gun and shoots her! (All the guys have a gun—They Don't Play!)

"Why would you do that?!" Gary yelled.

"We have to help her, she's just a child...I'll see if she's still alive" Gracie said. She gets out of the car and walks towards the girl.

"If you don't get back in this car right now, I'll shoot you too! She could be a zombie and infect you, and then you'll try to kill us!" Gary yelled (GRACIE GOT BACK IN THE CAR).

Behind them appears a man with a white mask on his face. Jim Bob shoots him! He gets up again...Jim Bob, along with his brother John, shoots him three more times (THE MASKED MAN STAYED DEAD). Three possessed looking wolf-like dogs come towards them...police sirens are heard (which is awesome and highly unusual because in these types of movies they usually don't come until you've done all of the work, and you don't need them anymore)! The little girl rises again... but Marcy was praying that the Lord would protect them, so she told the demon spirit to "GO! In Jesus' name!" and the little girl ran away. The policemen arrived in enough time to kill the devil dogs, because at midnight they'd be indestructible. One of the police officers got the car started, and they all drove home safely. THE END.

My girls like watching things like *16 and Pregnant* or *Teen Moms*—reality shows that follow the lives of four or five teen moms and their hardships and triumphs. I, being a mother of three girls, always jump into motherly teaching moments while watching these kinds of shows with the girls. I'd yell things at the TV, like "Why would you do this?! You know he doesn't love you if he got another girl pregnant at the same time! Why are you taking him back?!"

My girls are rolling their eyes and laughing at me. "Mom, calm down!" they'd say.

"Why is she putting herself through this again? Now she's bringing home another baby for her parents to have to worry about taking care of?... Yaw'l better not do that! That's just selfish!"

They'd say, "We know mom! Why are you trippin?! It's a TV show..."

"Yeah, but it's real and it could happen to you!" I'd say... "If you choose to start having sex and not to do things God's way...then you better use some birth control! Your dad and I are not going to be at home rockin no babies! We are going to be living life! We done raised yaw'l!" (I know it's broken English, but it feels better comin out that way!)

While giggling, they'd say "Wow! Okay, mom! We know...we know... you've only said this since we were three years old!" (that's an overstatement, but you get the point!)

Now, back to me talking to the TV... "Why won't you go back to school and use some birth control sweetheart? You can make it, tell that boy to go on somewhere, if he doesn't mean you any good! If he wants you, he'll get a job, a car, some savings, and a place to stay, and then think about dating you!" Yes, and I meant every word.

God uses me in Moments like these...it may be a little dramatic, and seen as a blessing for me to share wisdom, but to them...well, you can imagine.

Margins...Asterisks... Red Pens, and Ellipses...

Everything matters to me it seems, and it's exhausting. I overthink just about everything and it takes me long to make simple decisions. I realize that this can be very frustrating to those around me (I apologize family and friends...). Giving me a lot of options is dangerous! For me to go to a restaurant that has a plethora of delectable food items on the menu is like setting an array of newly found vibrant colors in front of Vincent van Gogh, and then asking him to only choose one quickly.

Red pens are A Must!!! If you were to borrow a book from me, you'd open it and swear that someone almost bled to death while reading it, because there'd be an abundance of underlined sentences, asterisks, and notes in the margins all done in red pen. When I was in college, I was instructed by my peers and some professors to take advantage of skimming and focusing on the main ideas of the readings, because there was just too much to read in light of all of my classes combined. This was so very hard for me; I wanted to know EVERYTHING!!! I did not want to miss out on anything in any class. It was ALL very important to me, thus all of the red ink on every other page!

It's frustrating to limit myself to focusing on only the "important" things. Wasn't it all important? If a person took the time to write it down in a book doesn't that prove that it was worth reading? I soon found out that it was extremely difficult to read everything that I wanted to, but I'm sure that I managed to read around 80% of everything. It ALL mattered to me. Oh, and the asterisks... you'll find them everywhere! I even have a system of how I use them. If there is one asterisk at the beginning of a sentence, it was important. If there were two, it was very important, and if there were three asterisks in front of a sentence...then Wow, it was life-changing to me!

As you can see by now...I absolutely LOVE using ellipses also, because I'm always thinking. Even when the conversation, the book, the movie, the musical, the argument, the message, the meeting, the play, show, the WHATEVER...is over! I'm still thinking about it and want to talk about it!

I have come to the conclusion that I have to be me even if it is a little overboard sometimes (well...most of the time). If I like to write my own mini book in the margins of an already written book, then I will. If I have panic attacks because I can't find a red pen anywhere when I'm reading, and I just can't manage to continue without it, then I'll wait. If it takes me an extra ten minutes to read a page because I refuse to turn the page until I've defined words that I don't understand, then so be it. If I read a paragraph three times to get everything out of it that I can, then that's okay. If I pause, stare off into the distance with a pensive look on my face, don't think it strange, because to me...almost Everything Matters.

Just the other day I told Charles that I had a surprise for him, and he and Tatiana started shaking their heads in fear saying "No! No! What is it, what did you do?!"

I told him I'd give it to him at 8:00 pm. I knew that would add to the suspense.

At exactly 8:00 pm I handed him a small pack of peanut butter M&M's. He doesn't eat sweets a lot—the day before he talked about having a taste for some, so I got them! Why all of the drama?!!! (Hee-Hee-Hee!)

AND NOW...

<u>Being Human</u>

Last night, my husband had just fallen to sleep...
he did one of those loud, short, snort sounding snores
(a little alliteration there...). He abruptly woke himself
up while holding his chest, staring at me in confusion,
and saying "What was that?! What happened? ..."
I said, "Nothing, that was you...you made a loud snoring
sound and woke yourself up!" He instantly fell back to
sleep, and all was well. IT WAS FUNNY THOUGH!

Chapter Eight
Just Thinking...

Ok, Soo...I think A LOT! This whole book is about thoughts—imaginative ones crazy thoughts, serious thoughts, dreams, hopes, fears, God, the Devil, men, women, children...you name it! The thinking never ends!!!! I'm happy about that, because once the thoughts end, I'm no longer me...and that's just sad. I'm kind of like that Twizzler commercial where the guy stares out of the window with a concerned, contemplating, look on his face and says, "There's just no easy answers. Am I too old to start skateboarding?" Yep, that's me! I'm always thinking about something...So, here's some more of my thoughts—Enter in, if you dare...LOL!

When I was little, I didn't understand why I had to make my bed every morning. I would think about it regularly—it just didn't make sense to me." I'm just going to mess it up again tonight, mommy" I'd say. Now I can't stand to leave my bed un-made in the morning, it bothers me deeply...my how things have changed.

Thinking...

I'm sitting in the dining room in front of a fish tank, with not quite enough water in it, which causes the sound of the water in it to be magnified.
I'm Thinking...
The sound of water can be ever soo relaxing and calming...it can also be repetitive and Annoying!

Bathroom Epiphanies

While in the shower this morning, I found myself complaining about the things we need fixed in the house. I started to get frustrated, I thought to myself, *The tub needs work, the kitchen ceiling is dripping, the piping needs done, the hallway wall is peeling, the door- knob is loose, the house is too small...* etc.
Then, I had another thought...
I have water to drink, a shower, and a tub to bathe in, shelter to protect me from the outside elements, a kitchen that I can cook in, a door that invites the fellowship of friends, a family whose hands have countlessly touched these cracked walls while imprinting timeless memories, and love that makes a home worth living in. Contentment and patience are the glasses through which change of mind comes.
Side Note: (Why is it usually in the shower, or on the toilet that I usually have some of my deepest thoughts?)

Sayings I Think About...

"For the love of Pete"
I hope the person who came up with this one didn't do it after "For the love of God" came out. What would be the point...who can top that?!

"What the Sam Hill?!"
Perhaps Sam Hill was a menace in a small country town who as a result of his behavior...procured a name for himself that became a saying that people used when aggravated by something or someone—kind of like Ernest T. Bass on "The Andy Griffith Show."

"Kill two birds with one stone"
I get the concept of getting two things done at the same time, but why would we want to kill them? Were they killer birds? Were they running after you and you needed to defend yourself from them?

"Any minute now..."
I have experienced many instances where a person said something would take place "any minute now..." and that thing happened three hours later! There should be a caveat added to that saying stating that if you're not certain that the situation at hand will take place in less than fifty-nine minutes, then you cannot use that saying—It is has now become an hour or more...

"Home...sweet home"
Uh...I'm sorry but some people would argue that—they're more like, "Phew! Home...do I have to go home...?"

"I'm right around the corner."
You're probably giggling right now...you know those people who say this regularly—they're always late! That must be a Loooong and Wiiiide corner!

"A bird in the hand is better than two in the bush."
Hmm...not if you're holding a boring looking little finch, and you'd rather be watching the two beautiful red cardinals that you see in that bush.

"It goes without saying."
Then why do we say IT, right after saying "IT goes without saying"?

"I'm lost for words."
Well...only if we actually say Nothing, after saying that!

"Now, enough is enough!"
But, isn't just saying "enough" actually... Enough said?

"You can't have your cake and eat it too"
Then…what's the point of having the cake in the
first place, just to sit there and look pretty?

"I Looked him/her in the eye"
Unless the person only has ONE eye like Mike Wazowski in
the *Monsters Inc.* movie, why would we do that? Shouldn't
we look them in both eyes? Should we ask the person to
cover one eye so that this saying can make sense?!

Why does Everything become STUPID when I'm frustrated? I'm like...

UGH…STUPID shirt! You're too small!
STUPID lady! Why did you dart in front of
me, then drive twenty miles per hour?!
I hate this STUPID store! They never have enough
cashiers… I need my Cheese curls!
I wouldn't have twisted my ankle if I hadn't
stepped on that STUPID rock!
This STUPID knee! Keep giving out on
me when I go up these steps!
STUPID hair! Why do you have to look
STUPID today? I have to take pictures!
(Dare I say, God is there in the STUPID Moments of life? Yep!)

"AAACHOOOOOO!!!!!!!!!!"

*Have you ever sneezed so hard and loud that you got angry
with your OWN self?... I mean, it felt like you cracked
a rib or shattered your chest cavity or something!*

WE STINK!

(Ok, so…this is weird)

Last night, I opened up a small notebook of mine that I keep beside my bed to write down random thoughts. I have so many notebooks like this lying around, that I wasn't surprised I had only written on the first page. It read…

12/25/18

Soo…it's Christmas morning, 8:30am. I (being my weird and silly self) was lying in the bed when I suddenly said to Charles, "You Stink! So, **I'M** going to take a shower." LOL!!! (Not that he really did stink, I just wanted to say something crazy, that didn't make any sense at all, to get a reaction from hm). Of course, he gave me that usual "My wife's insane…" look. We started laughing, but then I realized that that is The Gospel! WE STINK because of the sin on our lives, but God sent His Son to die in OUR place—to take a shower for us on OUR behalf, to cleanse us from OUR sins. WE STINK, so GOD sent JESUS to take a shower for us! It sounds really weird, but think about it…

My Wish List

1. I wish that sunrises and sunsets could last for hours, and that they'd always have shades of blue.
2. I wish that I could transport myself from one place to another in a matter of seconds so that I wouldn't have to miss things that I enjoy, nor the special moments in the lives of people I love, no matter where they are.
3. I wish that I could afford any piece of art that I desire and have a room large enough to admire them whenever I want to.
4. I wish passing gas was odorless and silent all of the time so that I could allow it to escape freely…uninhibited…often.

5. I wish that I were fearless at all times and possessed an equal amount of discretion and prudence to match it.

6. I wish that when we speak from our hearts, someone is always there to listen, understand, and help if that is what's desired.

7. I wish that I had the inability to think or speak negatively, though that may be annoying to some around me...or maybe even myself...hmm...I'll have to think about that one some more.

8. I wish that dogs didn't poop, pee, or shed, and that they'd always smell good, even when wet, then I'd probably get one. Oh! They can't NEED to be walked either...okay, so I basically want a stuffed animal that happens to be a dog, that can eat, sleep, cuddle, and play, and need walked occasionally, that's it! That's reasonable, RIGHT?!...

9. I wish that I didn't overthink, just about everything. It's exhausting!

10. I wish eating ice cream would cause me to become healthier and lose weight. I know this thought is not ingenious, but oh how I wish it to be so. A girl can dream...

11. I wish Sin and Death were persons that we could murder with a machine gun once and for all, and that ALL guns would vanish, never to return in any form whatsoever.

12. I wish that I could live in an actual wholesome, simplistic place like "Mayberry," (but with a few more people of color, Lol!) where everybody knows and trusts their neighbors, we go to church on Sundays, and purposefully teach what "the good book" says to our children. We eat supper around the table with our families, have picnics, church socials, and go fishing at the creek. Where going to the dance with your sweetheart, kissin', and writing your names on the old oak tree with a heart around it, was known as an awesome date! Where the worst crime is making moonshine, and where having a town drunk was soo rare that he'd be treated with tenderness, and respect, like Otis. A place where we all sit on the porch swing and relax in the evening, and later walk down to the corner store to get a bottle of pop.

13. I wish this Coronavirus would become best friends with Cancer, that Cancer would become jealous of it and kill it, and as a result of being around it... contract the virus and therefore be destroyed itself! FOREVER!!!!!

Allow Me This Little Rant...

Why do people who LOVE their cats, perhaps other animals too, but mainly cats... allow them to freely roam about as they please like everybody enjoys them? They sit on the porches of homes where they're unwelcome, lie on their outdoor furniture leaving unwanted fur, insects, and who knows what else... take naps on your swings and decks, and then get an attitude when you shoo them away, LOL! The Nerve! Hey, cat lovers! YOU bought the cat, you feed the cat, it "LIVES" with you...I don't hate them, and I've owned a couple myself, but at the present time I don't prefer to have a pet, so why do people insist on sharing yours with me against my will? Why won't you keep them in YOUR house? And don't use the "cute" excuse to make me feel bad: "Oh, well little Garfield likes to get out sometimes to get some fresh air and explore the neighborhood before coming home at night...he's a little ornery." "Well, can his exploration not take place in my trash, on my porch, on my roof, underneath and on my car, please?" (Lord, I know you made animals for us to love, take care of, and enjoy, but can I enjoy them when I want to—on my own terms? These cats be trippin' as bad as these squirrels do!) Lol!

TO ASSUME NOTHING

I was just thinking...in light of all of the shootings that are happening in our cities, and all of the riots, looting, and violent protests that are happening as a result of them...we should ALWAYS seek the facts and the truth first! It's human nature to react emotionally when we hear of, and see the loss of human lives, but we MUST get all the information possible before we come to a conclusion. 'Assume Nothing' is the mindset that I am trying to keep. I have to train myself to think fairly and wisely and not to allow my emotions to rule my judgment. I must wait until the evidence is fully presented from all sides. This is challenging at times, especially when what I see seems pretty cut-and-dry. I must remember that the "truth" is often muddied depending on the motive of the ones telling it at the time. Assume Nothing...

Sometimes Ya Gotta Laugh to Keep From Crying

I was just thinking about the moment in the car that my husband and I had with our grandchildren today, and I began to laugh again. Ali is eight and A.J. is six. We were on our way to Cracker Barrel, and we happened to pass a McDonald's. A.J. had just expressed to us how "some" people are afraid of clowns. "They just do not like them too much," he said.

This is how the conversation went down...

Charles (Paw-Paw): Hey, yaw'l remember Ronald McDonald?
Ali: yes... (she didn't sound convincing)
A.J.: No
Me (Nana): They probably haven't, because they don't talk about him the way they used to when we were young.
Charles (Paw-Paw): What?! Yaw'l don't remember Ronald McDonald?
A.J.: (with a nonchalant look on his face and his hands in the air) I think Corona probably took him away...
Paw-Paw & Nana: (we didn't know how to respond...it was an awkward moment, but it was strangely funny too. We Secretly gave each other the side eye, and Secretly started cracking up!).

While this was a serious topic, and we assured him this wasn't the case with Ronald...the look on his face was hilarious! We weren't laughing at the issue, but at his face and hand gestures! A.J. loves to talk, can hang with you on any subject, and he is quite comedic! "He has to talk and ask questions all the time like his Nana," Charles always says. Ali was just looking at him like "here he goes again, talking…"

We needed that comedic relief, even though it came in the strangest way. But… it also reminded me of how children need assurance in these times of uncertainty.

We all put our masks on and went into the restaurant. We spent time talking to them about people that they knew that had passed away recently from gun violence and/or sicknesses. We encouraged them to pray for people to stop hurting other people, and we asked them about good things they remember about loved ones who have passed away. We laughed a whole a lot, talked about Ali's dance classes, A.J.'s wanting to play basketball or soccer, and we all expressed our hope that we'd be able to be together again soon.

To Clap or Not To Clap?

I was just thinking…sometimes I get bored of just clapping when I'm excited about something or feel emotionally connected to something that is happening in the moment. Is there something else we can do instead of clapping? The next time we hear an awesome speaker or are enjoying a performance of some kind, could we stand up and jump in place, or maybe spin in circles instead of clapping? Perhaps we could burst out in song when we like something, but it has to be a particular type of song, let's see…how about opera? Yeah! Or better yet, we could just start yodeling right there in our seats. Yeah, that'll work!

Can you imagine that you're at a black tie, dignified event, and the speaker moves you so much that you start yodeling?! How freeing is that?! When asked (as you're being escorted out of the building), "Why were you displaying such behavior at an event like this? Don't you know how to act?!" your response should be, "Ya know, officer… sometimes ya just gotta do something different, and I'm tired of just clapping?!" And wouldn't it be so cool if the officer excitedly agreed with you and reacted by singing "Ave Maria" in a high, Pavarotti-like, tenor voice?!

You Never Cease to Amaze

Just thinking…does anyone else think that Sea Horses are some of the strangest, most fantastical, mysterious, coolest, little creatures ever?! Every time I go to the aquarium, I stare at them in amazement and wonder, What?... Why? ... How?... Then, I remember who God is.

AND NOW….

__Being Human__

Have you ever dreamed that you were playing in a swimming
pool, drinking an endless glass of refreshing water, or
sitting on the toilet emptying out what seems to be gallons
of water, only to wake up and find yourself still in the bed...
laying in something that is NOT water? TRAGEDY...

Chapter Nine
Things to Consider...

One thing that life is teaching me is to be more understanding of others: their experiences, opinions, points of views, and their beliefs. We are all different, and what we have gone through has shaped us, formed our ways of thinking, and many of our decisions. I count it a privilege to have been raised as a Christian in my teen years. I also count it a privilege to NOT have been around Christians my whole life. This has allowed me to experience all types of people, ways of living, different types of music, family structures, the good, the bad, and the ugly. All of it has made me better able to relate to people. Regardless of our personal stories, there is one thing that we can all do to make sure, that as human beings, we are all respected. Regardless of a persons' nationality, financial status, religion, sex, sexual orientation, or age, we can ALL give each other the right to be SEEN & HEARD. We all have a story to tell, and we all have a point of view. We all hurt, laugh, cry, bleed, make mistakes, change our minds, and have done things we regret. May these stories show our humanity and help us see ourselves and others.

Drive Unto Others...

I'm usually an on-time person...actually, I'm rarely ever late, so on the rare occasion that I'm running late, I get really aggravated when someone drives in front of me AT A SNAIL'S PACE!

I don't honk my horn at them (*that* can get you shot now a days), but boy am I letting them have it in the car! I'm not a yeller or a screamer, but I have been known to speak with great passion when frustrated. I say things like "C'mon! Why are you soooo slow! This is ridiculous... REALLY?!" things like that—nothing too alarming to the ears.

So, this happened the other day. It was like the driver knew I was running late—like she waited around the corner for me with evil in her heart! I got into the other lane, passing the driver up, but what I shouldn't have done was looked at the driver…it was a little short old lady with white hair. She could barely see over the steering wheel. *She probably has no one else to drive her around,* I thought to myself. I felt like the scum of the earth (well…not that bad, but bad)! I spoke out loud to the Lord in the car, "I'm so sorry for that Lord…I might be old one day and have no one to take me around. My own mother, or another older lady that I love, may be in this same position one day." She didn't know that I passed her up and angrily got in front of her, but I knew it! I kept looking at her in my rearview mirror apologizing to her in my mind. The irony is, I've noticed a lot more older people passing me up on the road lately—have you? Sometimes I've had to move over into the next lane…You reap what you sow. Oh, the Irony….

Mouth to Mouth Resuscitation

Why did they wait so long to revive her, to breathe life back into her parched existence? The same monotonous routine smothered her daily: Shirley slides out of the right side of her twin sized Cherrywood Victorian bed, making sure that her right foot touched the cold floor first, she found strange comfort in that. Fumbling around for her glasses to the right of her, she gropes for the tiny pink heart dangling from the end of the beaded string of the light fixture above the nightstand. There she finds her Louis Vuitton glasses framed in black, her favorite color. Shirley lazily drags herself forward, exactly twelve steps, to the bathroom. Making sure that the paste fully covers her brush in one smooth line, she brushes in a slow, methodic, circular motion giving each pearly white its due. After taking her four-jetted shower, she marches blithely to her walk-in closet fully alive now, and carefully chooses her clothing. It's Tuesday, so she remains faithful to selecting something in the blue family and gives close attention to her accessories.

Shirley insistently glares at herself while combing her thick red sunlit hair, always...always with the part on the right side like her mother used to part it when she was young. She can smell the coffee brewing on her automatically timed machine downstairs and begins to salivate. Adding three creams and two sugars, she grabs her coffee to go. She sets the alarm, slams the door and jumps into her black-on-black mid-sized Subaru SUV that she bought for its reliability. Shirley turns right out of her long winding driveway, right onto Main Street, drives exactly seven miles, and turns right into the parking lot of her job at the firm. Putting on her "I'm Alright" face, she smiles at everyone, even the three co-workers whom she knows constantly talks about everything she wears, how she fixes her hair, even her ruby red, well-manicured nails. Nothing is ever good enough. The air is getting thin...

She takes a deep breath and weakly exhales, releasing their poison once more, yet some remains—contaminated air in her lungs, transported there by words said and un-said. They began to rest inside the crevices, snuggling in like unwanted guests. They're not as strong as they once were—clear of judgment and the ugliness of sound—sounds that rode in amidst the winds of spoken things in the atmosphere—things that once upon a time, when inhaled... brought energy into her heart, causing it to beat on purpose. It used to be easy to breathe...the water was shallow then, and simplicity of life was her security. The words used to fly about her freely, like the dandelion seeds blown about by the breath of a little child on a summer's breeze. But the world is angrier now, and she's not used to this... kind expressions of thought that rolled off the tongue don't find their way to her ears anymore. Life has gotten too hard for Shirley—though to her observers, she's doing just fine. The words she speaks are free of charge, anyone can breathe them in, receiving life that they might live...breathe... anemically giving them what she desperately needs to live, they choose to drain. Like bloodletting, they take from her life supply to strengthen themselves, only to find the disease of discontentment remains in them.

Silence. The muteness of healing words, kind words, encouraging words, letters and syllables, consonants and verbs, sentences and vowels unspoken may cause one not to breathe anymore, exhausted by the weight of waiting... Then, one day...someday...that day too late to resuscitate—Shirley collapsed on the floor...she lied there gasping for simple sustenance—and finding none from familiar passers-by, she's now speechless...motionless...breathless.

Lessons from Movies

Have you ever noticed that in movies now-a-days, when people meet and are attracted to each other, they have sex either that day or before the week is out? Then, almost immediately after having sex, they start asking questions like, "Soo...how many women/men have you been with in the last year? Are you seeing anyone now? Why did your last relationship fail? Do you have a job?" Then, they start noticing things they didn't before they had sex, like...a pentagram tattoo on her back, dried up blood stains on the floor, the last five texts on his phone were from his mother, just wanting to know what he was doing, a bra underneath his pillow that does not belong to you, and Oh...she/he has six children!

HELLO!!!... Wouldn't it make more sense to ask all the questions that your heart desires over the span of at least six months to a year? Then, after finding out all you need to, from his/her family and friends, and establishing a stronger relationship based upon knowledge... you mutually decide to take the next step. It could save you time, mental and emotional anguish, and possibly your life... (unless it's a Life-Time movie/Ted Bundy-type situation where they psychotically covered everything up and you didn't have a clue!) In that case...Do what you gotta do and GET OUT FAST! If that's not the case, just ask yourself this—do I want...

Delayed Gratification -or- Prolonged Regret?

I've Never Been That Good in Cosmology, But...

I see that it's a new thing to consult, have communication with, trust, or even worship the Universe. I've especially heard athletes, actors, and entertainers say, "I want to thank the Universe for... (whatever the case may be)." Hmm...wouldn't that mean that it has a personality, personhood, and human-like qualities? Does the Universe have power, can it think or feel?... if "IT" can, then ask it to heal itself and stop all disease. The universe was formed: created—intelligently designed, just like humans. It was made for us to live in and enjoy. Therefore, how can I give thanks to, or worship what was created? Wouldn't it make more sense to worship the CREATOR of a thing?... Why would I build a car, and then worship it for taking me where I need to go? No...I should thank myself for being intelligent enough to create something that billions of people can use. If the car has power, personhood, and intelligence, then it can fix itself when it malfunctions, but instead…it has to be taken to the creator of it to be fixed.

We can never Totally trust the Universe! It will one day let us down—everything Created does!

The Universe cannot fix itself when it malfunctions—and we see that it is doing just that…so, it MUST take Someone greater than it, to heal it… It takes its Designer—GOD!

Understanding is Priceless

The other day a group of girlfriends were talking about different things that relaxes them. Frances mentioned, very excitedly "Fridays are my bath days!"
She instantly saw the looks of judgment, confusion, and disappointment (thinking I only cleansed myself once a week). Once she thought about what she said, she started to laugh, lightening the mood a bit, and then quickly expounded upon her statement. "Let me clarify what I just said, ladies…
Fridays are my days off, so I look forward to having a long luxurious bubble bath, with candles and music in the morning… usually I only have time for rushed showers."
Phew! Their sighs of relief, adjusted facial expressions, and "Oh's…" were priceless!

When Old School & New School Meet

New School taught her grandma how to use her new iPhone, how to look up old friends on Facebook, and how to access Netflix to see if she could find old shows from the 60's and 70's. It was quite a task for old school—it took much longer than she'd imagined it would and it took a lot more patience, but she learned it, for now… The next week, she'd forgotten how to do everything, so she had to drive thirty minutes to her house to show her it all again, and to add to that, Old School Grandma, asked her to show her how to use her DVR to record all reruns of *Matlock* and *In The Heat of The Night*. Old School listened very carefully and even wrote it down this time. The next week, New School asked her grandma how things were going, and grandma said, "Oh, fine dear...thanks for asking." It was not fine. Sometimes she forgot, and sometimes she remembered, and other times...she got so frustrated that she cried. But she dried her tears and thought of how blessed she was to be alive, healthy, and to have people who loved her. Old School found peace in knowing that these earthly pleasures are temporary and could not be compared to the treasures that awaited her in Heaven. She decided not to ask her granddaughter for help anymore.

One day New School Granddaughter lost, yet another, boyfriend and was crushed more than usual this time. She drove thirty minutes away to see Old School Grandma. She cried on her shoulders and screamed out, "Why does this keep happening to me?" Grandma listened, and sat calmly with her, holding her as she let it all out— Grandma's patience never grew thin. I'm so sick of feeling this way, Grandma! I'm not doing so well in school either, Mom is going to kill me," she sobbed bitterly. Grandma took her wrinkled hands, lifted her granddaughter's face towards her, and looked at her New School granddaughter with compassion and understanding in her eyes and said, "Wait on the Lord, baby...trust His timing for your mate. Tell Him the desires of your heart...but along with that, be strong enough to ask him to only give them to you if they fit within His will for your life. Love Him first, and He will teach you how to love yourself, and out of that knowledge... you will be fulfilled and not need any outside sources to fill you up, baby." She then smiled at her, kissed her on the forehead and said, "Now come on, eat some of these greens and corn bread and we'll figure out this school situation together later over some tea cakes and coffee.

New School Granddaughter realized that her knowledge and youthful energy was not enough to compare with the wisdom and experience of Old School Grandma, but that together they make quite the team!

Cool Things Older People Say and Sing About That I Love ...

"If the Lord be willin' and the creek don't rise." (Nothing will stop me from doing it or being there except these two things)

"I saw Betty's daughter the other day and she dun 'broke her leg.'" (The undercover way of saying she's pregnant)

"Evrythang shinin' ain't gold." (Don't be deceived, just because something/someone looks good does not mean that they are.)

"Yo eyes may shine Yo teeth may grit, but this right here, you sho'l can't git!" (Whatever I have right now before you—it can be anything from a sandwich the person saying it is eating to a $100 bill—forget about it, because there is no way in the world that you are going to get it!) k

"It's Tight, but it's Right!" (Whatever I—or somebody else—have just said, may be very hard for you to receive as truth, but it's still right anyway, so deal with it!)

"The barn might be old but it ain't nothin a fresh coat of paint can't fix." (Don't pass up a person or count them out just because of their outward appearance. You can fix up anyone with a little love, attention, and TLC)

"You crazy as a Betsy Bug!" (I still don't know what this bug is...and why it's crazy, but I do know that it means that you are REALLY crazy!)

"We livin' in the last and evil days!" (Watch and pray at all times because the obvious, increasing darkness of this world, that we didn't see back in the day... proves that Christ is soon to come!)

"I don't look like what I've been through!" (I have had a lot of hardships, trials, and tribulations in my life...so many that I should look like I'm crazy, beat up, broke down, and much older than what I am, but I don't!)

(Songs):

"There's a leak in this ole' buildin' and my soul has got to move to a place not built by man's hands" (My body is not doing so well so it's time for me to go on to my heavenly home and I'm okay with it.)

"This worl' is not my home I'm justa stranjah passin thoo." (I can't ever be totally comfortable and fulfilled here…I was created for heaven, my real home.)

"I gotta feelin' evrythang is gonna be alright." (No matter what has happened or will happen, I trust God, so it will work out fine, and if it doesn't down here…it's alright, because Heaven heals it all!)

"I…I…I…. know I been changed, the angels in heaven dun signed my name." (I know for certain that my spirit has been saved and I have Eternal life, so much so, that my name has been written in the Lamb's book of Life. I cannot be convinced otherwise—it's a done deal!)

Don't Mess with Mr. In-Between

Most things that truly matter in life are pretty simple. When it comes to loving someone, you either do or you don't. We don't kinda love them— if you think you can, I want you to try that out on your significant other, today. Go home to your husband or wife after work, grab him/her around their waist, stare them right in the eyes, and say, "You know what honey, I kinda love you." What response do you think they'll give? "Why thank you sweetie, I kinda love you too!" I don't think so.

Yesterday, my husband and I were on our way to church. I was acting my usually quirky (*which he calls phycho or insane*) self, and he looked over at me giggling at something I'd said or done, and said, "I love you…" When he said it, I immediately remembered what I'd written the day before about the word "kinda," so I did a little experiment. I responded to him with, "I kinda love you too, Charles." With a smirk on his face, he squinted his eyes, stared at me with evident confusion (*which was a little scary since he was driving),* and gently shook his head up and down as if to say, *"Did she really just say that to me after 26 years?"* It seemed like he did this for a whole two minutes. I know it was only about ten seconds, but even that ten seconds felt like an eternity in that moment! It got awkward, and I couldn't take it anymore, so I told him about what I'd written and how I couldn't resist my chance to try it out, and then I quickly declared my love back to him.

"Kinda" is an in-between word, it leaves wiggle room to continue to flip from one side to the other, it's lukewarm and unsure. Being in-between is ambiguous, and while it can be okay in some situations to be in the middle, it can be detrimental in many other instances. I find myself in the middle a lot! My mother and my husband both feel that I missed my calling by not pursuing becoming a public defender. I'm constantly defending someone, or something that is dear to me, or important to others. I'm hardly ever 100% on one side of an issue until I hear all of the evidence possible that's available to me. Let's be honest, we are fallible—imperfect, and biased in our reasonings, and we judge wrongly sometimes. Nowadays, judging appears to be the order of the day. We seem to constantly have an ought against something or someone in our society, don't we? It's become an addiction! We don't want to take the time to listen to the other person's point of view, or even consider trying to comprehend how they've come to their perspective. After each side has had their say, in the spirit of understanding, then hopefully, all parties can reach a happy medium, or at least agree to disagree peacefully.

During the 2016 election, I unintendedly, got into a few debates with friends, family, and acquaintances on our differing views concerning the candidates. It was extremely uncomfortable, and I knew that it could end negatively, but I decided to stand up for my beliefs, just as they did theirs. Some of the confrontations got pretty heated and I realized that they were not going anywhere because we were both adamant about our convictions. I'm learning that it is not necessary to state your opinion at every opportunity—sometimes it's better to keep silent. I'm learning to pray and ask The Holy Spirit if it's necessary or not, He never leads wrongly. Sometimes people are in darkness and need to be brought into the light on some subjects, as do I. More importantly, I've learned that animosity, resentment, hatred, anger, etc., especially amongst believers in Christ, should never be the end result of a disagreement. What matters is that we love one another with unconditional love like our Heavenly Father told us to do as brothers and sisters. Why would we turn against those whom we say we "love" over political views when we know, in the end, no human being can ultimately save us from what the Word of God says will happen in the End Times? There is nothing on this earth that should be able to separate us from genuinely loving each other, PERIOD!

However, somethings are non-negotiable. It's either Right or Wrong, Yes or No, Good or Evil, God or the Devil, Black or White—NO IN-BETWEEN...NO GRAY AREAS! These are the things that matter most in life, we can't mess with Mr. In-Between on these issues, decisions, and choices. The word of God is our guide in all of our day-to-day life situations. We can't decide to throw it to the side when it doesn't agree with our human way of thinking—how ridiculous is that?! So now we have "evolved" to the point where we don't need to follow Godly principles anymore? Look where that's gotten us as individuals, families, communities, cities, states, as a government, and as a nation! Messing with Mr. In-Between, when it comes to the fundamentals of living this life, can lead to total destruction if we don't kick him out of or thinking processes. Sure, he can come around if I'm deciding on where to take a vacation, where to eat dinner or what to wear, but whether I'm going to choose what God says over my own feelings, desires, or reasonings about something, just because I want to do things my way, because it makes sense to my little finite pea brain... then guess what?... Mr. In-Between has to go!

I realize that this can be very challenging at times, because our human nature WANTS WHAT IT WANTS!!! But, by all means, we must choose to do what God says to do—knowing that He knows everything from the beginning to the end concerning us and always has our best interest at heart, Sooo... DON'T MESS WITH MR. IN-BETWEEN

We have to love the next generation so much that we decide, NOW, to do the work of breaking curses off of our lives and burying them... so that they will not pick them up, and pass down to their children, the same things We've suffered.

Are You Sure About That?...

"What doesn't kill you makes you stronger..." It sounds good, but I don't think so—not all of the time anyway. I guess it depends on how we define Stronger.

If being stronger means that we've learned how not to make the same mistakes over and over again and have come out of our battles free of bitterness, confusion and anger... If it means that we've grown in our compassion towards others who are going through what we've been through and are now equipped to help them. If it means that we have gained wisdom, discernment, and understanding as a result of our sufferings. And, if it means that we do not measure our worth and value according to our past failures, then yes...what hasn't killed us has made us stronger.

Unfortunately, there are a lot of people who have gone through trauma and many terrible situations in life, and well...it didn't kill them. They are still here... broken, shattered, bruised and stuck. Many find it hard to get up some days, they fight to stay sane... to just keep breathing, and to even feel happiness anymore. They are chained to what has happened. They are numb and simply going through the motions--appearing alive, but inside... Zombies.

What makes you stronger is to admit that you have been weakened by life and need help to keep going and to live again, even if it hurts. What doesn't kill you CAN make you stronger, but if it hasn't, it's good to know that we can learn from those who have been through what could've killed them, but instead they held on and came through it, and discovered purpose in living again.

The key is not to give up on hope; if you are existing, you still have hope. Even if you feel no sign of hope, the giver of it will provide it as a gift. It's through our Weaknesses that God will show us His Strength. But... we have to be Strong enough to ask.

Jeremiah 17:9 Says...

"The heart is deceitful above all things, and desperately wicked: who can know it?" (KJV)

WHOA!!! This truth is challenging me to be more conscious about what I think, say, and do: I must hold my desires side by side to the word of God and make my decisions based off of what it says. If I begin to feel convicted or agitated while reading something in God's word that goes against what I thought was right, or with something I wanted to do... then that's an opportunity to listen quietly and intently to what God is telling my heart in that moment. What makes deception so tricky is that it usually agrees with something we already want, and it always has the appearance of truth. It seems justifiable or honorable on the surface, but after the deed is done, the plan is set in motion, and the words are spoken...the repercussions begin to unfold, and it may be too late. It takes great courage to tell the heart no when we want something so badly—to ask God to search our hearts when our minds are already made up. So, the next time we say "I feel in my heart..." no matter how innocent it may seem, it behooves us to check in with God's heart first.

AND NOW...

Being Human

In the African American church...who came up with the "hold up the index finger and all is well" rule? It's like the unspoken rule that allows you to leave the sanctuary during service with no questions asked. Does it work in any crowd?... Can I steal someone's wallet out of their purse on a crowded bus, look at them reverently, then hold up my index finger and all is well?... Will the crowd look at me thinking, "Oh...it's okay, she held up that finger and looked sacred as she left"?

Chapter Ten
The Mind's Wonderings

My love for the arts, trees, and sunsets, are obvious in my writings. Watching the sunset in the evenings through my office window is one of my simplest pleasures. Looking at all of the amazing blends of colors and the coupling of darkness and light into a marriage of pure artistry makes me wonder of your Glory more and more...Lord, you blow my mind! Experiencing closeness with you through nature, is a pleasure that I will indulge in and never get full of. There is so much about you and about life that I don't know, and will never know, but I love talking to you about it...I love allowing my mind to wonder. You gave me a wild imagination and boy am I putting it to use! Some of my favorite artists are Rembrandt and Monet for their selective choices of rich colors, and perfected use of light and dark, and Mary Cassatt for her use of vibrant colors and ability to capture everyday life narratives. Seeing the magnificence of these artists gives me more insight into how much you love beauty and are beautiful...and why you've made us to create and display it.

Picture Play

Sometimes I wish that I could transport myself inside of
a picture—I'd take adventures for a day or two, maybe
even a week...I'd do and see all that I dreamed of and
talked about with those who dared to dream with me.
As I sit here staring at the wooden pier fading into the golden
sunset and the waves resting peacefully upon the shore, I
wish that I could escape into that picture on the wall.
If I had that ability, I'd go to Italy for gelato from my
dining room table right after dinner, to Vermont to walk
amongst the fall trees from my living room couch.

And from my creative room to enjoying the sound of the rain dancing on my umbrella, while walking in Central Park lined with the lampposts' show of multicolored lights on the wet ground. I'd leave my bed dressed in my favorite pajamas to a quaint little lake at dusk while the glow of the moon is still lightly kissing the tips of the trees.

YELLOW

You give me hope when I see you…I sense better days are coming, and that the dimmed season I'm in is fading into You

True Ecstasy

Sometimes when I wonder about being in Heaven with God My Savior FOREVER…my imagination goes so far into the Breathtaking Blissfulness of it all that I can't take it anymore—I have to stop for a moment! I become overwhelmed by my spirit's Yearning and my body wants to know…to Finally know… what will someday be. Thank You Lord for what you have prepared for us who long an believe…

An Ode to Books

Books, to me, are like life-long friends that you can spend time with whenever you desire… you know…those kinds that challenge and lift you up at the same time… that give you that warm fuzzy feeling and then make you uncomfortable if necessary?

These friends bring laughter, escape, intellectualism, imagination,
truth, adventure, mystery, beauty, and so much more...
They always call you back to them and can
hardly wait to be in your presence again.

Black, Shades of Blue, and the Colors of You

My favorite color is black. Beautiful things, when outlined in black, seem to pop—they suddenly stand out in their loveliness all the more... adding flavor and dimension. Like a black frame around a painting of white, yellow, and red roses in a field of green, it gently demands recognition. Black is elegant, smooth, slimming, solid, strong, bold, and classy. When placed as the backdrop for diamonds in light, it causes them to dance. While black is still my favorite color, I've recently been turning my focus on blue, many shades of blue...particularly, medium to lighter shades of blue. I'm not sure why, but I find myself feeling comforted by its many hues.

When I was young, I remember coloring in a coloring book with a box of crayons that WERE NOT Crayola crayons. My finished product was always done with great pride and attention, but the waxy, mediocre, display of the under-brand sticks of diluted color, left me with a slight feeling of displeasure. Well, one day I had the pleasure of coloring with a new box of Crayola crayons beside me. It was exciting to have all of these choices to create with, *and I'm sure you figured out by now* that the shortest crayon in the box was the black one. I outlined all of my pictures in black, because, to me...they deserved to be presented Grandly. Unexpectantly, my eyes lighted upon this soft, pretty, pleasant-feeling, shade of blue...its name was Periwinkle. Periwinkle?!...I'd never heard of this color before, it changed my coloring life, forever! A shade of blue had introduced itself to me that day. I found every opportunity possible to use that color. The thing was...I only wanted to use that shade of blue if it made sense. For instance, if it was a bowl of fruit on the page, I wouldn't dare color a piece of fruit any shade of blue, especially

Periwinkle! Now, I've pushed myself to "create outside of the box" and to use any color, on whatever I want, although it is still hard at times when your brain is equally analytical and creative.

It may sound strange, but when I look at shades of blue, I feel peaceful. I also feel happy when I see shades of yellow, and green *(a color I never used to like, unless it was grass)*, a color that brings thoughts of life to me. So, what am I really saying? Maybe nothing much at all, except… don't be afraid to use all the colors at your disposal: colors that add peace, happiness, and life to you. Make sure that you use them to the fullest—get as much out of them as possible. Then, enhance them by outlining them in black, so that all can see their beauty through you.

<u>Renew</u>

Looking at the ocean, feeling the breeze… hearing the sound
of seagulls, and listening to the laughter of families around me
enjoying the beach, gives me pleasure and joy. Seeing the sun
giving its approval to the busyness of the waves…inspires me
to lean back in my chair, look up to you in gratefulness, breathe
in the smells of the air and say, "Thank you God for giving me
this moment and for being in it—experiencing it with me…"
God In Every Moment.

<u>Of Trees and Lamp Posts</u>

What is it with this affinity I have for trees and lamp posts?
It started when I was a little girl. I'd watch through the screen
in the window on a rainy day, smelling its earthy scent. I'd
study the way the trees would sway back and forth in the wind
like a Baptist church choir down the aisle on Sunday morning.
The rustling of the leaves was intriguing to me, drawing me in
closer as they gave praise for the rain. During the storm, though,
all was quiet. It seemed as if it were their time to speak—to
express themselves to whomever would listen. I would listen…
In stately grandeur, the trees stand firm and stretch out their
arms reaching out to give refuge and life. I tune in as they
forecast their mood through their whistling songs—most times,
sweet and calm, and sometimes harsh and confused. Proudly

displaying their statuesque trunks of warn and tattered existence, they show the wisdom of the ages within each earned crevice. They have stories to tell of history and present things still growing in their roots: healing roots that support each other by sending nutrients to those that are sick around them. Their textures, tones, and moods change with the temperaments of the sky and earth. If they could vocalize what they know of our world— what they've seen and heard for thousands of years—they'd share without withholding... and all would be better for it.

Like with trees, I also have a love for lamp posts. Their works enhance the beauty of the scene they're grounded in. Their expertise is bringing light to dark places, and in the day, to give a glimpse of what's to come. When standing amongst the trees they appear to feature these kingly ones, particularly at night when the darkness sets the backdrop of their luminous dance together. With unique degrees of embellishment and purpose, each lamppost plays its role in making the grand, and the mundane, better in its presentation.

Spring's Thing

It's still a little crisp in the air...but that's
okay, I know how you think.
You like to change things up a bit, keep us guessing.
You enjoy giving us snippets of what's to come.
Today, you decorated my yard with pink
and burgundy blooms on a bush...
Just yesterday there was no sign in sight.
You like to sneak things in... I like that!
The trees are teasing us with their vibrant bright
greens on the tips of their branches
Only giving us enough to whet the appetite of
our eyes—anticipating a total unveiling.

Our imaginations are swelling with thoughts
of walks, and talks, and gatherings...
You woo us, casually: tantalizing our emotions as
the sun warms and the earth fills our nostrils.
The scents you bring excites our senses
and ushers us into newness...
Your rain refreshes our souls.

Fulfilling the Senses

I've always enjoyed the sound of birds outside my window, but
now... I listen a little more intensely to the melodic nuances
of their songs. I take in the crisp nutty smell of the leaves as I
walk through them and take note of their rustling chatter in my
path. Sometimes the scent is so strong I can almost taste it. I
purposefully opened the front door today, just to feel the cool
breeze on my face... to breathe it all in. While listening to the
soothing lull of the wind chimes, my eyes took notice of the
Japanese maple tree planted against the left side of the house. It
was tenderly waving all of its tiny dark red hands at me—as if
hoping that I'd notice its frolicking. I looked for a few seconds,
but soon the chill advised me otherwise. Not wanting to lose
that moment... I closed the door, walked over to the window,
impatiently pulled back the curtain, anticipating another look...
the leaves were still soliciting my attention. I took a moment
to oblige, and for that short time...my senses were content.

MONET'S ASPIRATION

*I'm watching you through my window as I perfect my
writing craft. Creativity flows when you're around—giving
me inspirational aid. You changed your mind right before my
eyes... from yellow, orange, and touches of white, to purple,*

pink, and gray. Ah... there you go again—morphing into a
particular shade of blue in harmony with one another...
How you amaze me every evening
This free gift of beauty—brush strokes by hands unseen...
Monet has nothing on you...

Some may think it strange, but I find it profitable to go
to funerals; they are uncomfortable reminders of how
short life is. The wise will adjust their plans and manner
of living with this in mind... and ponder their eternity.

EDIE BOWMAN

Expectation

My inner wonderings coerced my eyes to open this morning, 5:45, Virginia Beach, Virginia.

Exhaustion was bullied by desire once again, "wake up," my longing said to see whatever would be seen—differently this time… for Your expressiveness is unabating.

You rose slowly above the horizon like a crocodile's head stealthily coming out of the water—fiery eyes glowing with purpose and passion.

You brought me pink, blue, grey, and white.

You reflected upon the ocean a runway from you to me…

Soon you ascended further into your heavenly position and changed your mind, and said… "I'll show you even more, see…?"

You took away the pink and grey and gave the most glorious golden yellow beams that widened out across your stage.

I waited in expectation to see more, raising my hands in praise to The One who commissioned you to come—And I gained strength in the waiting of the Sun's rise…

The seagulls joined in with their insistent cries and wings that soared like fancy letter *v*'s.

I imagined your Son taking me up someday like this—in this kind of magnanimous display, at least something like this…

You'll come back in the clouds and Rescue us—bring us to yourself. It could be evening, night, or like this…

But for now, as I look up, I'll remember your personal performance for me—from your heart to mine, reminding me that you are right here, and you hear Me…and are wooing Me…Still.

Maranatha…Even so Come, Lord Jesus

What If Inanimate Objects Could Talk?

Would a doorknob say, "Leave me alone, you twist and turn me all day...can I just have a moment to myself?! Please, I just need a day without anyone touching me, okay? I just feel so violated sometimes... you know?"

Would a mirror say, "Okay now... you're way too into yourself! I can see checking yourself three to four times a day, but ten?! Look, I'm gonna be real with you...I didn't wanna say nothin' but look, you're not that cute, so why keep torturing yourself several times a day?"

Would nails say, "I feel soo beat down all the time..."

Would a toothbrush say, "NO! Don't you to put me away yet! You need to go AT LEAST two more minutes or so...and going in circles is not working! Your breath STILL stinks! Try going in squares or somethin'! Yeah...try somethin'' different."

Might a rash say, "Every time I clear the garbage out of my life, here comes someone bringing more garbage. I can't get a break!"

Would toilet paper...NEVERMIND!

Might a book say, "Let me read you today...tell you what I-I-I-I see. Allow me to study you for an hour or so."

Might walls of your house say, "Man... yaw'l crazy up in here! If everything wouldn't fall apart...we'd detach ourselves and leave!"

Would paper say, "I used to be a beautiful tree...now look at me, I'm just a fragment of myself."

Might a bed say, "There is too much goin' on in here! I can't get no sleep, and it's supposed to be my specialty!"

Would eye-glasses say, "You only want me for ONE THING...I feel so used!"

Might windows say, "I do have eyes you know...and Man, have I seen it all! I have an idea...try keeping the blinds closed once in a while or put up dark curtains. Unfortunately, I can't UN-see some things! If they only knew..."

What The Tree Says...

There's a tree outside my creative/prayer room window—standing tall above the houses in front of it. It touches the clouds and moves with the leading of the wind. It looks as if it's there just for me at times...beckoning me to take notice. It waves at me and sways, showing me God's wonders. It seems to say, "Look at me, I'm still here...I've made it through decades of wind, rain, snow, and disasters, and I am still here...standing strong and beautiful, and so will you, Edie... Look at me!"

What I said to The Tree...

You still had green leaves just two months ago;
you were telling a different story...
Now, as I look out of my window...I didn't
realize that you had lost something.
How did I miss it? Did I get too busy?... Did you
beckon me to sit, relax and take a moment?
When did you change?... Why didn't I notice?...

Chasing Sunsets

I was sitting at my desk reading a book, when a glimpse of the sunset caught my eye. It wasn't very much to see between the houses and trees—just a hint of blue and pink, and a little bit of faded orange. That was enough for me! I jumped up, went to my husband to see if he wanted to go with me to see it from a higher place. He wasn't in the mood. I ran to my daughter to see if she wanted to share this experience with me...she wasn't feeling it. So, I grabbed my purse, put on my crocs and darted out of the door like I was about to miss the changing of the guards or something. You see, the thing with me is...I love to share experiences with people. There are very few things that I like to do alone, so for me to do this, especially as it was getting dark, was out of the usual. I drove looking at the sunset on my way to the higher place. I was enamored with it...captured by the beauty. Once I got there, I parked my car, turned off the lights, and waited. I waited because it grows more and more gorgeous the darker it gets, and then...it's gone!

I learned something about chasing sunsets—you have to be patient and you have to pay close attention to every nuance that they bring. The colors change moment by moment, and I don't want to miss a thing! I also learned that sometimes you have to do things alone—sometimes you're supposed to experience things for yourself. I felt the presence of God there as I watched his handiwork, and I know it might sound cheesy but, I began to cry. The sky was a very dark grey and greyish blue, sitting on top of a darkened pinkish color. What was captivating though, was that between the clouds was this small area of yellow light piercing through. I felt like God was looking at me through that yellow...like he was saying "I'm here, I see you."

God knows what we like. He knows that I like imagery and nature, so that's how he speaks to me. This is how he shows me love—he shows me through his artistry. I learned that if I really want to feel him, be close to him, commune with him...I will even jump in my car, alone, at night, to chase a sunset.

EDIE BOWMAN

AND NOW...
<u>Being Human</u>

Have you ever seen someone fall asleep in church and then wake up shaking their head up and down in agreement with the pastor? They start looking around hoping that they're not busted, and then begin saying things like, "Amen... Amen...that's right pastor...Mmm-Hmm...Hallelujah!" The rest of us are like, "Huh... Hallelujah?!...What's he sayin that for?... Sis. Jones is just reading the announcements!"

Chapter Eleven
Nostalgia...

Winter's Snow

Walking to The Store (that really was the name of the store) in the evening from Grandma's house on Mahoning Road, you glistened and glimmered on the ground reflecting the streetlights along the path ahead of us, showing me your wonder, giving my mind a futuristic scene upon which to remember.

I felt safe and protected nestled between my cousin Patrick and my sister Beanie, who were being their usual overly comedic selves:

cracking jokes and seeing who could do the craziest, silliest walk. We ran, then slid, then threw you up in the air, feeling your cool refreshment dazzling on our tongues.

It was such a short distance from Grandma's to The Store, but what a long-lasting memory of joy, love of family, and the playfulness of youth you bring back to me each time I walk along surrounded by you in the evening.

You left behind three sets of footsteps on the sidewalk on our way to see *The Polar Express* at the Palace Theatre. It felt nostalgic… your giving me this moment again, walking with two more people that I love, now over thirty years later. Tatiana, Autumn and I were in no rush: we elongated the moment, enjoying every step, and every word spoken as the smoke from our breath continued to quickly vape away.

I showed them for the umpteenth time, Timken Sr. High, the school I loved so much, as we walked by. I glanced at two churches that I always wanted to attend when I was little, but they were not our church (they know those stories too). We turned around and looked at the footprints before we crossed the street and I took a snap with my phone. The three sets of footprints didn't look particularly unique, but in that light dusting of snow, that night…it meant a lot, for it framed our story, our presence, our having been there in Winter's Snow.

The Good Ole Days

The kids in the neighborhood are playing basketball in between the cars passing by…it's interesting to see how upset they look as their game is interrupted every five minutes or so. I wonder if I looked that way while playing kickball in the street when I was younger? Nah…my parents didn't play that! We'd get in trouble for grimacing at adults, especially for driving where they were supposed to—as a matter of fact… the adults in the cars would tell us to straighten up themselves, and then tell our parents if they knew them!

We took a walk today down by the park and I heard the sound of the swings going back and forth with their squeaky, nostalgic sound. Suddenly, I was a kid again at Maple Park, with my head hung back looking into the moving trees above, gliding with the wind and feeling Free

<u>Simplicity</u>

Iced tea in a mason jar
Good neighbors to holler at across the street
Feet propped up, Old Glory waving in the evening sun,
And you beside me—Ahhhh…

Play Another Slow Jam, Please

My husband and I chillin' in the room listenin' to old school jams
"It's so good lovin' somebody, when somebody loves you back..."
It's not 70/30...not 60/40...talkin' bout 50/50 Love...Yeah..."
—Good ole Teddy Pendergrass
Need I say more?...

Sounds...

My focus was turned to the sound of the fan the other day—the old-fashioned kind. Remember the big, basic square fan with a thousand little white rectangles on it? You know...the one we used to put it in the window before we had air conditioning? The mild breeze felt soo good coming through the window mixed with the ambient sound of the fan. The sound of the cars going by and the sound of the neighbors talking and laughing made me feel at ease, for some reason. When I was little, its consistent calming sound filled the living room and was one of the first things I noticed when I came in from school—it immediately soothed me. My sister and I would rush in the door, quickly finish our homework, get a snack, and then rush into the living room in front of the peaceful sound of that fan. We'd turn on the TV, lie on our bellies and watch shows like *The Munster's, The Brady Bunch, Looney Tunes* and *The Flinestones*. It's crazy how simple sounds can take you back to moments in life.

Refreshing

Sometimes when I listen to the old school singers like Guy, Whitney Houston, Michael Jackson, and Boys 2 Men, it makes me feel happy and nostalgic. It brings back great memories of sitting around the picnic bench at summer camp with my friends and seeing who could sing the latest songs the best, I'd always choose **"The Greatest Love of All"** or **"You Give Good Love."** My mind goes back to having family cook outs where we'd sing our hearts out while holding a fork or spoon in our hand as a microphone—if we were in the house... then the curling iron was the best microphone. We'd laugh, play, and dance until we were exhausted. **"Ain't No Stoppin' Us Now"** by Mcfadden & Whitehead was my favorite cook out song—it had such a good vibe to it! "Ooo...I can hear it now..."

It Felt Like Christmas Morning...

One day I was sitting across from my husband watching him figure how to play with his new toy: A Star Wars Battleship Drone!!! It is, literally, giving me joy right now (*well a little fear too, because it looks like it's gonna take off and possibly hit one of us in the head any moment*). The ship has flashing lights on it with its own techy looking stand that also lights up, kind of like the look of the Rock -N- Roll Hall of Fame. It has a high functional remote control that talks and plays music...Oh, and it also lights up! Wow! This is like watching a little boy on Christmas morning opening up that last gift; that gift that he hopes is the one he wanted most. We all remember THAT gift, the one we knew we were most likely NOT going to get because it was too expensive, not for playing with in the house, or like the mom on *A Christmas Story* said... "Will Shoot Your Eye Out!

His eyes are full of wonder and excitement as he's figuring out just how to work this thing. Whoa... something else just happened that I think you should know... he's placing the stand in its own clear acrylic box! It feels like I should hear Angelic music as he does this—something like

"Ahh...Ahh...Ahh..." (Angelic music)

Allergies

The grass was my friend and enemy growing up: swollen eyes and runny nose...sneezing and wiping and running in and out of the house for relief. The yard meant freedom to play, and not to be bored in the house all day...it meant laughter and imagination, friends and adventure...then why is it fighting me this way!

Hey! Remember when just a blanket, a ball or frisbee, a few hotdogs and burgers to put on the grill, a little fishing spot for the parents, and a radio, equaled a wonderfully fun day at the park?

Musical Memories

I listened to a lot of 60's and 70's music growing up, even though I wasn't born until 1973. My father played and sang these songs often. My favorites were The Temptations, The Stylistics, The Commodores, Earth Wind and Fire, and Ray, Goodman & Brown. These songs still really get me excited today! But it's funny to me how a lot of the male groups have long monologues that go on for a while? Even some of the 80's and 90's groups did it. They go something like this...

"You know I really, really love you baby...and I know I haven't been everything you needed me to be...I want you to know I need you baby...Pleeeease forgive me baby...I can't breathe without you in my life...The sun doesn't shine any more, the wind doesn't blow... My food has lost its taste... I can't even see any more, my eyes are blurry from crying all night long..." (You get the point). Then, there's a lot of adlibs of extreme begging, some soul filled _Oooh_'s, and finally, the rest of the group comes back in.

I do find this funny, looking back... but at the same time... I wouldn't change a thing!

Winter Memories...

Making Snow angels as the snow falls softly upon my face
Gliding down that particular hill on a piece of cardboard
Building a snowman in the yard with friends from your street
Watching the snow scurry by my window
illumined by the streetlights
Snowflakes melting with their unique
designs on the car wind shield
Hearing the giggling of children ice skating on the square
That gentle kiss by the fireplace and a Christmas movie

Summer's Promise

Saying your name comes with promise, even Olaf
from *Frozen* gets it! (Remember his song?)
The world cannot wait to bathe in your
presence—to partake of your glory.
Soo many dreams you hold in your hands that
we're counting on you to deliver.
Please don't let us down...
Nine months we wait for you; there are
some things only you can do.
This year we're not sure of our plans with you,
but we know you'll still show up.
An invisible enemy is looming, and it fiercely
longs to steal our time together.
We'll fight it with eagerness and persistence,
knowing that you're waiting on us...
Waiting on us to come out and play...
Is this too much for you to bare, our drawing on your consistency?
You deliver what we expect: sunny days
with soft breezes by the lake...
scoops of ice cream, boat rides, and vacations on the beach...

Blankets strewn across the grass and sandwiches
eaten to the sound of soft jazz
And we only have a three month's date
So, we wait…and so, we wait…

You Don't Know Nuthin'!

Have you ever played the "You Don't Know
Nuthin' bout dat there!" game?
It's when you see, hear, sing, or know something from old
school times, and someone who's significantly younger than
you, knows nothing about it, so you tell them about it with great
nostalgia and excitement! If they have heard about whatever it
is, you're so shocked that you still feel inspired to say… "You
Don't Know Nuthin' bout dat there! Gon' Somewhere!"
You usually laugh during all of this, because you get to
share something old with New School, and it feels good!
"Boyyy, You Don't Know Nuthin' 'bout walkin' to
school ev'ry day, with snow up to yo knees, with your
parents' car in the driveway! Gon' somewhere!"

`Those Were The Days

Remember walking to the corner store to buy Boston Baked Beans,
Dog Eyes, Mary Janes, Now & Laters, Fun Dip, and Coconut
Bars (chocolate, strawberry, and vanilla) and still have change?…

Summer Time…

I just listened to "Summer-Time" by Will Smith, in the car.
I immediately had visions of me playing Chinese Jump-
rope with my sister, cousins, and friends in front of the old

house on 7th Street northeast. I still remember the words
we used to say to stay on task while jumping… "jump in,
jump out, jump side to side, jump on, jump in, jump out!"
Ponytails, barrettes, and colored beads were bouncing
up and down with us—making their own music.
Good Times …

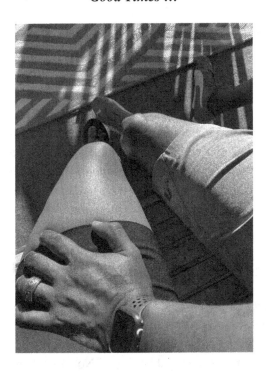

Swingin'

The fan on the porch complimented the
breeze as I read poetry to you
on the old wooden swing, and you cared enough to listen.
Our feet touched happily, gliding back and
forth with a subtle knowing.
We shared a glance here and there…
It was familiar and it was home—our finding comfort in the Now.

Pursuit

Dream the most fantastical dreams and
fight to make them all come true.
May your faith in them give you strength to keep on pursuing...
and may your "Timonergy" never run out.

An ode to the #2 Pencil

*Sometimes I just want to write with a good old-fashioned
number two pencil! I want to feel it in my right hand—
between my thumb, index, and middle finger. I want to
hear the sound of it against notebook paper with the holes
on the left-hand side...to see the smooth pencil sharpener
shavings fall to the ground...to wipe and blow away eraser
leftovers from the page, and to remember simpler times...*

"Bill's Store" Down on 6th Street Southwest

Now, I'm not a promoter of smoking cigarettes, but remember back
in the day, when someone in the neighborhood would give you
a couple of dollars to go down to the corner store and buy them
some cigarettes. They would be like, "Now look here... I want
you to go on down to the Sto (not store... but "Sto!" Lol!!!) and
get me a pack of Kool Super Longs cigarettes, and you can keep
the change." Oooo Weee! Keep the change?!... Whatchoo talkin
bout?! I was one happy kid! That meant I could buy a small bag
full of penny candies and a bag of chips, and maybe even a pop!
Do you remember that corner store?...

Schoolin' In The Late 80's

That teacher that everyone liked…the laughter and chatter echoing
in the halls, Monster Chews (old school candy) in your book bag, the
boys making beats on the desks with pencils or their fists while beat
boxing, the class clowns crackin' on people, and making us all laugh…
Feelin good when the "Cool" principal comes to visit your
class instead of the boring one, going to the school dance
and forming a circle around the really good dancers as
they bust a move to the latest songs, and girls standing
around in small groups talking about the cute boys…
Passing notes, spitballs, and smackin' gum, running outside
after school to see the fight everyone was talking about,
after school suspension for talking in class for the third
time, the smile on your face when the popular students
signed your yearbook, and stressing over your outfit for
Spirit Week (Remember Pee-Wee Herman day?!)

The 11ᵗʰ Hour Kind of Faith

EVEN IF "THE FAT LADY" HAS SUNG!

It was the fall of 2016—The eleventh hour! We were down by 3 (If
memory serves my girls and I well). The Canton Mckinley side was
looking sad and faithless. All hope seemed to be lost, some people were
packing up, while others were leaving. "What are they doing?!" I said,
"The players are still on the field" Why are they leaving?!" I refused to
give up. Before I knew it, I stood up, looked around at the other people
near me, and to my daughters (who were crackin up, and embarrassed
at the same time) and said, "It's the eleventh hour, don't give up yet!"

My girls were like, "Mom! Sit down…what do you mean it's the
eleventh hour?"

I said, "It means you don't give up when it looks hopeless, God
can still turn it around and give us a miracle at the last minute!"

"Okay…but we're not in church Mom, you're always trying to make something spiritual," they said while laughing hysterically, because now I was making my usual game noise—I cup my hands around both sides of my mouth and project with all of my might (in a male type, deep voice) "Yeah! Ye-Ye-Ye-Yeah! Yeah!" several times until I feel it!

There were four minutes left on the clock, the team huddled up to make their final battle plan, the kicker did his thing, and all of a sudden…Dominique Robinson catches the ball!!!! He literally, ran forward like lightening, did a leap that looked like he'd been trained in Classical Ballet (I guess classical ballet is a thing…I don't know, but it sounds good), and then… catapulted over the heads of all in front of him to an unforeseeable TOUCH DOWN!!!!!! By this time my girls were acting crazier than I was, the buzzer ran out, AND… I think you can imagine the thunderous roar of the crowd—those who maintained the faith to remain to the end, that is! We will never forget that moment, and no one can tell me that God was not in it! We learned something that day… And it felt MIGHTY GOOD!

Score 32 to 28!!!
(Again, if memory serves us well…anyway We Won!)

Heart Pictures

When the girls were younger, I used to watch them washing the dishes, playing with toys, or even doing homework, and I wanted to keep those memories in my heart so that I could recall them when they were out of the house someday. I also desired to do this with my husband and other loved ones that visited my home. One day I was watching one of my girls doing the dishes (I miss that chore being done…) and I squinted my eyes really close together, almost shut, until she was like a dream-like vision. I allowed the feeling of that moment to sink deep within my heart, and I captured it! I called that moment, "Taking a Heart Picture." One day they all caught me doing it while they were dancing around and singing in the kitchen, and they asked me what I was doing—they just thought that I was acting my normal, weird self! I explained to them that I was taking Heart Pictures, and then I taught them how to do it. They thought it was so fun to do! When my husband catches me doing it, he says, "What are you doing, weirdo?"

I tell him, "Taking Heart Pictures of you."

Even to this day, when my girls catch me doing it, with love in their eyes, they say, "What are you doing mom, taking Heart Pictures, again?"

And often, with tears in my eyes I say, "Yes, I sure am."

It's Funny How the Mind Works: one minute you're basking in the joys of what was, the next you're wishing what was never was.

Saturday Afternoon Drive

Riding in the car with the windows down on a Summer's day, soul music on the radio, licking vanilla ice cream cones from Mickey D's in the backseat, my sissy and I picking at each other, tube tops, matching shorts, and ponytails... and no particular place to go.

AND NOW...
Being Human

Let's be honest...Have you ever thought to yourself, "Man... Jesus got me all messed up?! When you need money, He tells you to give. When someone takes your coat, He tells you to give them your shirt also. When you are weak, that's when He says you are strong...and if you want to be great, He tells you that's the time to be humble." WHAT?! C'MON JESUS, YOU GOT ME ALL MESSED UP!!!

Chapter Twelve
Wounded...While Healing

I miscarried you, my first and third child...that was, and still is, an unusual, lonely, indescribable type of pain—to know you were growing inside me, and then you were not. It's been well over twenty years, and I still think about you both: what you look like, if you are both boys or both girls, or are you one of each, do you have your father's big beautiful dark brown eyes, do you have my smile?... The sorrow isn't as strong as it was then, but I have my moments, especially when I see others going through this mysterious loss. What gives me hope and healing is to know that you're in heaven waiting for me. I will see you, and hold you, and spend time with you, smell your necks, squeeze your chubby legs, and nuzzle my nose close to your cheeks. I'm so glad that the scripture says that before you were even formed in my womb, God knew you. Based upon the truth of that word...it proves that you existed in the Heavenly Father's heart and mind before I even met your father. WOW!!! You were wanted, you were loved, you are loved, you were created by God, and I can't wait to meet you both.

I'll love you for Eternity, Literally...
—Your Mommy

Faith is not *Denying* that you feel fear, sorrow, or pain... but it's *Knowing* that you have help and hope Through it all—that you will overcome.

(One day, I was staring out of my office window at work, and the fall tree in all its glory captivated me! The colors of the leaves demanded my attention as they waved at me. I was going through a difficult and confusing time at the moment, which inspired me to write this poem—God was there in the Moment.)

EDIE BOWMAN

Autumn's Tree

I look **beautiful**...people often tell me so as
they walk by. The thing they don't
know is—Just one more strong **breeze** will reveal my true **colors**;
I'm barely hanging on to these **leaves**...
one by one they **Fall**. Life has
taught me well to put on **colorful** clothes while
quietly dying inside, BUT DON'T I
LOOK GOOD?! Putting on airs are second **nature**
to me—Just one more **wind** and I'll be exposed. I'm
standing Tall, after all... Appearances are Everything!
Oh, but if they only knew... that just one more
gentle breath would
Tell It All
But I Will
Not Fall
I Will Not
F A L L
I 'LL GIVE IT TO THE LORD, FOR HE
KNOWS AND HEALS IT ALL

LOL!!!... What does it really mean?

SINCE WHEN DID THE ACRONYMN "LOL" (Laugh Out
Loud) GIVE US A PASS ON SAYING THINGS THAT WE
USUALLY ARE HESITANT TO SAY? ARE WE REALLY
LAUGHING OUT LOUD EACH TIME WE TEXT OR POST
IT, OR ARE WE JUST USING IT TO SOFTEN THE BLOW
OF TRUTH? "LOL" SEEMS TO FIX EVERYTHING...IT
MAKES HARSH OR NOT SO PLEASANT SITUATIONS LOSE
THEIR STING A BIT... SOMETIMES IT MAY EVEN COVER
UP A CALL FOR HELP. PEOPLE SAY THINGS LIKE...

"THAT OUTFIT YOU'RE WEARING IS CUTE,
BUT IT WOULD LOOK MUCH BETTER ON A
SLIMMER PERSON LIKE ME, **LOL!!!**"
OR…
"I KNOW WE'VE BEEN DATING FOR A WHILE,
BUT I'M STARTING TO HAVE FEELINGS
FOR YOUR BEST FRIEND, **LOL!!!**"
OR…
I CAN'T COME HANG OUT WITH YOU GUYS
TODAY, MY MIND IS GOIN' A LITTLE CRAZY
TODAY, **LOL!!!**" (INTERPRETATION: "I NEED
SOMEONE TO TALK TO, I'M HURTING)
OR…
"I HAVEN'T HEARD FROM YOU IN A FEW WEEKS,
I GUESS I'M NOT ON YOUR PRIORITY LIST, **LOL!!!**"
(INTERPRETATION: I MEANT EXACTLY WHAT I SAID
BUT PUTTING "LOL" AFTER IT MAKES IT APPEAR
FUNNY AND PERHAPS WON'T OFFEND YOU)

*"There is no one in this world who is exempt from
hurting me in some way once I accepted this, I was
able to totally rely on you alone for unconditional
love and was therefore free to love others fairly."*

Questions That Bring Answers

Her arms were made for caressing, but he bruised them

Her face was made to be adored, but he grew to despise it when adored by others

Her hands were made to be lovingly held…they were cut in defense of herself

Her eyes that he complimented that morning, were blackened by noon…

Her beautiful feet are now hardened from the many long walks in the night to escape his terror—

One child on her hip and the other at her side trying to keep up the pace...

"Where are we going, mommy? I'm getting wet."

"I don't know, honey, but we'll be okay...the Lord will provide... He will..."

As she courageously took her next few steps in the cold down pour, she realized that he did provide.

He provided the other night when the little old lady opened her home and begged her to stay

He provided when her sister and brother-in-law offered to pay for an apartment

He provided when her pastor and his wife prayed for her to get a good job and a lawyer—and God did...

He provided when her police officer friend said he'd personally arrest him the next time he raised a hand to her.

He provided through soft whispers of instructions as she lay in her bed—a bed that became a place of dishonor...

He provided by keeping her alive when hands of death gripped her throat that day

He said he'd never do it again... but he did that almost deadly night—the night she ran in the rain with her children

She courageously said within herself—against all the voices telling her to go back...

"Wait, aren't I the King's daughter?... Then, why am I settling for less?"

"Didn't he promise that he'd make a way of escape for me?"

"Has He made ways for me already? Have I dismissed them out of fear?

The screams pouring out of her baby boy's mouth and the looks of exhaustion and confusion on her daughter's face gave her the answers.

The "Good" Life

She made him breakfast every morning at 6:00 sharp, packed his lunch—making sure to add a pickle wrapped separately in a sandwich bag, checked the weather to decide if he needed an umbrella, snow boots, and to pick out the right coat or jacket. She kissed him on the lips, gave him a hug and sent him off for the day with a smile.

She made sure that his dinner was hot and on the table at exactly 6:45 pm when he'd walk in the door, faithfully, every day. They'd sit and talk at the dinner table with the children where she'd monitor their behavior, not to cause him too much aggravation. When they were finished eating, she'd send the kids away to play, and create time to listen to his day. She'd laugh at his corny jokes, wash the dishes, and then scurry up the stairs to prepare his clothes for the next day's work. She made sure the children were quieted at night so that he could rest, and she never refused his sexual advances.

What a great wife I have... he thought to himself as he leaned back easy in his recliner. He could smell the sweet scent of her perfume on the pillow she had just fluffed for him before going up the stairs. "I have truly found a good thing..." he said with a satisfied sigh.

Oh, but he lost her ten years ago with his sexist undertones, stifling words, soft intimidation, and firm touches.

Silence encourages Secrets to Fester—festering secrets,
allows Darkness to Remain. But Light...it Expels the
darkness, and implores secrets to be Revealed—
And Now, as painful as it may be...they can finally be Healed.

Peace is Worth It!

Eager to please, she became distressed
Longing to be found, she lost herself
Inclined to nurture, her heart became calloused

Addicted to loving "love"… she hated herself
Yearning to be held, she received abandonment
Searching to be filled, she remained empty
Hearing the Voice of Salvation, she desperately chose to listen
With barley enough energy to crawl, she forced herself to walk
Running into The Light, she began to leave the darkness
Broken, she finally realized that Peace…is Worth It!
Needing mending…she sought The Designer
While Healing…she helps others to heal
Lips often kissed with bitterness, sings songs of Freedom now
She knows that Peace was worth it…Peace is worth it all.

SafE/EfaS

She looked in the mirror trying to practice "her" smile, but it wasn't hers.

She widened her eyes, opened her mouth broadly—teeth apart, almost like she was laughing with no sound.

The smile was beautiful, it even looked good on her, but it was not hers to wear—

She didn't have the story behind "her" smile.

She didn't know the pain that came first—that produced That smile "she" wore with such grace, which "she" earned.

Her teeth weren't as attractive as "hers"—they were off-white and average,

"hers" were strong and perfectly lined like ivory keys, but HERS brought invaluable comfort to those who were hurting when SHE opened HER mouth to speak.

And when SHE smiled, HER smile, for them… they were uplifted, and inspired to embrace their own.

In time, through many joys, trials, highs and lows, SHE came to enjoy Her own smile—SHE got used to it, became comfortable with it, encouraged Herself with it, and finally owned it!

Afterall… SHE, was the only one that ever could.

Spiritual Resistance

I will allow my pain to build my spiritual muscles—
to push me to pray more sincerely.
I choose to take the hurt I'm going through
cause me to look to you.
I will not resist your guidance in my life
anymore, but humbly yield to it.
I choose to follow your word for direction for
decisions I have to make, I will not trust myself.
I will exercise my spiritual muscles by lifting all
of my cares upon you—you care for me.
I will build my resistance as I press into your
presence, to worship you IN my trials.
I choose to lift my hands in surrender, as weak as
they are, from fighting your will for my life.
I will walk in righteousness against the opposing
pressures of sin and distractions—
I'll keep on walking with you beside me...
strengthening my legs of faith and trust.

Do It for Someone Else!

I wanted another joint so bad I couldn't think, but
I suddenly thought of you and flushed it.
I wanted that one-night stand, but I knew one
day you'd ask me, so I withheld...
I wanted her... but she wasn't my wife,
and you were always watching.
That drink was calling my name, LOUDLY...
but I walked it off and asked for help...
It's my fifth time getting clean...I will make it my sixth.
They say that God's not real—I looked around
at the orderly creation and knew better...

EDIE BOWMAN

I thought I couldn't live without him, but I
thought of you and left anyway.
She was beautiful but her character was ugly,
I didn't want you to model her...
Before we do whatever we want to do...
let's think of our future sons and daughters,
grandchildren and great grandchildren.
How will our decisions today affect those
around us and those who are to come?
If doing what's right for our own good is not motivation enough...
Then let's do it for someone else.

TIRED!!!

I'm tired now...I give up my way.
I'm tired now...Please Lord, forgive me.
I'm tired now...I'm listening, Lord...
I'm tired now...I let go of old things, I'm open to the new.
I'm tired now...I'm on my face!
I'm tired now...I don't care what anyone thinks now.
I'm SOOO TIRED NOW...it's only what you want!

Burden

I did it again...but here I am.
I wanted it, I sought after it, I got it...I'm disgusted.
I relied on myself and didn't ask your opinion.
I keep on falling, turning away from you—knowing the outcome.
I feel I've gone too far this time...
The voices are closing in on me: they're louder than ever!
Regret and sorrow are my closet friends:
sticking with me...accompanying me.

This is too much for me—I can't bear it...
this constant cycle I've created.
I thought it was the last straw, but then you said...

"Come to Me, all who are weary and heavily burdened (by religious rituals that provide no peace), and I will give you rest (refreshing your souls with salvation). Take My yoke upon you and learn from Me (following me as My disciple), for I am gentle and humble in heart, and YOU WILL FIND REST (renewal, blessed quiet) FOR YOUR SOULS. For My yoke is easy (to bear) and My burden is light."
Matthew 11:28-30 (Amplified Version)

AND NOW...

<u>Being Human</u>

Have you ever gone grocery shopping, paid the cashier... then headed straight for the door leaving your bags on the counter? It wouldn't have felt so bad if you'd remembered before you got to the door, or the if the cashier had stopped you, but if you got all the way home before you even remembered...UGH! It feels like you have to drive to AFRICA now, to get yo stuff! even if it's just around the corner!

Chapter Thirteen
All Things Marriage…

Back in 1992 I was at a youth service in our church in Massillon, Ohio. The minister speaking was a man named Bro. Darryl Glass. He was a man known for being a prophet—a man who speaks the heart of God to people. That day, towards the end of the service, he called my name out, and told me to stand up. I didn't know what to expect. This is what he said, "You might like this, but the Lord is saying that you are going to marry a minister…" I was devastated! Not only was I afraid of marriage and thought that men only brought pain and hurt into your life…I REALLY didn't want to marry a minister!

I went up to Bro. Darryl after the service and asked, "Is this something that has to be. Do I have to do this, do I have no choice in this?" He began to laugh, and looked at me with kindness and understanding, and said, "When God tells you something, he doesn't make you do it, but it is in your best interest—it's something that is good for you." I left that day with a feeling of fear, because I didn't see a lot of good marriages in my life, but I also left with a spark of hope and expectation… after all, God hadn't ever led me astray.

I prayed about this word of knowledge, because we are supposed to judge what is said by prophets. I knew that in my heart I desired a relationship but was too afraid to think about it. I had pushed that desire to the back of my mind. I was only nineteen, but my mother taught me to pray in advance for a husband, I didn't want that at the time, but I did it anyway. I continued to spend time in prayer, go to bible college, hang out with wise women, and serve in my church. Later that year, I was introduced to a young man named Charles Bowman in the basement of our church. He was very tall, dark, handsome, and had an amazing smile…I love a nice smile!

We talked on the phone a couple of times, but it didn't go any further because I was just too afraid to move forward. But a year later he started going to our church and was made the youth pastor and later an elder. One night, at the North Canton skating rink, he asked me, through my friend Tracy, to go on a date with him. It was so funny because she kept going around and around in circles, Literally, with me trying to convince myself to just give him a chance. I was soo scared! On Sweetest Day, Saturday October 16th, 1993 we went on a double date with my friends, Tracy and Eddie Kolbs. We were married a little over a year later in 1994…and the rest is history!

The Lord taught me how to overcome my fears with his help. Charles has been the balance that I need in life, and I have been his.

EDIE BOWMAN

Us

For all I desire now . . . is your smile, a twinkle in your eyes when you look at me, a touch from your hand on mine, a word of comfort to ease my mind, a gentle kiss from your lips, a loving embrace, and to see your face each morning as my eyes awaken. For now, I know what matters most—to let go of the small things and hold on to the big thing. Quality time is more favorable than quantity, but consistent quality time makes all the difference. Listen a lot, laugh a lot, understand a lot, and compromise even more, for Intimacy grows naturally when the ground is fertile with honesty and Unconditional love.

<u>My Charlie Pooh...</u>

It's 12:56pm, Thursday afternoon, and I just received a text from Charles. It's a song called, "It's You," by Kem, from his album *Promise To Love*. It's very refreshing...those who have been married for at least ten years or more know what I mean. We're still going through the coronavirus, so being cooped up in the house has its romantic challenges. We've been through many personality clashes, disagreements, misunderstandings, and financial struggles, but I have to say, it's gestures like these that remind me of my choice back in 1994...I chose you. I choose you, and I'm still choosing you each day.

Morning Grace

We had a horrible argument last night...
We said we'd never go to bed angry at one another...
We both said some pretty harsh words...
This morning, I glanced down at my hand, and
yours was lying lightly across mine...
I looked at our rings sparkling in the morning sun, and I smiled.

Laughter Does a Marriage Good

My husband and I were reading the Proverbs the other day on an app that allows other friends to join you with posts that talk about what we've read together. When we got to chapter 19, verse 13 it said, **"A foolish child is a calamity to a father; a quarrelsome wife is as annoying as a constant dripping."** He posted this with a laughing face and a silly face after it. My comedic, loving, submissive response to this post came after reading chapter 21, verse 23, **"Watch your tongue and keep your mouth shut, and you will stay out of trouble."** (followed by a laughing face, of course).

Taters & Coffee

I was watching this cooking show and I realized that this particular dish called "Lyonnaise Potatoes," sounded similar to what I like in a man—A little rough on the outside (doesn't look like a push over), tender in the middle (kind, and loves God), and full of flavor (dresses nice, likes to have fun, and intelligent)!

I also realized that the way I like my coffee has similar characteristics—Dark roast (strong physically, mentally, and in character), Sweet (shows tenderness, and loving), A lot of cream (comforting and warm to be around), and Hot (has a stable temperament, BUT...will take care of business if he has too)! Before you think this strange...I could've said I like my men the way I like my doughnuts: Big, Round, Soft, too sweet, and sometimes with Cream Filling!!!—I'll leave it up to your imagination to figure those out...

Wow! Is God Funny!!!

Only God would put a person who has a Doctorate in Leadership Education and Master's in Business, is a Math teacher, an Introvert who doesn't like crowds, hardly ever overthinks anything just does it (weird...), is quiet, gets excited thinking about what he will build next in the garage and what he will cook next after watching the Cooking Network (also weird), and enjoys staying home...TOGETHER!!!...
with a person
who loves writing plays, overthinks everything, acts ridiculously silly/crazy (most of the time), is often Loud, receives energy by being around people (most of the time), doesn't like cooking, would go to a musical or play every month if possible, talks to strangers daily, and doesn't like to be in the house much unless I'm exhausted from a long day of fun and talking with others.

"Peanut & Noonie"

(Nicknames...)
Our parents never dreamed that these nicknames given to us while we were young would one day take root, bud, and then blossom...forming a couple who are unique in their union, creative in their giftings, strong in their differences, and forever growing in discovery of themselves—developing into what was already meant to be planted.

"The Marriage That Prays, AND Laughs, together...
Has a Better Chance of Staying Together"

EDIE BOWMAN

BLACK CHRISTIAN WIVES LIBERATION THEOLOGY

(Just warning you...my husband and I have a strange
sense of marital humor. I made him this way—
he used to be so sweet and NORMAL!)

I was in my living-room having a mini-concert by myself. I was
singing *"Be Lion"* from the musical *"The Wiz"* and I was singing
with all of the passion inside of me, after all... that song and *"Home"*
are my favorite songs in the musical, I had to give it my all. It was
9:45, and my husband was upstairs and ready to chill for the night,
so he hollered, "Hey, Ms. Motown Soul Liberation, can you be quiet,
please?! (As if adding please would make it better) ... And he yelled it
just when I was getting to the good part—you know...the part where
the Lion really feels courage rising up inside of him and begins to
sing with this newly found strength and revelation?...

HOW DARE HE?!...

I knew he really did want me to be quiet, (I can sing dramatically
and loudly as if on stage!) but I also knew he was being funny, so
instead of being mad I started to laugh! And I, being my quick-witted
self, immediately said, "When are we black Christian wives gonna
be liberated, huh?! When will we be free in our own homes with our
husbands? When will we be free!? I should start my own movement
called the Black Christian Wives Liberation Theology! When will
I be loved like Christ loved The Church, huh?!" He laughed so hard
that I could hear him downstairs! I began to crack up also...He brings
out the "Best" in me, particularly the crazy/funny side. Thank God
for the crazy moments!

An Ode to My Husband

*Oh, how my eyes never did see, a man who'd
plan a friends' trip for me...
With plane, hotel, and rental car—all free,
and money to spend limitlessly...
And Oh, the pleasure my heart would feel, if
my husband would one day do my will.*

Ode to My Wife

By Dr. Charles Eugene Bowman Jr.

"Picture this," the famous line from the Golden
Girls. This is my life in a nutshell
with my wife. She is constantly picturing
something, and then inserting me into her
thoughts. There is never a day that passes by when she doesn't
ask me, "have you ever..." or "what if...." Her mind is a finely tuned
orchestra playing the most complex Beethoven musical piece.
Her "have you ever..." is the wind section, "what if..." is
the string section, and "picture this..." is the percussion
section. They are orchestrating all at once.

You would think, how is that possible? How can
someone think and juggle so many thoughts,
ideas, and questions all at one time? Just like Beethoven, he
worked endlessly until the last chord or musical arrangement
was constructed. This is my wife! She is conducting while
she's sleeping. While she's watching a TV show. While she's
writing another thought or idea. She's conducting 24/7. I'm
exhausted! Now you may ask, "How are you exhausted?"
Let's go back to the beginning of this ode. My wife can't
conduct all by herself. She solicits co-conductors (that means

me!). I am her peanut butter to her jelly. Her gravy on rice, or dressing. Her butter on toast. Her ice in iced tea. Her cream to her coffee. I can go on and on, but I won't. Wait I think I sound like her! Oh no! I have been converted into a "picture this..." person. Well, if you can't beat them, you simply join them!

Comedic Passive Aggressiveness (CPA)

(It's sounds deep, doesn't it?! It's not a real thing... (I think).
I made it up, but you have to admit, it sounds good!)
Soo... I was missing my husband today and I was in one of those dramatic, theatrical, silly moods. once he sat down, I walked over to him, put my arms out towards him, like a little girl reaching out to her daddy for a hug, and I began rocking back, side to side, in a slow motion. He looked at me and said with a slight giggle, "Oh No...what do you want?" I said, in a baby- like voice, "You saw me, sought me out, pursued me, dated me, married me on Dec. 17ᵗʰ 1994 and brought me home...So Here I AM! You Got Me! It didn't work that time... he actually had a lot to do, BUT sometimes it does.
I often struggle to be me, out loud...I wonder
too much about what others may think or say...
But I'm learning to Trust what God has breathed in
me...I'm different...and He expects me to be.

My Wife is Nuts for Talking to a Squirrel

(I let my husband choose the title for this one)

I talked to a squirrel the other day right outside my kitchen window. We both froze and stared at each other for a while, to see who'd be the first to make a move. "Hey Mr. Squirrel, whatcha doing?"

"Oh, you know…I'm just a squirrel out here tryna get some nuts for me and The Fam, tryna get it done before old man winter git here," (*he was a squirrel from the hood*). "Whatchoo doin?" "Me?… Well, I was just about to make me some lunch, read a little bit, maybe watch a little TV or something…" "Oh, yeah?" "Yeah…" "Coo." The squirrel scurried off of the picnic table on the back deck, up the pillar, leaped onto the garage roof, and before jumping into the tree, he looked back at me. We briefly shared a parting glance, and I'm sure he gave me an "Aiight, then" head nod, and like a flash, he was gone.

Communication Styles

Why won't my husband answer me in Chirp? Oh, I know…we have our Twitter tweets and such, but I mean whistling that sounds like birds chirping. I just asked him a question in Chirp across the dining room table, and he refused to answer me. I asked him why won't he answer me in Chirp? He said, "I refuse to answer you in a language that I do not understand…with your psycho self!" Then he left and went to the basement for a moment. Oh well…I guess some people just want to stay small… to stay in their own little worlds of letters and words… consonants and verbs, they don't want to grow…to experience new things…new ways to express themselves…to join in with the chirpitty, chirp chirp, chirpness of the birds. Huh, some people are soo uppity…

Selective Sleep

Whenever I ask my husband a question, he immediately closes his eyes, falls over, lands on whatever is beside him, and starts snoring! If he's already sitting down, he just drops his head into his chest and acts like he's asleep! It's really scary when he's driving! He even has my daughters doing it! He constantly says... "Edie, stop asking all those questions...you don't have to know everything."

You Be the Judge...

Sometimes my Husband looks over at me, especially at bedtime, with a face of compassion, confusion and often times frustration, and says, *"Turn it off Edie, just turn it off. I wish you had a switch on the side of your head that I could use to turn your mind off to make it stop thinking so much!"*
I wish I had that power too sometimes, but the problem is...If he's the one in control of the switch, I'd always be in the state of nothingness because he'd love the silence, Lol! You see...I also have the problem of talking and teasing him too much, so he wouldn't be able to overcome the urge to just leave the switch off! I'd only have a working mind from 5:45-ish in the morning when he leaves for work to 7:30ish when he gets home from work. Well...perhaps he'd be gracious enough to allow me to ask questions and have some brief conversation before he turns me off, so let's say...9:00 pm. Soo sad.
(Ahh...the beauty of marriage)

An Ode to The Remote Control

(In honor of my husband)

Oh, how he holds me like no one else can...I know my purpose, whilst in his hand. Though he sleepeths, it suiteths me fine, for as long as he grips me, his heart shalt be mine.

M   A   G N E TISM

Opposites do sometimes attract.... BUT later can make you want to kill each other IF.... You don't patiently, and purposefully... Seek to discover the Power and the Purpose in the coming together.

AND NOW...

Being Human

After the coronavirus scare, I feel that all marriage counselors, during premarital counseling, should now be required to have a mandatory teaching called "The Quarantine Scenario." This experiment pushes the adoring couple to imagine living with each other for three months without leaving the home or premises (of course this is considering that you don't already live together). The counselor MUST ask questions like, "If you can't stand her breath, or her smacking while eating, Now... will you be able to for three months?!... If his feet stinks and he talks too much, Now... will you be able to take it for three months?!... If he/she doesn't like to clean up Now... and he/she runs at the sight of a dirty dish... (You get the point!)

Chapter Fourteen
Thankfulness

At Thanksgiving time, we usually go over to my grandmother, Mama Bertha's, house for dinner. Before we eat, we go around the table and say what we are thankful for...Mama goes last. She graces us with her strong, passionate, faith-filled voice, coming through such a tiny body, as she reminds the family of the goodness of God, and how He's been with us through it all. She prays for all of us to know God and to develop a close relationship with him. She proclaims that all of her children, grandchildren, and greats, etc., will be saved! She never lets us forget that we should always be able to depend on family, come what may.

Thank God all Mighty for those grandmothers who have lived a life of faithfulness to God, and who have lived long enough to pass it onto their families. I have listened, Mama...and I see your strength and faithfulness—you have modeled it well. It is not in vain.

Simple Things

*I was feeling a little down today I was stuck in the house,
and there' was nowhere to go anyway it's chilly outside,
and I didn't want to walk I was running out of ideas
to write about, and I needed to do laundry. I know big
deal! People are starving in Africa and there are homeless
people in our city, so why am I whining, right?...
I went upstairs and there was a brightness in the hallways and in
the rooms, shining through the sheer curtains of teal blue, black,
and white. The sun was giving me a gift, reminding me to be
thankful for the small things the simple things of life. I suddenly
felt better, and all because my husband had opened the blinds.*

Unity

I'm in my new creative writing room today—
envisioned by Me and Created by You.
Looking out of the window, I'm inspired to be
myself and use God's gift he gave to me,
made easier by the gift he gave to You.
This haven of creativity is filled with glorious golden yellows,
peaceful blues, touches of vibrant reds and greens
And a feeling of beauty and wonder...
Thank you Charles for making a dream come true.

Each day that we are able to awake, get dressed, have a cup of coffee, go to work, drive back home, and see our families...should not be taken lightly. Let's be Thankful, because someone didn't come home today, somebody lost a loved one, and somebody didn't wake up...

SUNDAY, DECEMBER 8th, 2019

It was a wonderful worship service today. The praise team sang my favorite song, and I felt the presence of God strongly. The words, "Your grace and mercy has captured my heart..." rang over and over in my ears, filled my heart, and came pouring out of my mouth in worship to God. As I was singing, I whispered something to the Lord... "When I'm with my sister and my mom today, please do something that brings us closer together and brings them, my sisters, closer to you..."

Later that day, a couple of my nieces, and my mother enjoyed putting up the Christmas tree, singing and listening to carols and old school music. We had food, cookies, punch, etc. We laughed, talked, reminisced, and just enjoyed each other's company. We rarely have all four sisters together, so this was special! My mother really looks forward to our putting up her tree each year.

After the festivities were over, I took my oldest sister Marie, my sister Doretha, and my niece TOR E'ZHA, home. On our way, we were on Walnut and were crossing over 12th street.

All of a sudden, my sister Doretha hollered "That car is not going to stop, it's not going to stop!!!"

I, in what seemed like slow motion said..." Whaaaaaat Caaaaaar." As I was saying that, a long white car flew past us, at what appeared to be 1000 miles per hour, and remember, I'm IN THE MIDDLE OF THE ROAD!!! I promise you... and everyone who knows me knows that I am honest and would NOT lie about something like this, but I PROMISE YOU THAT CAR WENT THROUGH US!!! I was still in the middle of the road, and there was no way that car could've gone around, in front of, or behind us! IT WENT THROUGH US! I sat there for a moment until I came to myself. I slowly creeped across the road and was facing a church called Community Life.

The car was eerily silent for a moment until I said "Did what I think just happened, happen?

Doretha said, "Yes, that car went right through us."

Marie said, "Yes it did..."

I said, "Thank you Lord, there is no way that that car should've missed us!" I was in the middle of the road. I never even saw it... the only thing I saw was a white blur going through us..." We were all in a state of disbelief, and silent. I drove them home, told them I loved them, and then I cautiously and robotically drove myself home.

When I got in the house, I began to ask God, "Did you just do what I think you did?" This was my analytical side talking. "Did that car go through us?" As I stood there in my kitchen, I saw a vision: I saw the whole thing again, right before my eyes, but this time in HD! I saw the truth...it really did happen! That was the Lord confirming it to me. He knows that I will explain away something if it doesn't make sense. I began to thank him and to cry uncontrollably. I called my mother to tell her about it, and while we were on the phone she began to cry and thank him also, saying that she knew it was the Lord who protected us!

I continued to cry and cry and cry…I called my sister Sylvia and told her what happened—she knew it was a miracle! I told my husband and children. I told my congregation that next Sunday, I even told my customers at the salon, and other people's customers! I will continue to tell it! The Lord still does miracles. A few weeks later I was on that same road after dropping off someone.

I was driving, and my daughter was in the passenger's seat. I began to cry again… "What's wrong, mom?" Autumn said.

"This is where the car almost hit us," I said.

"Don't cry, you're going to make me cry..."

"I can't help it... I've never experienced anything like that before."

My mind often goes back to the prayer I whispered to the Lord that day in service. I asked him to do something to bring me and my sisters closer together and closer to him…well, he did! Not in the way I would've chosen, but it worked in my life. Whenever I'm feeling down or ungrateful, I will remember this day. The day the Lord showed his mercy, grace, and protection, and favor towards me and my family.

Your Strength helps my Weakness

I love to see people who just roll with the punches—they keep right on movin' no matter what comes their way! I need these kinds of people in my life because they encourage me. Just by watching them, I feel like I can make it too. This type of fortitude does not come naturally for me: I have to work harder at it to get there. I have to fight through the "what if's" and the "I don't understand's" going on in my head before I move, sometimes. I am so very thankful that the "Roll with the Punches" people, are there to balance me out, but remember…those strong personality types need times of rest, refreshing, prayer, and balance as well.

EDIE BOWMAN

Let's be thankful that we are all at different levels
in life and have different strengths that we can use
to balance one another out when we need to.

Memorable Compliments I'm Thankful for as a Playwright:

"Thank you, I understand now…I never really understood
the true meaning of what Christmas means for me, but now I
really do. It changed my heart" (***The Gift***, Christmas Play)

"I felt joy and healing flowing through my body while I
was laughing. I couldn't stop! I had to excuse myself from
the theatre." (***Good Like Medicine***, Comedy Show)

"Kingdom was my son's first play and we just wanted to
pay homage to you by blowing up and framing the playbill
and putting it in my dining room. Thank you for giving him
that opportunity." (***Kingdom***, Play on Fatherlessness)

"Edie…You're Sick!" (***Good Like Medicine***, Comedy Show)

"Much like your play, ***Kingdom,*** the message in ***The Gift,***
changed my life, and my family's as well!! Bravo Edie! Bravo!!!"

"The play, ***Good Like Medicine***, was a success! It was
a blessing after the show to be told by two older women
that one was having health issues and hadn't laughed
so hard as she did during our skit, Side Effects.
"Maaaan, the play was suuuuper dope. I was laughing
from backstage. Huge shout out to the ever so talented
Edie Bowman for her vision. Can't wait to see how far
the Father takes it. Big shouts to the cast. I loved every
moment!" (***Good Like Medicine***, Comedy Show)

I Met a Man From Hungary Today...

I met a man from Hungary today... he stood in front of the downtown parking meter in front of the salon I work at. He was looking quite confused.

I asked him, "Do you need some change?"

I already had fifty cents in hand just in case, but he said, "No, I'm trying to find The Cultural Center." I told him how to get there and then we began to talk. I asked him where he was from and he told me he was from Hungary and had been here for over sixty years. I was shocked because his accent was so strong!

He was going to see the art exhibit. "They're featuring art from my country" he said.

I asked him, "Is it from the Renaissance or Impressionism period?"

He said, "Yes! Impressionism." At this point I was glad I studied a little bit of art history in college, and LOVED IT! Look at me being well rounded! I was so excited to have met him—even for that short Moment In Time.

I wish the world was not so crazy and untrusting, because I would've followed him to the art museum and enjoyed the beauty and conversation of art with him that day, and possibly...gained a new friend. I'm Thankful for being me.

Psalms 91

It's was Easter morning and we are at home because of the coronavirus. I was just thinking about how when I was in high school, I missed the first Easter service that I could remember. My family went, but I had to stay home because I was sick. While lying in the bed feeling sad about what I was missing, I decided to read Psalms 91. It was one of my favorite Psalms. I also decided to memorize it that day. It wasn't too hard because I read it often. I struggled with fear, so this was my "go-to" chapter; I'd read

it aloud, often, to get through whatever plagued my mind at the
time. By the time my family returned, I had memorized it all lying
there in that bed. It sustained me through so many dark times…
This morning, I felt a little saddened that we wouldn't be
at church for Easter: I was missing my church family, my
mother, daughters, and other precious family members,
but then my sorrow quickly changed to thankfulness.

I had a revelation…that same Psalm echoed in my heart and in
my mind, reminding me of how it was still sustaining me even
thirty years later. It was still my covering during this plague
of the coronavirus. It was still calling out to me to trust In
God, for protection, to call upon Him for everything I need.
Your word is timeless, limitless, and eternal…it's alive!

Thank you that I will never go through
THIS again… for I have learned.

<u>Beautiful Darkness</u>

I met you there… though it was the most
horrible time of my life, I met you there.
You heard my shallow cry for peace, came
right on in, and sat with me
asking no questions right away…just there…
You began teaching me how to see things
differently, I fought you at first.
I felt comfort in the pain. I didn't want to be free…not yet.
Anger was my friend…we understood each other
well—an unstable relationship built on fear.
He came in uninvited, but you…you came
tenderly—a subtle, sweet conversion.
Like a burnt orange harvest moon in late October,
you overwhelmed the sky of my haunted soul,

EDIE BOWMAN

Filling it with new things that never existed—
leaving little room for anything else.
You met me there...like a gentleman you took my
hand, and beautifully led me out of the darkness.

Controlling My Narrative

Thank you for controlling the narrative—
you speak life between the lines.
Thank you for entering My story—giving me a new perspective.
Thank you for some fairytales—often life has
groomed us to expect the nightmares.
Thank you for teaching us to hope...of
wonderful, beautiful things as we dream.
The pages of my life are already written in your book
And I'm still walking them out...
I may not know each sentence, word, comma, or period
But with you as my co-writer, at least I know where I'll finish.
I thought I went too far this time... but when I looked up from
my fallen place, I wiped the dirt from my face, and you were
there with your hand outstretched to pick me up once more...
--THANKFUL

On Being Extra!

Ok, so I'm a little extra, I admit that...but it's not like
I'm the Barney Fife from *The Andy Griffith Show* or
Dwight Schrute from *The Office* kind of Extra!
They are hilarious though...
They both take everything seriously and want you to know it!
They will make you laugh and think that they're
doing way too much at the same time!

They insist on things to be their way, because
it's the best, even to a fault!
They have an extreme passion for excellence in all that they do!
Now I'm not quite that extreme, but when it
comes to comedic extremes...I'm close.
I'm thankful for how God created me...
comedy can be invaluable at times.

<u>Thankfulness</u>

Thank you for your Mercy when I deserved to pay for what I did.
Thank you for your Grace that empowered me
when I didn't have the strength to do it.
Thank you for your Justice...you are the one
who repays and sets things right.
Thank you for your Faithfulness—you never
let me fall or stay where I am.
Thank you for Gentleness when dealing with me when I'm hurting.
Thank you for being a Good Father—you
know me personally and intimately.
Thank you for Kindness, Lord...you bless me just because.
Thank you for Joy unspeakable, accompanying
me even in the time of trouble.
Thank you for showing me your Unconditional
Love by sending your Son.
Thank you for Healing me physically, emotionally, and spiritually.
Thank you for your Presence—for being there...In Every Moment.

EDIE BOWMAN

The Power of Using Your Gift

Many graves are filled with songs, books, paintings, movies, businesses, and such...Because fear of failure kept them back. I have that same fear...but like my favorite Author and Speaker, Joyce Meyer, said in her book *Do It Afraid*; that's what I'm doing...
Thank you, Lord for using others in the body of Christ to use their gifts to heal, encourage, teach, and bring joy.
May I do the same with my gifts as well.
Thankful...

AND NOW...

Being Human

Have you ever been in your car and needed to concentrate on parking or how to get somewhere you haven't been before, so you turned down the volume on your radio, or turned it completely off to help you accomplish your goal? Do you notice that we hunch our backs and raise our shoulders, or take on this weird kind of walk when we're caught in the rain...as if that makes us get less wet?

Chapter Fifteen
Community: We Need Each other

I've always been a peace maker—I couldn't stand to see someone done wrong, and for them not to have their say or get justice somehow. I've learned that peace doesn't come without some kind of confrontation, un-comfortability, pressure, or struggle. When I was younger, I used to look at hurting, addicted, broken people around me, and wonder why they were hurting, and what happened to them to make them this way? I'm the same way today. I love to see people who may disagree with each other, who have an ought with another person, or who are finding it hard to forgive another person, work things out. It brings my heart joy to see healthy relationships of all kinds, functioning in harmony. We need each other in this world: we need families to be healed, communities to work together despite differences, healing in our government, nation, and the world. The truth of the matter is, it all begins at home. That may sound elementary, but just think…If families are healthy and whole, then communities will be. If communities are, then cities and states will be, and so will nations, and ultimately our world. I need you—what you have to share and teach. You need me—what I have to offer that you didn't know you needed. We need each other—to build up, encourage, and strengthen, not to tear down.

Divided we cannot stand.

The Fishbowl Epiphany

I was standing in front of our fish tank today watching all of the four little frogs and the thirteen fish swimming back and forth, up and down, going in and out of the playful things we placed inside for their pleasure. Suddenly, I was drawn to the expression on my face—it had a slight grimace—a look of frustration and contemplation. I also began to ask myself about the feeling I was experiencing in the moment. I often have these kinds of expressions on my face without noticing. Someone usually draws it to my attention and asks me, "what is the matter?"

I realized that I was frustrated with seeing the same old fish day after day! There are only black fish or white fish with black spots swimming around in there! I was tired of seeing them! The only enjoyment I get out of looking at that tank every day are the playful frogs—they are quite entertaining. I WAS BORED! I needed to see some more color! Red fish, yellow fish, green fish, multicolored fish!!!!

I had an epiphany…that's the same way God felt when he created man: he wanted to see many colors: red, black, brown, white, yellow, and red—beautiful faces, interesting cultures, diverse personalities... he didn't want us to only be around what we are familiar with—he wants us to enjoy and learn from our differences. He hates boring things—One way He proves it is by creating a new sunrise and sunset each day and each night.

EDIE BOWMAN

Praying Hands

Mr. Worthington picked up his money clip that was lying on the dresser and began to put it in the back pocket of his favorite, well-worn jeans—left pocket like always. Before he jammed it in, he glanced down at it for just a second and noticed the twenty-dollar bill that enclosed all of his lesser bills, had a name written on it. The name was carefully written sideways in the center of the right-hand side of the bill. It simply read… "Jason."

He, being a man of fervent prayer, began to imagine who this Jason was and call out Jason's name before his God, daily. In his vivid imagination, he had an ingrained picture of what he was like, and what he even looked like—tall, lean, clean-cut, dark, handsome, and in his early thirties. One day he realized that he had pictured Jason a lot like himself—minus him being in his thirties part.

"Jason is a good man…" he said to himself. "If I had a son, I'd want him to be just like Jason!" He imagined, a God-fearing man… strong, smart, hard-working… Intensely engrossing himself in the story of this now, very real, imaginary being, he prayed for him more purposefully and endearingly, as if he knew him intimately somehow.

Lord God, please bless Jason today…shower him with your blessings, bring him to the place that you want him to be. May he walk right into your purpose for his life, order his footsteps, Oh God! Show him your grace and mercy, prosper him, and protect him. May you lead him down the path of righteousness, Oh Lord! Show him your will for his life, and may he never stray away from it, in Jesus' name, Amen!

Today, felt particularly joyous to him—he had showered, eaten breakfast, read his bible, and gotten up from his knees in prayer like he did every morning. He slowly walked over to grab his coat off of the back of his favorite chair when the phone rang. He doesn't get many calls, except for telemarketers, so he almost missed the call.

"Hello?"

"Hi, Dad!"

"Natalie, what a pleasant surprise! Are you okay? I haven't heard from you in a while."

"I'm fine Dad, I just have something to tell you, is all…"

"Okay…now I'm really nervous, Nat."

"Don't be nervous. Can you meet me at our special place in about 10 minutes?"

"I can…are you sure everything is okay?"

"I promise it is, Daddy."

"Okay, I'm on my way."

"Thanks, Dad! See ya soon!"

He nervously hung up the phone, grabbed the keys off the counter, and paused. Scratching his head, he released a sigh, "Hmm…"

On his way to their place, he had memories of the two of them sharing sodas, burgers, and ice cream cones—mint chocolate chip for her and chocolate for him. He remembered how Natalie always wanted a little taste of his also, and how he'd take great pleasure in allowing her to have his leftover waffle cone, but only if she'd give him her last two fries. He gave a nostalgic giggle as he pulled up.

As he walked into the small, damp smelling, cozy place, he saw her sitting in what used to be their favorite spot. They embraced, and she began to tell him of how she had finally found the job of her dreams, and a nice apartment that she'd love for him to bless. He was so proud of her. She was a lot like him—hard working, strong, God fearing, kind…

"Oh, Daddy!" she said nervously.

"Yes," he said while enjoying the final licks of his chocolate cone "You want my cone?" he said with a smile.

"No, Dad I…I have one more thing that I want to tell you, someone I want you to meet."

"Well, who is it sweetheart, and why are you so anxious? That's not like you. You hidin' some tall, dark, and handsome guy around here somewhere?" he said jokingly. "You know no one will ever be good enough for my Nat, right?!"

"I…I know, but I found someone, and he makes me extremely happy, and he's so much like you, Dad! It's what drew me to him!"

"Yeah?... Well bring him out! Where is this young fellow that's so much like me?!" He said, looking around with much excitement.

Rising up from the booth behind him stood a slim, strong, handsome, God fearing, black man with his hand held out to shake his.

Natalie's father's, strong hands, began to tremble—much like they did when they were up lifted in prayer every morning.

"Hello, Mr. Worthington, my name is Jason, I've heard a lot about you. I'm very pleased to finally meet you, Sir."

His strong, fervent, praying hands, became weakened, numb, and cold...

The Eyes See...The Heart Remembers

I remember when I was a little girl, I lived on the southwest side of Canton, Ohio for a while. Our neighborhood had both black and white people in it. I never remember focusing on it though...we just all played and had fun together. My next door neighbor was a little white boy named Darin, he had blonde hair, and we were best friends. He'd come over to my house sometimes, and I'd go over his house and sit on the porch with him. We'd talk, play, laugh, and share snacks together. He was so nice to me—that was the biggest thing that I remembered about him, well...that and the day that he shared a bowl of radishes with me. I didn't like them at all! Oops! I also remember that he couldn't say my nickname very well...it's Noonie, but he'd always call me Noodie. He would come over to my house, knock on the door and say "Can Noodie come out and play?" and we would laugh. I don't remember if we moved away or if he did, but to this day, I do remember the pain of losing that friend.

God Uses People

We all are given gifts, abilities, and talents. I thought about this the other day when the icemaker on our refrigerator broke. My husband acts as if the world is coming to an end if he doesn't have 1000 glasses of ice water a day, so this was a major problem (well, at least an 8 on a scale of 10)! It felt so good to call a friend who has his own business and the expertise to fix appliances like these, and to have the situation remedied quickly. That was a great ability and a gift to us! Sometimes, we may need someone to listen to us or to talk to… if we have such a person in our lives, he or she is an amazing gift to you! They were able to give you comfort and release. Sometimes we may need to be entertained without hearing expletives and covering our eyes…God gave me the ability to write and produce plays that give us these escapes through entertainment!

I desired to have a place in my home to get away—a place to pray, read, write, and just relax by myself. I wanted a window seat, a desk, a bookshelf, and pieces of art on the walls that I chose. I told my husband the colors: a particular shade of blue (Blue China) to paint three of the walls, a particular yellow (Golden Promise) for one wall, a mustard yellow for the curtains on the sides, sheer white for the middle, white venetian blinds, and accent colors of red and green through pillows, plants, my chair, rug, etc. He thought I was crazy when I told him all of these colors.

"That sounds like a kid's playroom, Edie!" he said, but I had a vision inside. Long story short…I have a beautiful little getaway room that he absolutely loves. God used the talents he has to bring the vison I had into reality. It gives me much joy, peace and relaxation.

I just got done watching the show, *Hoarders* a show that helps people who have mental/emotional issues that make them believe they have to hang on to things in large quantities regardless of if they need the items, if they cause health hazards, or even if it may cause them to lose their home. It totally invades their lives, hinders their ability to move forward, causes family problems, and even health problems. It's heart wrenching to see them suffer needlessly when there is help available, but their mind tells them that they can't let go. Seeing the people who come in and counsel the hoarders, clean up everything, and ultimately give them a new perspective and way of life is encouraging to see! Those helpers are gifted with patience and compassion!

EDIE BOWMAN

We may pray to God and ask Him for help in time of need. He can miraculously fix our refrigerators, talk to us audibly, give us visions in our imaginations that entertain us, and even give us an amazingly beautiful room to relax in, but he usually chooses to use people. Why?...

Because He's a Good Father and created us to live in community—to need each other, and to one day dwell together eternally with Him as his children.

An Art to Perfect

Listening is an art of its own...it is not something you do audibly only, for some cannot hear...It is something done with the heart and mind—a willingness to understand and then decide what to do next with that knowledge. It behooves us all to perfect this art— All healthy relationships depend upon it.

I Don't Agree... But I Listened.

If I possessed a super power, it would be the ability to stop people from talking and thinking about anything else except about what the person they're listening to is saying. Once that person is finished listening and thinking ONLY about what the speaker was saying... he/she is now able to respond, while the other person is now listening and given the same powers to listen. This would be specifically useful during debates, interviews, marriages, politics—in overall communication.

The inability to stop a person who disagrees with you as they're talking, and the inability to think about what you want to say in rebuttal when we're feeling strongly about an issue, may feel uncomfortable in the beginning, but once it's practiced for a while, even if the parties disagree...at least both sides were heard, understood, and received the respect they both deserved as unique individuals with opinions. This is extremely difficult in cases where something is clearly right or wrong according to the truth that is available to the opposing side, and when the word of God says so. In these cases, we have to be like Jesus: tell them the Truth, shake off the dust from your feet, and move on.

Irrational Rationality

Friend #1: A cup is something that you wear around your neck for beauty

Friend #2: Uh...No-o-o, that would be a necklace

Friend #1: Well, that's your opinion

Friend #2: It's not my opinion, it's the truth. The dictionary proves that a cup is not something that you wear around your neck, it's something you drink out of.

Friend #1: Like I said...that's your O-PIN-ION!

Friend: #2: No, it's not. It's reality!

Friend #1: Well, I choose to believe differently!

Friend # 2: You know what?... I can't even have an intelligent conversation with you. You're irrational!

Friend #1: And Again...that's your opinion!

Friend #2: UGH! I can't!... Let's just move on

Friend #1: Yeah, let's. I think that would be a good idea. I don't think we're going to agree on this one.

Friend #2: (*Yeah, because you're insane...* he thought to himself) Would you like a cup of coffee or something?

Friend #1: Sure.

<u>The Wisdom of Proverbs 18:17 That We All Need!</u>

When it comes to making well informed decisions concerning relationships, solving problems in the workplace, family situations, business, and even who we choose to vote for during election time... remember the words of who God said is the wisest man who ever lived, King Solomon:
"The first to plead his case seems right, *until* another comes and cross-examines him."
(The Amplified Version)

"The first to speak in court sounds right—
until the cross-examination begins."
(New Living Translation)

WOW!!! SO...
In every situation, it's wise to listen carefully to all sides, do our own unbiased research—without already having our minds made up, ask questions to get clarity and understanding, Then... prayerfully make a decision based on God's Word as the final authority because in many situations, we may never get the whole truth?... This is especially important when voting. In my extremely dramatic mind, I can't imagine the Holy Spirit of God turning his head or jumping out of the booth as we're voting, like He's trying to give us privacy or something—that would be absurd! Afterall, He is with IN you, telling you the Father's heart on every issue on that ballot.
He's God IN Every Moment.

20/20
(In Light of Our Differences)

He KNEW he was right
And then, he heard the other side of the story.
She was TOTALLY convinced,
But ten years later, she saw things differently.
They STOOD on their truths.
Unfortunately, the heavy boulders of life cracked their foundations.

Let's face it…no one knows everything.
We can always learn from others even in our fields of expertise.
Saying something emphatically before
we've had time to KNOW it's true
USUALLY ENDS UP MAKING US LOOK PRETTY BAD!
Conclusion: observe, think, listen, study, then speak if necessary.

Conflict

She caught his eye that first day of school—
he secretly made soft glances
She had a way about her he'd never seen before.
She was different very different—he liked the difference.
He wanted to ask her to sit with him at lunch he didn't.
She smiled a smile of white clouds set against the darkness of night
He painfully quelled his desires to get to know her—
and felt sickened by his weakness.
She was free she knew who she was and walked in it.
The next semester he saw her with his best friend
Sitting together in Seminary class.
"When did he change his mind?" he thought.
"When did he become so strong?
Why didn't I?…"

EDIE BOWMAN

Human Interaction PLEASE?!!!

I NEED to interact with people outside of my house! It would
be a delight to go to Belden Village Mall and greet people that
I haven't seen in months… to go to Starbucks and shoot the
breeze with a friend or two…to walk at the Monument Park
with a different face beside me to look at, and a different voice
to listen to…to have movie night over at my Mommy's house
and kiss her face as I hug her…to sit next to a stranger and share
expressions of awe as we enjoy a musical at Playhouse Square…
to scream alongside my daughters at an Elevation Worship or
Lecrae concert…to experience my first cruise with my husband
while risking internal combustion as a result of the bubbling
over inside of joy as I interact with people all around me!!!…….
WHOA! I think I just almost fainted with Futuristic
Excitement Overload (F.E.O. it's a thing!)
I do realize that I don't actually NEED these things, but I do
miss and desire them greatly, as I'm sure we all do during
this time of social distancing, BUT this too shall pass…
and when it does: hug a little longer, say I love you
more often, call for no reason at all, give without
being asked… and appreciate the small things.

A Declaration Over Our Youth

I call forth a righteous generation of young men and women
who will rise up and take their positions as warriors. They
will stand against the powers of darkness that are sent out to
destroy them through deceptive, cultural and societal norms.
Our young men will not fall prey to drugs, gangs, violence, and
creating children out of wedlock. They will know the worth and
value of women and treat them like the daughters of God they
are. They will know their Heavenly Father whether their earthly

fathers are present or not. Anger will not rule their hearts and actions, but love will—Agape Love that only God can give.

Our young women will not have sex before marriage because they know who they are as daughters of God and will not settle for anyone who does not believe as they do or love them enough to wait. They find their identity and security in knowing their Heavenly Father whether their earthly fathers know how to show them love or not.

Our youth WILL know their God and do Great exploits for His Kingdom! They will discover and develop their gifts and talents and use them to bring God glory. They will learn from the wisdom of their elders. They WILL be strong and courageous to stand up against the false ideologies of this world and follow Godly principles instead.

They will be Godly fathers and mothers that train up their children in the word of God. They will not compromise who they are to follow the ungodly ways of this world. They will be pillars for the next generation to model and will never stop being the Light in this dark world.

GIFTINGS
I Fell…

GARY ran over and picked me up, SHERRY told me, "It'll be okay…" HENRY prayed for me, GRACE took a band-aid out of her purse and put it on my knee, MICHEAL told me how not to fall next time…CRYSTAL told me how she also fell once, EDDIE told a joke about it to lighten the mood, JOYCE gave me money to buy new stockings, JOE hugged me, MARY called later to check on me… they ALL helped.

EDIE BOWMAN

—For what I fear is that while we all long to be seen, heard, understood, and loved... many may never get to experience this—to have their basic longings fulfilled.

<u>Things We all Can Do Better</u>

- *Take the time today to listen to someone and try not to talk about yourself much at all, just listen...*
- *Do something nice for someone and expect nothing in return.*
- *Talk to someone who has different interests than you, learn something about those interests, then share it with them later.*
- *Ask about another person's story with the motive to understand them better.*
- *Say an encouraging word to someone today, whether they seem to need it or not.*
- *When someone shares their problems with you, don't compare them to yours—it's not a competition, you'll have another time to share yours.*
- *If you see someone at work, school, church, etc., who is usually alone, invite that person out for coffee or dinner—take a risk...*

(Unless, of course, you see strange or scary Lifetime movieish tendencies in that person that tell you to do otherwise— "Momma didn't raise no fool!")

AND NOW...

<u>Being Human</u>

Have you ever heard someone's voice on the radio, and then when you saw them on TV or in person, you were like, "Huh! I thought he was at least 6'5," weighed 300 pounds, had a beard, AND a mohawk... and here he is lookin' like Barney Fife wearin' in a hoodie, some joggers, wit' some Nike's on! WHAT?!!!

Chapter Sixteen
The Power of Christmas

<u>The Power of Christmas</u>

I just got done watching a Christmas
movie, and it's the end of March!
What I realized while watching the movie was that the wonder
and the majesty of Christmas never ends—it stays in our hearts all
year long. It just takes a spark to ignite its presence in our lives.
The Coronavirus is still affecting us right now, but the Lifetime
Movie Network keeps playing Christmas movies. Do you know

why? Of course you do… because the ability to uplift and inspire us to love, give, and to think of others is what Christmas brings. Despite the fact that nine times out of ten we already know how the movies will end…we don't care, because the lights, singing of carols, romances, parties and such, keeps our minds on good things—kind things. These movies help us remember what's important. And even in these times of uncertainty, somehow, the Christmas Spirit is still calling out to us to remember… remember its power is in Christ, and He brings hope at all times.

Christmas 2019

(The Joy of "Presence")

This Christmas was busy…a good kind of busy though…but still busy. Our family had a Christmas Spectacular show at the theatre and a wedding all within a week apart! Talk about biting off more than we can chew…that we did! We bit it, chewed it, and committed to seeing it through. It was now Christmas eve, and we were sitting in the living room, exhausted. No Christmas eve dinner was planned this year, No awesome smells coming from the kitchen flowing through each room to our nostrils and into our salivation glands and memories...No loud family voices of laughter and joy filled our eardrums and our hearts. No stories of old, and the men debating over their favorite football teams. No stepping over each other because the rooms are soo small yet overflowing with love. Nope! Not this year.

Now, we knew the real meaning of Christmas in our hearts, and we declared it, but something still felt off...then, she showed up!

"Bama!" as the girls called her...

"Mommy!" I screamed, as I opened the door and hugged her lovingly. She entered with her broad, open, bright smile, with that gap between her teeth, and her buttery, creamy toned skin that makes her shine like the warming sun. We were soo excited! We quickly took her things, put on our jammies, gathered our pillows, blankets, and snacks, and Picked a movie (A Christmas Carol). We giggled, cuddled, and talked a little through the movie, but it was okay...

She brought what we needed that Christmas...at that moment in time. She brought warmth, joy, and that presence of comfort and stillness. She brought gentle tones of voice, peaceful gestures, and cozy heart memories. Yes, this Christmas season was very different, in its busyness, but boy how one person's "presence" can change the whole atmosphere.

A CHRISTMAS 2020 & 2021 PRAYER

I pray, this Christmas, I'll warmly embrace
and kiss my loved ones on the face—
that peace and joy may rule our streets and
bring prejudice and hatred to its knees.
Let anger and fear be hushed by hope while
Christmas carols fill our homes

and ungloved hands actually hold, others'
hands… instead of phones.
I pray the Christmas table will hear sweet
songs of worship—dispelling fear…
words of praise, and not politics or talks of
things we cannot fix without your grace.
Christmas 2020 and year 2021 will definitely be
new, but one thing that will never change
is spending it in honor of You.
Christ has come, let's focus on Him and
be mindful of what we say…
This is a time of Holy remembrance, give
thanks this Christmas Day!

"God Rest Ye Merry Gentle Men" is one of those
Christmas songs with a gentle, yet commanding tone. It
instantly captures your heart within the first few notes—
drawing you into the moment, imploring you to listen with
awe and remember the timeless miracle of Christmas.

A Christmas Prayer for Today

*O Come, O Come, Emmanuel and ransom captive Israel
That mourns in lonely exile here, until the Son of God appear
Rejoice! Rejoice! Emmanuel, shall come to thee, O Israel.*

This song still speaks to us today…our world is suffering
from racial tensions, a pandemic, financial instability,
political upheaval, and a spiritual drought.
We need you Emmanuel…Please come to us!
Heal us, revive us, bring peace…Save us!

EDIE BOWMAN

We are in Exile to our own way of existing, and
being left to our own devices—we have failed!
We have not depended on You, and we are
now experiencing the repercussions.
This Christmas, Come to us... that we may Rejoice!

A Christmas Song for the Hurting

Light in the darkness, come rescue my soul.
This day at Christmas, I give you control.
My heart is broken, but you can heal.
Savior of the world, your love I feel.

So now I sing with the angels' chorus, "Hallelujah to the King"
And I rejoice in you for the joy that Christmas brings.
Light in the darkness, you shine within me
Healing my sorrow, thy peace renews me.
Carols of promise, filling my tongue
While singing through me, chains are undone.

Emmanuel come and live within us, fill our emptiness with love
Overflowing...peace arising... celebrate this day of joy.

So now we sing with the angels' chorus, "Hallelujah to the King"
And we rejoice in you for the joy that Christmas brings
Yes, we rejoice in you for the joy that Christmas brings.

*I was feeling a little down today but then I heard a Christmas
song. . . and its magic filled my thoughts and immediately
changed my perspective—I began to long with expectation
for the season of Joy to come again, and it's only June!*

The Christmas Blues

Isn't it crazy how boring our neighborhoods look a couple weeks after Christmas?...I mean, it literally goes from lights and wreaths, Santa and his reindeer pulling the sleigh in the front yard, huge snowflakes dazzling in the trees, angels blowing trumpets, inflatable snow globes and snowmen with pipes, decorated trees, doors that look like presents, lighted lampposts, and holly all around... to one day you're driving down your street, and you feel this emptiness inside...your eyes are experiencing depression, and your heart is void of joy—it's only left with the memories of what was.

There are only houses left that have decorations and lights that never come on again or deflated Santa's laying around on the ground, which in my opinion, is an equivalent to the third degree murder of Santa and the owners should be arrested! (TRAGEDY!!!) Sure... there may even be a couple houses still lit in the neighborhood, but let's be honest... "The Thrill is Gone" and let's face it... "You Lost That Lovin Feeling." It's Gone...Gone... Gone...until next year!

Christmas NOW!!!

IT'S NINETY DEGREES OUTSIDE—IT'S SOO MUGGY
I CAN HARDLY BREATHE! EVERYTHING IS GREEN
AND IN FULL BLOOM...AND I HAVE THREE
CHRISTMAS MOVIES SAVED ON THE DVR WAITING FOR
ME, AND I'M SINGING CAROLS IN MY HEAD RIGHT AT
THIS MOMENT! HURRAY FOR CHRISTMAS IN JULY!
OH, HOW I LONG FOR THEE...EVEN AS
THE SUN BURN-ETHS MY FACE.

EDIE BOWMAN

Excerpts from "*The Gift*" Stage Play

(Scene Nine)

<u>Narrator</u>
A soul that once was filled with darkness
has now accepted the light
A heart that once was lost, is found, and beats with new delight.
A mind that searched for rest and peace,
has ceased, it gropes no more…
For now, the secret that had never been
hidden, has opened up the door.
Receive it now, embrace its coming…this Christmas gift is free!
Its ribbons are love, its wrappings, joy, given to you and me.

Listen to the voice of Christmas, He's speaking all around,
Receive this Gift not purchased, His worth cannot be found,
So forget your gold and silver, and be free from pain and strife,
In case you haven't noticed, this gift is eternal life.
Jesus! Is the voice you're hearing, it echoes loud and clear,
He's The Gift, that keeps on giving, all throughout the year,
Will you heed His calling? Will you dare to try once more?...
Listen, I hear Him knocking, open your heart's door.

Christmas Jammin!

"*Carol of The Bells*" when performed by The Trans-Siberian Orchestra, is a song that is absolutely impossible for me to be still on! Even if I'm sitting in the car, I have to at least fake like I'm the world's best drummer or electric guitar player… I mean you can't just sit there and do nothing!!! But if I'm at home or in an open place, it's Goin' Down! There will be jumpin' on couches, running, dancing, head bangin' and a lot of Rock-N-Rollin'!

The Thing About Light...

Light shines in darkness and brings direction
Light gives clarity and understanding to our minds
Light refreshes us after the storm
Light produces life and sustains things connected to it
Light draws attention to itself...
This can be good, but it can also cause problems.
Jesus is The Light of the world:
He came to bring peace, but also a sword.
He came to bring righteousness, as well as justice.
The manger, that day, was filled with Joy and coming despair
When God placed his Son in a lowly manger
to bring the light of salvation...
He also he had to die in darkness on a cross to do it.
The light shines greatest in dark places
Jesus...the light shining through us in this world.

A Letter to Christmas...

*JUST KNOWING YOU'RE COMING FILLS
MY HEART WITH ANTICIPATION
AND KNOWING YOU'RE NEAR PUTS A PEP IN MY STEP.
I'M PREPARING FOR YOU—GRADUALLY
PICKING UP THINGS HERE AND THERE...
I SING YOUR SONGS AT ANY GIVEN MOMENT
AND INSTANTLY, I FEEL JOY!
I WISH THAT YOU COULD STAY LONGER
EVERYTIME YOU GET HERE
I FEEL A LOSS WHEN YOU GO...BUT HOPE
IN KNOWING YOU WILL RETURN
BRINGING THE GIFT OF YOU AND SHARING
YOURSELF WITH THE WORLD.*

EDIE BOWMAN

AND NOW...
<u>Being Human</u>

Do you ever catch yourself still doing things you made up as a child that are totally ridiculous? For instance: "step on a crack and break your momma's back." Do you subconsciously avoid stepping on the cracks as you walk on the sidewalk? Or, how about punching someone beside you when you see a Punch Buggy roll by? Well, we don't see those much anymore, but for the sake of making my point...
"Punch Buggy, Blue!"
Remember that?... LOL!

Chapter Seventeen
Something Serious to Remember...

I've always been a person who not only thought about what was going on in the present, but who also thought about things that are to come, especially serious things. I want to know the facts—I want to know them now, and I want to know as many details as possible! This can be a rewarding thing at times, because one can feel better prepared, but it can also cause stress to know a lot of information. I never liked mysteries too much, because by already being an overthinker, they leave me wondering what actually happened. As a child I used to wonder if God was real and if he really loved me... if Satan was real, and was he going to get me for doing wrong? Death was something that plagued my mind, particularly at night while lying in bed. I would dream that I was falling into a deep, dark, demon filled ocean that never ended. It was kind of like that scene in "Get Out" when the guy was falling backward in darkness.

I am so thankful that now I know that, yes, Satan and God are both real, and they both want me. I know that sounds weird, but as I mentioned before...They both want our souls for eternity. One wants it to enjoy life with you forever, and the other wants your soul to torment forever! I am happy that I have accepted the right Ruler of my soul! While God has given me eternal life and wants the best for me in this life as well as the next, Satan has his plans for me also, and for you.

Knowing that Satan is going about like a roaring lion and seeking who he may devour...it behooves us to prepare and protect ourselves from his tactics. For a year straight I kept seeing **the number 1010** wherever I went. At a hotel I would see it on or close to our room. I'd see it on clocks in different places, at times when I wasn't conscious of the time. I'd see it on pictures, hear preachers say it more often than usual. People would send me text messages at 10:10, or I would send them messages at that time. It was happening very frequently.

So, I decided to ask God about it—He's God IN Every Moment, Right? He revealed to me that I was to write about the scripture **John 10:10**. I was to write from Satan's perspective—how he wants to kill us, steal from us, and destroy every area in our lives, by any means necessary!

I know that I didn't come close to the evil, twisted, perverted mind he has, or his hatred for us, and I'm sure that's a good thing, but I do believe that God granted me a measure of how he feels towards us. He has allowed me to tap into Satan's plans for us…read and take this seriously. Our lives depend upon it!

(10:10)

Have you ever watched a movie that left you with a strong feeling of unfulfillment, or even anger? You know, those type of endings where the person(s) who were wronged never got a chance to get even? Allow me to set the scene: a nice loving family of four is murdered by three men while the youngest son is off at summer camp. The son (let's call his name Jack) returns home to the bloody scene that has now changed his life forever. Jack makes a righteous vow to one day hunt the murderers down and make them pay!

Fifteen years later, and after much searching, he finds out that two of the men are dead and the last one is on his death bed in a nearby hospital (convenient, right?). Finally, Jack has his opportunity to kill him, to finally unleash his life-long hatred upon this one person that is still alive to feel his wrath. But, for some reason the man's being so close to death already, made his desire to annihilate him diminished. And, because of the man's condition, Jack didn't even have the opportunity to ask him why he did it. So, he leaves the hospital with no resolve, angry with himself for having an ounce of compassion for not killing the man, and a whole lot of unanswered questions burning inside of him. But that's not all… did I mention that he has a family at home? Two daughters, Darcy and Madison, a son, Jack Jr., his wife Jenna, and his dog named Max. Perhaps he thought of them before deciding to kill the man. Perhaps he thought that he'd be caught and have to be away from them forever. Perhaps he thought that knowing what he did would be too much for his family to carry for the rest of their lives. After all, he knew how it felt to carry years of pain, loss, frustration, and even survivor's guilt.

He slowly walks to the door trying to compose himself to greet his family, who thinks he's been working overtime. He places his hand on the doorknob, twists it with forced happiness, and says, "Hey, I'm home!" Silence. Jack walks into the living room to the left of him, and flashbacks from that day, that horrific childhood day, overwhelmed him again as he saw his wife and children slain on the couch, the chair, and the floor in front of him. As he's screaming out in total despair, to say the least, his dog Max walks over to him with a note attached to his collar.

The note read: Hi Jack, I saw that you stopped by today. You had your chance, and you blew it. And in case you're wondering why we killed your family...Because we can!

Who in the WORLD wants a movie to end this way?! I definitely don't! I hate it when an intruder can just come in whenever he wants to, wherever he wants to, and at any moment in our lives, wreak havoc, and then get away with it, satisfied at your utter demise. How dare he?! Why is it that this evil one can kill, steal, and destroy and leave behind lives that are violated, shattered, fragmented, and empty? There are so many more words that I could use to describe the spoils of what's left behind after this intruder's contravention, but these four will suffice for now. Now, I know that it doesn't come across as very loving, forgiving or nicey-nicey, but a good revenge movie is one of my favorites to watch. Why? Because it balances the scales somewhat. It diminishes the weightiness of evil a bit. In my imagination, I picture this golden set of scales. On the left side there is a pile of black, shiny lumps of coal, representing the bad things in life, and on the other side there are several nuggets of pure gold, representing the good things in life. The scale is drastically leaning to the left. Well, I'd like the scales to at least be evenly balanced, so, in my mind, I see this huge hand place a few more gold nuggets on the right side. Sometimes I force my imagination to place this humongous lump of gold on the right side that totally tips the scales so far over, that it causes the black coals to fly up into the air and crumble into tiny pieces of dirt on the floor, the fragments are then blown away and scattered by the wind. Wouldn't that be great! Unfortunately, life isn't like that most of the time, and life cannot be manipulated by our imaginations, thank God!

Did you know that we all have one Ultimate Enemy? This enemy studies us, learns our habits, our likes, and dislikes. He knows what ticks us off, and what brings us excitement. He fixates on us like a lover does to his beloved watching her every move that he may please her. On the contrary, his strategic attention is not to bring pleasure and delight, but to take it away while you think that you're enjoying what he's bestowing. By any means necessary, he devotes his energy to not failing at trapping, then devouring his prey.

His beauty was not to be compared; he was created to be amazing in every way. He exuded glorious sounds of music that the ears have never heard still, they were too pleasurable for us to even endure without exploding. A worship leader all by himself, he'd serenade the King of Kings and Lord of Lords and all the heavenly beasts. As he walked the music flowed out of his very being, jewels and pipes were interwoven into his structure. An anointed cherub (not the little chubby, cupid babies we see on Valentine's day!), an Angel of music (not the Phantom of the Opera), powerful and full of everlasting life.

As the Light Bearer, he carried Truth within himself—the Truth about who God is in all of His Glory. He was filled with radiant colors of light and brilliance wherever he appeared in the heavenlies. Smitten with pride, he tried to usurp the throne and lost. Fallen to earth now in fierce anger and nefarious determination, he vows to rule the world's system: the way we think, operate, make decisions, and what we value here. People run the system, and people who are not purposefully guided by the love of God and His Holy Spirit, are therefore open to the power and control of him. Therefore, he must use whoever yields—gives access to his devices to achieve his goal… Sounds too simplistic? Because it is…most things worth believing in usually are: it's God or the devil, right or wrong, good or evil, yes or no. Don't mess with Mr. In-between, it's too risky. This is not a Hollywood movie that complicates things by presenting multiple ways around the truth, and makes evil seem so attractive that you want to see it played out over and over again on the big screen. This enemy—Our Enemy, is real, and no matter how fantastical and exciting the movies make our enemy out to be, they are created to appeal to our senses, to desensitize, and divert us from the real truth that there is a Real Entity who is alive and active, with our destruction in mind.

This evil one is working behind the scenes: like a lion he roams about seeking whomever he can devour, one by one, home by home. Communities, cities, states and nations fall to his intellectually crafted, well thought out, systematic and individualized schemes, and tactics of demise. As an evil genius, our utter destruction is his daily sustenance; he survives each second by feasting on us.

If I had to describe a dream to you, or perhaps I should say a nightmare... where I was in hell and Satan forced me to write one of my greatest works, and it had to be about him, the dream would go something like this:

He chained me to a chair with a desk in front of me and commanded me to write out a strategic plan on how he could deceive the most people possible. He told me that I had to do it within 24 hours, I could ask no questions, and take no breaks. He said if I didn't accomplish the task, I'd be stuck there with him for eternity! But not only that...he also told me that my whole family would join me if it wasn't good enough! He forced me to write from my own perspective-- from what I've experienced and what I see him doing in people's lives on the earth. He sarcastically said, that if I were a great writer, it shouldn't be a problem. He looked at me with a horrifying stare and said, "Write! Write MY dreams, MY goals and aspirations, My Masterpiece! Your life depends on it!"

I felt increasing fear...My whole body went into shock! But then, all of a sudden, I felt the presence of God in that moment with me- He was guiding and empowering me to write! I didn't tell Satan that! My mind began to race. I was thinking to myself "how can I write a diabolical plan for him to deceive the nations AND make it into this evil memoir?! God be Will Not be ok with this?!" Then, I sensed God's peace, yes, even there, IN hell! And so, I began...the first thought that came to my mind was this scripture:

Revelation 12:12

Therefore, rejoice, O heavens! And you who live in the heavens, rejoice! But terror will come on the earth and the sea, for the devil has come down to YOU in great anger, knowing that he has a little time. (New Living Translation)

The enemy has great anger, and his greatest desire is for us is to spend eternity with him. He licks his fingers as souls enter his insatiable, unholy realm. There is no satisfaction where he dwells.

Holy things are what he despises the most. We were holy... separated, set apart for God alone, and created for His purpose. We were His pleasure and glory: to be loved by Him, and to love Him of our own free will.

He lost his place with the Holy One by making pride his companion—carrying it around in his bosom. So now, this Chief One, unable to return to his former splendor, has unleashed his wrath on all creation—working desperately to destroy what God has lovingly made. I thought about all of this as I began. Then, I thought...since this is a strategic plan, I should write it in sections. I can categorize his areas of attack! But first...I'll talk about his insatiable appetite.

Insatiable

Multitudes of souls are coming...Hundreds by the hour! Young, old, rich and poor, Republicans, Democrats, all colors, faiths, religions, and sexes. He would bask in the aroma of their torment. The flames dance and sing as they taste their flesh. "Tis, soo sweet..." is the song the demon choir sings as they endlessly indulge. They elongate their lusting tongues to enhance the sensation of taste and to extend the erotic flavor. "Never Satisfied, Never, Never Satisfied..." is the chant his demon spirits sing. It rings in Satan's ears constantly to the gloriously maddening beat of screams that penetrates his total being. He swells un-holy gratification as they fill him up again and again with the rhythmic chorus of their pain, but he still wouldn't be full, for the increase of souls is insatiable to him.

Our eternal deaths are praise to him! It fills him up with praise: unfulfilling praise that is—It's never enough! He will do whatever he must to steal our destiny and drag us there with him! He Enlarges his dwelling place, again and again, to accommodate the influx of souls! And he laughs manically knowing that Greater is Coming... Greater is Coming...

Women

He particularly receives the utmost enjoyment in seeing women cry. He mocks at how they worry about everything, and he calls it annoying! He watches as they worry about their children, their parents, their friends who are hurting... And most of all, what really gets them going...MEN!

He laughs at how easy it is for some, how all it takes is to steal their hope that things will get better.

The single ladies say, "I'll never find someone who 'TRULY' loves me. I'll never get married. I'll be alone forever!"

The devil calls them pitiful babies—whiners and pouters! He understands that man cannot fulfill them and knows there will always be a void if they trust in humanity—always waiting on a man to do what only God can do in them. He loves it! He can easily steal their hope and joy at the same time with this same old tactic: He'll just convince them that they're not good enough, pretty enough, smart enough... He could go on, but that'll get the job done! Or... He'll convince them that they've waited too long and just need to settle for any ole good for nothing, controlling, cheating, lying, abusive, egotistical, narcissistic, lazy, money hungry (you get the point), Man! Impatience will drive them to the type of person that will ruin their lives, or at least mess them up enough to never recover. He knows this will cause many of them to begin to see men, and God distortedly. But he doesn't want them to find that out. He'd rather they find out after it's too late for them to repair the damage. By then they'll be so jacked up that they'll fail at every other relationship or be unhappy in the one they're in and still be miserable. He knows that misery loves company, which for him, means expansion, which produces more emotionally charged bad decisions, which in turn brings more misery, and even more expansion of his domain! He loves Expansion...so it's is a win-win! He HATES WOMEN! It was through them that The Anointed One came, and he *LOATHES HIM!!!!*

Sexual Abuse

The devil boasts about how he'll bring some to himself through sexual abuse. He likes this one because it's self-loathing, it loves darkness, and grows in silence. He encourages secrets! He's the Great Deceiver, and this is one of his most skillful ways to deceive: He makes you feel unworthy and unwanted...dirty. He steals your innocence through molestation, rape, and incest. He uses all types of sexually confusing, power-driven monstrosities as these. While the abuse is happening, he'll tell the abused that there must be something wrong with them... or this wouldn't have happened. Most don't know this, but he brings along with him many, many, more demon spirits to attach themselves to their souls (mind, will, and emotions). This is the big secret... they attach themselves during the very moment of their abuse. And again, He Laughs, for now he knows that they will not only suffer with fear, but with issues of intimacy, sexual identity, promiscuity, lust, self-hatred, distrust, guilt, confusion, suicidal thoughts, ETCETERA!!!!! These spirits are already present IN the violators, which gives him and his demons the open door to be present while the violation is taking place. They are now able to follow the violators and the victims, hopefully, for the rest of their lives. He knows that if a person chooses to engage in things that go against God's Laws... He and his demons are invited to increase their influence in the situation—like increasing the pain and after-effects of the abused!

He absolutely adores this form of abuse. Why? Because for the rest of their lives he'll ask the abused questions like: Where was GOD when this happened to you? If He cared, why didn't He stop it or prevent it? He'll make them blame God for EVERY bad thing that happens to them. Satan will never let it cross their minds that it's HIM behind the scenes—that it's HIM influencing the violators, that they are using their own sexual desires to hurt others—operating in their own free will. AND, for some that he Really wants to destroy and confuse—those whom he knows that God wants to use for His kingdom...He'll make sure that these "unfortunate situations" happen to them over and over again. He'll bring people in their lives to, purposefully, hurt them until there's nothing left in them but emptiness and self-loathing. He hopes that they will destroy their own selves before God gets a chance to reach them. That's evil, but GENIUS! ARE YOU ANGRY YET?!

Oh! And about the Violators... he wants Nobody to care about them! Anyone who harms a child, rapes, and molests...are the scum of the earth, Right?! That's what he wants us ALL to believe! He wants us to Never allow them to be forgiven, to Never find out what drove them to do such horrendous things. WHO CARES! They don't deserve Forgiveness! AND WHAT KIND OF GOD WOULD FORGIVE THEM! RIGHT?! They should go straight to HELL! That's how Satan feels... Who cares if many of the violators themselves were raped, abused, molested multiple times, and was left Alone to deal with it as a child! So what if they had no one to come to their rescue to heal them...to tell them that it wasn't their fault when it happened. We should leave them to Satan, Never come to their defense! The sad part is, he'll turn their torment into a cycle of abuse, it goes something like this: they'll get abused and never tell, so then they'll abuse others and tell them not to tell, then they'll do it, then their victims will do it, then they'll do it. And if one does tell...He'll convince those they tell to dismiss it or make it a small thing, or worse yet, take the violator's side.

He wants us to ask this question, "Why are we even talking about the violators?!" He wants us to think they shouldn't even get a seat at the table! He knows that soon we'll have whole families full of secrets, lies, deceit, hurt, and abuse...Just All Messed Up! It sounds good to him! "Once an abuser always an abuser, they'll never change... No Redemption for them! Jesus has no room for those types of people on the cross! His blood isn't powerful enough to cover them... The Dirty Rotten Bums!

The End. PERIOD."

"Saints"

Oh! I can't forget this... He especially likes Stealing "Saints" or "Saved" people Straight from the Pews of the Church to the Pulpit—from the Stained Glassed Windows and Sunday School Classes, from little girls' Shiny Shoes and Choirs Singing Songs...he wants us to fall! Some are already spending eternity with Satan: they're the sweetest aroma of all to him! He sees them as the most Deceived. Deception is one of his best strategies because it's so subtle. He just tells them that they're okay, that all they have to do is continue to go to church every Sunday, do good deeds, put an extra $20 in the collection plate here and there, and make sure that their good outweighs their bad. He finds this hilarious! He knows that many appear to know God: looking impressive to those around them, saying and doing the right cliché churchy things. They LOOK like they know Him, but their hearts are far from Him. Continuing to see no difference between the Saints and themselves...those who don't know Him (the UN-saved), are turned off. The unsaved watch the

"Saints"party in the same night clubs as they do, cuss people out, drink, fight, sleep with their boy/girlfriends, or both, then get up and go to church the next day and usher, sing in the choir, preach, and then sing "Oh, How I Love Jesus, because He First Loved Me." Satan absolutely LOVES this!!!

He scoffs at them wondering, "What are they "Saved" from? If there is no change in their hearts, that shows through their actions, then what's the point, why did Jesus even die? So that those who are supposed to KNOW Him can stay the same?!" He sees that they have the appearance of being Godly on the Outside, but don't allow His power to change them Inside. Even Satan knows this, and sneers at the hypocrisy. He gloats in the fact that some of them are not deceived at all, they just refuse to allow God to change them because they enjoy their sin. SIN…many hate that word. It makes them uncomfortable, and no one wants to feel that way. After all, he loves that we don't want anyone telling us what to do! He hopes that we will fight against hating that word—it's a wonderful word to him. And a life of no restraint is the best kind of life—the life he's counting on us to live! He speaks to our minds and tries to convince us that we should be able to do whatever we want and not have to answer to anyone! He counts on us thinking, "Why should we have to listen to this…this unknown, unseen God who we don't even have enough proof exists?!" He's betting on us to keep up with our ritualistic routines of "Goodness." Keep performing for the approval of those around us in the "Christian community" while the one who truly matters, weeps over us. He wants us to share his sin of pride by boasting of our own good works, thinking that we will get on the good side of "The Man Upstairs." The Man Upstairs… WOW! That's hilarious to Satan—we don't even have enough respect to call Him by His name! He wants us to continue to go through the motions of "Churchy-anity" while at church, and then do whatever we like after we leave those four walls. "SAINTS"… LOL! I can literally imagine Satan laughing out loud. We're like modern day Pharisees to him! I'm done!

Family

YES! It's thinking like this that destroys entire families. Families... that's an easy one for him. All he does to destroy families is convince husbands that their beautiful, committed, supportive wives, are not enough anymore. He highlights to them, that they just don't have what they used to have, and that they just don't do it for them anymore. "The Thrill is Gone, Baby!" He tells them that the only thing left to do is to find fulfillment outside of the home. He speaks to their minds and the husbands began to say things like, "She just doesn't understand me anymore, all she does is nag and put me down all of the time, and I deserve to be happy! Marriage only works until it doesn't, it's time to move on." And let's not even start on the topic of SEX...he'll convince them to think, "It's soooo boring now...she doesn't satisfy me like she used too. It's okay to watch pornography to sustain myself." And other things like, "She'll never know, and if she does find out, I'll just tell her 'It's a Guy Thang, you wouldn't understand.'"

He really finds it amusing when he hears the wives say, "But I thought he was 'The One.'" He knows there is there is no "The One!" He'll say things to her like, "You're not attractive anymore, and he doesn't want you." And, if she finds out he's into porn, he'll convince her that it's because she's not sexy or exciting enough in bed. That gets them all the time—unless they're both into it, that's even better in Satan's eyes! He persuades them both to keep this in the center of their marriage, convincing them that they need it to keep things fresh. He knows that at the same time, he's sneaking in other perverse spirits to attach themselves to their marriage bed and cause more damage: lust, perversion, emptiness, and a false sense of intimacy love to tag along with pornography. They'll make sure that you're never fulfilled, that you'll always want more, and one day do the unthinkable-something you thought you'd NEVER do... only to come up empty again once the sexual deeds are done—always wanting...More.

He whispers to the wife, that her husband spends more time at work, on his phone, and watching TV, than he does with her.

EDIE BOWMAN

She knew he was a cheat and a liar before she married him, but she thought he'd change. So, when opportunity presents itself, she thinks, "It's okay to go on a few 'innocent' lunch dates with my male co-worker. I deserve someone to listen to ME sometimes!" (*knowing in the back of her mind where this could lead*). Then, He'll seal the deal by influencing her friends to give their blessing on it... "Girl Power!!!" Satan is so sneaky! He knows that all it takes is a little seed of doubt about your mate, a little compromise, AND the okay from friends...BOOM! DECEPTION. It works every time.

The Poor Children...

The Children...Satan has a fierce passion for them! His goal is to focus on their self-absorbed, self-defeating, good-for-nothing parents! He sees that many are soo preoccupied with their own desires, that all he has to do is consume their offspring with...with... just about anything that they THINK will fill the void and hurt. For example: take poor little Julie...he'll bring a boy into her life to fill the Daddy void and have him show her just enough attention to get what he wants. And Lord help her if he showers her with a lot of attention and things. The skit goes a little like this:

The phone rings (*Ring-ring-ring*)

Julie: Hello

Kenny: Wassup, baby girl?

Julie: (Giggly) Oh, hi Kenny...

Kenny: Wanna hang out at da crib tonight, jus you and me, around 8:00?

Julie: (Still giggling) yeah, but I don't know how I'll get my parents to let me go.

Kenny: Leave that up to me, baby girl, jus let me talk to them, they trust me already, cuz I told them I go to church every Sunday. I'll come over a little early, act all sanctified and stuff, and before you know it, I'll have them wrapped around my finger. I'll tell them, I'll have you back around 10:10, and we're out the door!"

Julie: You miss me that much?

(She's STILL giggling!!!)

Kenny: You know I do, Boo...

Julie: Okaaay...

(Long story, short):

They meet up, have Sex, NO condom, Pregnancy, Arguments, and he hopes on Abortion, or Single parenting, Life of Regrets, Hurt, Pain, Cheating, Unforgiveness, Guilt, Shame, Silent tears... *ETCETERA!!!* Satan LOVES ETCETERA., because, in this case anyway, the destruction goes on and on and on...from generation to generation. It never ends until someone breaks the curse and passes the truth onward. Julie's children are more likely to abort or have children out of wedlock, her grandchildren will do it, and on and on. Or... if anyone does get married, they'll marry someone who doesn't know what it means to be a provider, protector, loving, strong, patient, or God fearing. She'll marry out of her own need to be valued, treasured, and fulfilled, but she won't find that in any human. Satan knows that only God can fulfill, but he won't let her in on that Truth!

His Sole Purpose

Satan's sole purpose is to **Kill**, **Steal**, and **Destroy**! He kills dreams, influence, character, hope, ETC.! He finds it pleasurable to see the light God breathed into us seeping out of our hollowed souls like a flame slowly losing oxygen...dwindling...dwindling...dwindling... And then, *Poof*! Nothing but smoke remains, smoke that has soon, itself, vanished. ! He knows good old Solomon was right! Our lives are like vapors—here one moment, gone the next. He deceived the Wisest of all too: turned his heart from God to idol worship. Good Old Solomon... but in the end, Solomon got it right:

"Fear God and keep his commandments, this is the whole purpose and duty of mankind," he said. Satan realizes that our lives are like vapors—here one moment, gone the next, and he wants to be the one who captures it!

He delights in convincing many suicide victims that things will never get better, that the only way to end the pain is to not feel it anymore, and that the only way to do that is to end it all. He makes sure that they can't see that just around the corner, is a brighter day—that they had a purpose in staying here. And, if someone tells them that things will get better…he makes sure that they don't believe it! Oh… and the ones left here to mourn them… boy does he takes great pleasure in destroying their peace. He has mastered filling them with guilt, by making them believe that they could've prevented it—that they should've seen the signs if they loved them. He really gets the Mothers, because they can't help but think that they should've known their child's thoughts. And the wives of victims… He tortures them too, Reeeeeal Good! Mothers and wives hardly ever forgive themselves, "I should have known something, I just talked to them!" they say.

Ahhh…MUSIC!

Murder, violence, hatred, racism, strife, and discord of any kind… these are at the top of his list also. Let's face it…EVERYTHING'S at the top of Satan's list…Everything Matters! Sex, money, family, and MUSIC. He uses this tool to heavily influence people. Since music was his creative purpose in heaven, he uses it on earth to lure people to himself—using it to seduce people into all kinds of evil. He's convinced many to even sell their souls for the "Love" of making music; they love fame and fortune more than life itself. This is sooo HUGE!

He uses music to influence many people to murder: they listen to certain songs to hype themselves up to do the crime, not realizing that he's the influence behind the creation of that particular song. He uses it to get people in the mood to have sex outside of marriage, and even to commit adultery. He uses music to worship himself through the vessels that write it, sing it, and produce it—they become his instruments! He likes to use people like puppets; they will do anything to be worshipped in the music industry. It's PRIDE, that age old sin, again. It's Satan's worst enemy and best friend—it destroyed him, but it also gives him pleasure, through US, at the same time! He enjoys it when people in the industry finds out that it doesn't satisfy that empty spot they have inside: the voids that money, fame, fortune, houses, cars, vacations, groupies, "Friends," ETCETERA... could not fill. By then it's usually too late, He has them! They kill themselves, go mad, destroy their relationships, lose everything! Or better yet... stay the way they are and remain caught up in that lifestyle. In their false happiness, they'll destroy those around them and help bring them to destruction also. MULTIPLICATION...

Murder and Cycles of Violence in the Black Community

Murder...it's soo easy nowadays. He influences people to kill groups at school, churches, movies, stores, synagogues...He's involved. The murder of innocent babies in the womb by the millions...He's in the room. Bombs, 9/11, terrorist acts that kill soft targets like women and children...it's Him working through people! The mass murder of God's chosen people, the Jews, during the Holocaust, the Anti-Semitism that still exists...ALL SATAN!

Black-on-Black crime?... Now that's one of his masterpieces. These people of deep spirituality seemed to always have an affinity towards God! Even while bound in chains they called on Him: singing songs of hope and faith in the midst of unthinkable oppression. Satan was the one who inspired their oppressors. He used the same old tactics that he often does—Pride, AGAIN! He doesn't have to work too hard. It doesn't take much to convince one people group that they're better than another, especially if they're jealous of something they have or just don't understand about the others' culture. Instead of learning about or taking an interest in others that are not like ourselves, Satan and his demons influence us to believe that we are superior, and that those who look and live differently should be beneath us. He uses Fear instead of Understanding—it's easier, and most are too lazy to take the time to seek understanding. But, with Black-on-Black crime, he sent his best demons to influence them to turn on themselves! And he laughs!!! He lies to their fathers—deceiving them to leave the home, and like the domino effect, the walls of their homes come tumbling down from that one, destructible, move! He makes the mothers bitter, overworked and frustrated, then their children become frustrated, full of hurt, and anger. And guess who they'll take it out on?... Everyone: their mothers, fathers, teachers, principals, anyone in authority... *(because their fathers weren't there to model it for them, so they reject it)*. The boys will take it out on their women when they get older, repeating what they saw at home. Then, feeling trapped, they'll take it out on their children, and their communities...it's called CYCLES, and they work extremely well! It's hard to focus on schoolwork and having a better future when your father's not there to set an example of discipline and love, and when your mother is too exhausted from trying to make ends meet. She fights to keep up with the children's day-to-day needs while she's exhausted, mentally, physically, and emotionally. Satan is very crafty in all of this...he keeps the cycles going. Sure, there are a lot of mothers holding it all together, but Satan knows that God's way—a whole family with a loving mother and father—flourishes and is stronger in every way.

Satan has deceptively presented our black communities with a "better way" to use that anger to blame everyone else, except yourselves, for the predicament that we're in. He wants us to keep killing and allowing the horrors of slavery, that HE designed, to cripple us and totally paralyze us, STILL! He uses our own hands to kill more and more of our men and fathers with guns, influences us to sell drugs, our youth to not take school seriously, thus perpetuating staying on government assistance—believing that we can't make it any other way. He wants us to stay impoverished and keep having unprotected sex. Kill our unborn—the next generation... and the next, and the next... and one day, we might look up and find most of our men dead or imprisoned. Satan is the method to the madness, but he keeps us blind to his tactics and instead we turn on each other or continue to blame others. And the cycles continue.

He is counting on our black children to use that hurt and confusion on ourselves. The people who once danced and sang the praises of their God! Decades ago, we loved Him, we looked up to Him as our Savior, fathers could be counted on, mothers took care of their children, and together they went to church and prayed. Martin Luther King Jr. was our hero. He heralded the power of faith and justice in your communities. We, the People who once believed in non-violence, because our leaders believed in God, but today... Our enemy, the devil, is proud that we're the furthest we've ever been from God! What happened to US?! We once were proud to be called Black or African American, now we'll laugh when called a derogatory name associated with our race! What happened, you who once called on the name of Jesus out of despair, and He was faithful to answer and set you free?...

"SATAN HAS TURNED OUR STRENGTH INTO WEAKNESS..."

He continues to work on us to keep God out of our families, to drink to escape, to party until we lose our minds, act like animals so that the police will treat us like animals! Sex it up, sleep with multiple people, have multiple "Baby Daddies" and "Baby Mommas" and think it's cute! That'll confuse the children, weaken their self-esteem and security... mess em' up real good! He wants us to drug it up, sell those drugs for the man (*who ultimately is Satan by the way... not the white man*), lose ALL control, live as if we're free of ALL restrictions, side effects, and consequences to our actions. Destroy our lives and those in your communities, hate truth, love murder, deceive to get money and more drugs. Steal from sweet, little old grandma for more drugs—you know... the woman who raised most of us and our siblings and prayed over our hard-headed selves, and dragged us to church when our momma's couldn't get off drugs and wouldn't stop having four, five, six more of our sistas and brothas?! So, Cheat, Pervert and Lie... join the devil—do whatever he tells us to do, keep passing the blame, and he will win!

<u>Why He does What He does...</u>

He is Lucifer. He once carried light within him, but now he's the destroyer of it. His most valuable deception is... I hate to say it... to convince *us* that our creator is not real, and if He is, He doesn't care about us. He wants us to believe that God caused or chose not to stop all of the pain in our lives. He MUST persuade us to believe that He does not exist—that He is a myth. His goal is to constantly tell us that living in this fallen world, having a free will to do evil things, make bad choices and self-pleasing decisions, has nothing to do with WHY we suffer. He has to make sure that it never crosses our minds—that He, this fallen world, and our own brokenness, just might play a part in our misfortunes. He has to be excellent at this or we might accept God's son, JESUS, as our savior—He MUST make sure that we keep blaming God and keep us blinded and confused as to who we are—God's Beloved.

But even he, The Thief, has to obey The Way, The Truth, and The Life. He has to do what God tells him to do, and he passionately hates it!

And... unlike an unfulfilling movie, the end for believers in Him is everlasting life in heaven, regardless of what happens to them on earth. What happens to believers on earth, is nothing to be compared to what awaits them in HEAVEN. God has tipped the scales in their favor. But, for Satan...his end is the Lake of Fire. His sweet, sweet, delectable reward is drawing ALL who will follow him STRAIGHT TO HELL, "By Any Means Necessary."

(JOHN 10:10)

The Thief comes only in order to steal and kill and destroy. I came that they may have and enjoy life, and have it in abundance [to the full, till it overflows]
Amplified Version

Chapter Eighteen
Family Ties

There are NO perfect families, and there never will be...but we can strive to become better. Because we are all broken and have to deal with our sinful natures, family relationships will always have some struggle. While I'm thankful to have a family that loves me, there will be disagreements, misunderstandings, arguments, and even times of deep pain that we may cause each other. These moments will happen in a family, but what has kept us together is our faith in the creator of relationships. God created us so that we could be in a loving relationship with Him. He knew that we would disobey him, turn away from his laws, and reject him, but he still made a way through his son to bring us back to him. If we keep looking to Him—the Master of relationships, He will instruct and direct us in every relationship we allow him to be a part of.

(An Ode to My Parents)

The smell of his cologne on a stranger walking down the street
You turn around discretely to see him pass
by, and deeply breathe in...
Visions of hardworking hands with a gold ring on
the steering wheel on a Sunday morning.
And those nurturing words you spoke of me
over that Christmas Eve dinner table
twenty-four days before you departed.

Her daughter placed a yellow dandelion in her
hair as she lay in the grass, tanning
She smiled widely with her teeth apart and a sparkle in her eyes

A face that matched the beauty of the sun glowing in Autumn's
morning, and her tone... deep, sweet, calming...stern.
Arms and hands that reach up to God on behalf of
others in prayer with tears of supplication.

The way he leaned his head to the side and stood
like a confident cowboy ready for a duel
His high soulful voice sang songs of gospel, rhythm and blues
his home was his stage, pleasing all who gathered in close
to share his crock-pot cooked food and company.
A born entertainer, a mysterious man I
still long to know...to hold on to.
The way your eyes lit up when you saw my face and
said with great pride, "That's my baby!" as if you
had to make it known—I needed to hear it...

Thank you all (Mommy, Daddy, and Pops)

Love, Noonie (Your baby girl)

An Ode to Grandma (Ella Smith)

*Though she never seemed to have enough, she managed to feed
all of the grandchildren, and anyone else that stopped by.*

*She told the funniest childhood stories that made you
laugh, and wonder how she survived, at the same time.
She'd kick yo butt playin checkers, and then had the
nerve to whistle, and sing happily while doing it!
When you sassed her, she had the strange ability to
throw anything within her reach at you, and somehow...
managed to hit you upside the head, even if you
were in another room! (How did she do that?!)*

She could have up to seven grandchildren in her house
at one time, mix all of their names up, constantly,
and we'd still know who she was talking to.
Most of all, Grandma knew how to show her love for
each and every one of us with a song, a story, a taste of
homemade food from a worn-out pot, a smile, or simply
a sparkle in her eyes when she looked at you.

Ties That Bind

You know sometimes your Spiritual Family—those who share
the same Christian values and principles as you do, may
actually be closer to you than your Biological Family. Our
brothers and sisters in Christ are the ones that we will be with
for eternity in heaven, because we have the same Father.
It's sorrowful to think about it but there may come a
time when our beliefs and lifestyles will separate us from
the ones we love here on earth—just love them all.
Jesus said, after being told that his mother and brothers
were unable to get to him because of the crowd of people
around him, "...My mother and brothers are all those who
hear God's word and obey it." -Luke 8:19-21 (NLT)

The Man in the Window...

I pull up and I see you sitting there with your head hung down.
I wonder what it is that you're thinking about.
Slim-figured with that familiar white T-shirt, dressy
brown pants and that twitch of the eye.
What was life like when you were younger?...
Were you like your father?
Did you model him or try hard never to be like him?
Were you just like your mother, or a mixture of them both?
I'd ask myself these questions about you at home
on my bed at night, as tears flowed.
It was a nagging ache of my heart trying to
figure you out, but I had to know more.
There had to be more than just singing,
working hard, and drinking...

EDIE BOWMAN

But boy were you quite the entertainer...your
whole body, every fabric, exuded music!
Your voice was full of soul—high tenor and
smooth as a hot knife through butter.
I remember sitting on your knee with my sister
and singing with you to your friends.
I could feel the energy in the room as they
listened with excitement and joined in.
You'd make them laugh, sing, clap, and even feed
them—you were an entertainer for sure!
I know you passed that gift to me, and I'm so,
very thankful...it keeps me going.
I'd sit in the car for a moment and stare at you in the window...
What were his hopes and dreams? Did trying
to reach them cause The Sickness?
Did you drown yourself in the sorrows of
disappointment and unfulfilled hopes?
I tried to ask you these things in several
ways, I even wrote you a letter...
But again, your response was vague and
short, leaving me wanting more.
Finally, I learned that your life was not a subject
that you felt comfortable sharing with me.
I'm sure you had your reasons...maybe they
were too painful to talk about.
Twelve years after you died, I asked your baby
brother to tell me about you in more detail.
I quickly found out that it was just that...
way too painful for you to express.
That moment gave me closure and understanding of who you were.
Sitting there with my uncle and my girls,
hearing YOUR story, was life to me!
I wasn't the only one who needed it, they did too,
because they heard me speak of you so often.
You...this mysterious Man in the Window...

The man my heart longed to be closer to.
We connected in the greatest way
That Father's Day... I led you to the Lord,
the greatest conversation EVER!
The moment I'd prayed many years for...
Our eyes and our hearts connected
in a way only dreamed of.
We understood each other.
You spoke no words...
You listened to me.
We cried together.
You shook your head in acceptance.
I kissed your head.
Stroked your hair.
And I knew I'd see you again,
Fully Known.
Daddy...

A Word to Mothers

Hold On!!!! But Let Go...
Hold on to them in Prayer: lift them up to God continually,
but let go of Control.
Give them advice, but not often.
Ask for discernment and wisdom when relating to them.
Don't say, "I told you so..." they already know.
See what they shall be, not what they look like right now.
Entrust them unto the one who loves them more than you do.
CAUTION! It Will NOT Be Easy.

EDIE BOWMAN

The Woman of Prayer

Your words were softly spoken but held authority when needed.
You put in me the desire to read books, upon books...
You would read to us when we were little, with
such mystery and dramatic effect.
Those were some of my best moments with you as a child.
My favorites were *Charlotte's Web* (because you'd do all
the voices so well) and *Someone is Eating the Sun*.
I see now that those moments inspired my craft
of writing and telling stories...Thank You.
Later in life you taught me through word and action,
that The Bible is the number one book.
It was not some ancient relic that had no relevance for today,
but a living, life-altering treasure to be cherished above all.
My sisters and I would laugh at how your Bibles
looked—tattered and torn, highlighted and ripped.

It's because you diligently searched out each page and stood
on its promises through every situation in your life.
You Read it, Teach it, Pray it, and Walk it out!
Do you sometimes stumble or fall?...
Yes, that's what we do at times, but I watch
you get up and continue on.
I saw how your relationship with the Lord changed
negative circumstances around you.
I witnessed miracles, restoration, breakthroughs,
healings, and coverings of protection over you
and your family as a result of your prayers.
Many do not realize how your prayers have kept them safe
and prospered them in multiple ways, but God knows.
I know for a fact that I have been delivered, uplifted,
carried through many tough times, healed and restored
because of your intercession for me and my family.
You have a smile that tells the story of laughing through it all...
Your smile still brings me joy, and your laugh is delight to my ears.
I realize, now that I'm older, that keeping
them was not easy... but you did.
I have seen many tears stream down that beautiful golden face.
Most tears were shed for others in prayer...
there's a reward in heaven for those.
Those hands that joined with others, anointed, and were
lovingly laid upon the heads of many... may they reap what
they have sown in abundance on this earth, and in eternity.
My prayer for you is that you'd live a long, joy-
filled, healthy, and prosperous life,
As promised in Psalms 91
For you have dwelled in the secret place of The Most-
High, so may you abide under the shadow of The
Almighty...and under in His wings have you trusted.
Therefore, with long life may He satisfy
you and show you His salvation...
My dear, Mommy

EDIE BOWMAN

Forgiveness

She's caused me too much pain, I can't just let that go!
She didn't fight for me...
He's missed way too many birthdays; I don't even care anymore...
He's on his seventh child with his sixth girlfriend,
why would he find time for me?
She chose a man over me, again!
I'm her child...shouldn't I come first!
He doesn't love her...why does she keep
picking these types of men?!

Lord, please help us to forgive while it's still hurting...
Our hearts are finding it hard to let the pain go
Our minds remember as if it were yesterday
And holding on is stealing our peace.
Give us our daily bread, Lord.
Help us in every moment that we feel it again...
Help me to see with your eyes when I look at him.
Give me the grace to overcome the anger when I hear her voice.
Retrain my thoughts when I think of him
And strengthen me through this process of forgiveness.

A Family Tree

I have Great-Grandma's smile and Great-Grandpa's tenacity
Grandma's eyes and Grandpa's gift of gab
Momma's singing voice and Papa's hands
I walk like Daddy and talk like Mommy
I laugh like Auntie, get over emotional like my first cousin,
and get my sense of humor from my great uncle.
I wonder from whom I 've received these big chubby toes?...

A Note to My Daughters

Jazzmin

She has hands that love to jump in and pull you up—while intentions are pure, it will sometimes sting when the results aren't good. Hands that are All-In, willing to lend help and lead you to a better place. Like the sweet smell of Jasmine, she leaves an aroma when she enters the room. She presses through the pain while managing to bring the fragrance of joy and excitement to the atmosphere. As she grows, she will blossom and gain strength: enabling her to expand her reach to empower others while opening herself up to grand possibilities and the beautiful, wonderful things she deserves. Keep helping, keep giving, keep restoring, and keep pressing. Allow God's wisdom to guide your decisions.

Tatiana

Her heart beats friendship, closeness, and healing. Once she sees you, the beating gets stronger and stronger—never wanting anyone to ever be alone in their pain. Compassion is her food and weakness—she gives it freely even when it's not returned. She has a smile that welcomes and mesmerizes you, and she laughs like there's no tomorrow. Sometimes these traits will not be appreciated display them anyway. She writes out of her overflow of emotions: the thing that keeps her going and restores her soul, and others as well—these are your gifts. Keep writing, keep smiling, keep laughing, and keep being a friend. Pray for and use God's direction to weed out the thorns: those who seek you out to use.

Autumn

Her words are spoken with conviction and honesty something that is welcomed and sometimes disregarded. They often heal and give direction to the listeners and challenge them to change—this can cost a lot. Going against the grain seems to be her natural way of being it takes strength to do that. She has your back once she finds out that you have hers and will be there through the thick and thin. Time and experience will develop her gift to see God's beauty in people that many do not see, and His word will help her know what truths to follow and which to share. Keep listening, keep speaking, keep trusting, and keep seeing for others that they may see. Trust His discernment and timing.

IF...

(In Memory of Uncle James, A man
of interesting conversation)

If I know you're in life's storms with me
     Then I'm alright.
If I can look across the raging sea, and See that you're there...
     Then I'm alright.
If thick darkness overwhelms and the search for light comes to
a close
     You will become the Night.
When questions unanswered weary my soul
     You'll train my heart to fight.
Life will hurt, abuse and sting
Relationships?... They come and go
You stabilize my footing still...
     Gently lead and I will follow.
If you're not in the calming wind, in that place I shall not stop
to rest.
But If on a daunting road We find ourselves, then there is
where I'm best.
And I'm alright...
     I Know that I'm alright.

EDIE BOWMAN

We Are Sisters...

(With Funny Nicknames)
I, Noonie--your little sister, would like you
to know what you mean to me:

Beanie, you make me laugh until I cry... you were like a
second mom while we were growing up: loving, forgiving
and protecting me. You are hospitable and giving.
Bobbie, you were a great homemaker, a comedian, and
a joy to be around...like a breath of fresh air to all who
visited your home. You are a priceless jewel...believe it!
Chuckie, you were a wonderful mother: caring
for and nurturing your children—you put them
first even when you needed to be loved yourself.
You have hands and a heart that heals.
You have all imparted something inside of me...
I've watched you and learned the wonderful
attributes of selflessness, love, and sacrifice.
May the Lord cover you with His hand of protection
and prosper you. May He give you peace and joy. May
he bless your children and grand-children, and may
you find rest and safety in knowing Him as Father.
Thank you for believing in, loving and encouraging
me. I love you all so very much!
Love, Noonie.

My Uncle Buddy

Uncle Buddy, you have been a man of respect...a man that I admire.
There were not many men in my family that I looked up to for
serving God—you were one of the few. There are some people that
can never say that they had a pillar of their family, but I always saw
you as that! You are a pillar in the church, in your home, and in the

lives of so many people that you've helped over the years. To me, a pillar is someone who is stable, reliable, has good character, works hard, loves God, and takes care of the people he loves. You have been all of these things and more.

Your heart is so big that just loving your family isn't enough. You have touched the lives of foster children and given hope to those in need. I will never forget that day when you took out the time and sat with me and my children to tell us more about my father, their grandfather, your big brother. That was something that I desperately needed to heal my heart. I remember hearing your voice as you sang in the pews at church when I was little. Your voice rang above the crowd...it was powerful, peaceful, and gave me hope. I remember thinking, "That's my uncle Buddy singing!" Even today, whenever I mention your name to people that know you, they get a smile on their face and always have something good to say about you.

You make a difference...never forget it!
Love your niece, Noonie

AND NOW...

Being Human

Have you ever had your front door open and happened to see one of those people with a chart, a name tag, and a chipper tone, talking to one of your neighbors? So, you slowly closed your door, turned out the lights and the TV, slumped down in the chair you were sitting in and stopped breathing? Huh?... Anyone?... Don't leave me out here all by myself, now!

Chapter Nineteen
Random Thoughts

Do you ever have crazy or serious random thoughts that come to your mind? Well, I do all of the time! I also do randomly crazy things all of the time, which I'm sure you know by now. It doesn't take much for them to be activated in my head: it could be a movie, a conversation, a song, a piece of art, a person walking down the street, a book, a piece of paper, a smell, a bug, a piece of lint, a cloud... there is no end to my randomness of thought. I might regret writing them in a book for all to see though...

A Random Thing

Sometimes when I'm feeling excited, frustrated, or just plain ole silly, I let out a few loud, high-pitched barks and I feel...well, I feel... Strangely, Better. Hey! If people can yell and scream at each other when they're angry or take off their shirts at a football game and run around like they're crazy...why can't I bark?! (Don't judge it, don't over think it, just try it! IF YOU DARE....)

Crazy & Not So Crazy Things
I'm Thankful For...

1. I'm thankful for arms that are long enough...how else would we wipe our bottoms after having a boom-boom?
2. I'm thankful for toenails...if my legs or feet itch at night while under the covers, I can scratch them without disturbing my upper body.
3. I'm thankful for hot sauce, Frank's Red Hot cuz it helped me out of a lot of unpleasant food situations—it didn't taste so good... but you saved me!

4. I'm thankful for windows...can you imagine if you could not see the light of day in your own home, especially in these dark times? Pulling back the curtains and opening the blinds to see the sun is something I've taken for granted.

5. I'm thankful for flowers...their colorful beauty surrounding me, and my neighbors' yards bring joy and comfort to my senses as I sit on the porch, limited to the places I can go.

6. I'm thankful for ears...of course they're great for hearing, but they also make it a lot easier to wear these masks on my face every day, and I wouldn't be able to talk to Charles' right one while in the car and bed. (Did you forget...?)

7. I'm thankful for the sound of the ocean...it seems to drown out all the inside voices, cares, and stresses of life...at least for a little while, and makes me reflect on the creativity, wonder, and power of God.

8. I'm thankful for birds...even though at times they may wake us up a little too early, somehow they give me the feeling, through their song, that it's a new day so I start off with a "Thank you Lord... I'm still here and there is hope."

9. I'm thankful for pencils...though computers are the easiest way to go as a writer, I still like the sound of the pencil scratching the paper and the feel of it in my hand.

10. I'm thankful for a soft cool breeze across my face in the Summer

11. I'm thankful for remembrance...of things that brought goodness and kindness into my life and those that brought pain, that I may choose to learn from them.

12. I'm thankful for butter knives...they make good screwdrivers.

13. I'm thankful for the clouds...they give us something to do on a long drive—giving us a free game of the imagination to play as we try to find the pictures the other person sees.

14. I'm thankful for sidewalks...without them we'd have to walk in the street, heighten our possibility of getting hit, AND... we'd have to walk with the annoying people who refuse to walk on the sidewalks.

15. I'm thankful for the needle of the earring...they're great for taking knots out of tangled necklaces.

The Perfect Conundrum

Sometimes it's hard to tell if it's God talking
to me, the devil, or myself…
If I want that third scoop of ice cream, is it God saying,
"Every good and perfect thing comes from above."
Is it the devil saying, "You won't surely die."
Or…is it me saying, "God wants me to enjoy the fruit
of my labor—Eat, Drink and Be Merry…?"
Well, I guess since there are no objections…
I can proceed as desired!

Wisdom of the Decades

You remember how in your Teens (and clueless…) you were like, "Well I think…*Blah, Blah, Blah…*" then by your 20's, (Still clueless…) you were like, "I Know…*Blah, Blah, Blah…*" By the time you reached your 30's you were like, "What in the world was I thinking?!…" and now that you're in your 40's you're like, "I didn't know anything!" I guess in my 50's and beyond I'll be more like, "Whatever…Let's just wait and see… it might be…it might not be… Let's go on another cruise, life is too short!

Ignorance CAN be Bliss

Carl needed to lose weight, so he ate a whole meat
lover's pizza with extra cheese and washed it down
with a 2 liter of pop! But…it was DIET pop, so…
There you have it! All is well.

Things I Hate!

(Well, maybe not HATE...that's a strong word—it should only be used in extreme cases! So, let's say... things that annoy me!)

1. When people cut you off when you're talking to them: I understand that this happens, sometimes, during heated or exciting conversations, but it shouldn't happen fifty percent of the conversation!

2. When people promise things and never do them: if it happens every once in a while, then okay...but when it happens regularly, there's a problem. It's better to just make sure that you can actually do it before you say it.

3. When people are REGULARLY late without a good excuse! UGH!!! Things happen...but not ALL of the time!

4. When someone else's time is more important than yours: both of our time is important, let's compromise.

5. When scripture is used to manipulate others to get our own way: Not Good...Scary!

6. When someone speaks in a demeaning, belittling, intimidating, know-it-all tone, to others. Everyone's deserves to be heard. Listen... you may learn something.

7. **When I don't practice what I preach or find myself doing the things that I hate!!!!! Lord, help me to do what I expect of others!**

Beautiful Uncertainty

Who said having all your ducks in a row was best? Didn't
they know that Good is often found in the mess?
And knowing that the path ahead is clear doesn't
necessarily mean there will be no fear...
There is purpose in the struggle—a
cocooned caterpillar would say...
For it knows those wings are painfully,
but beautifully... on their way.

Sort of a Beatitude?...

*Blessed are the Patient... for they shall not LOSE THEIR
MINDS when people walk SLOWLY, in the MIDDLE
of the street, instead of on the sidewalks, like they are
CARS!... and expect you not to get UPSET!!! (Smiles...)*

*"Now I lay me down to sleep, I pray the Lord
my soul to keep. If I should die..."* (**Loud Snores**)
*Uhm...I think it might be better to just know
where you're going in the first place.*

(1 John 5:13) KJV

Now Wait a Minute...

While pulling into our drive, a cat who was resting on a chair on
OUR porch began to run away. But he suddenly stopped, lifted up
on his hind feet, and stared at us with aggravation and intimidation.
He meowed, rolled his eyes, then proudly walked away like an
exhausted lion... as if to say, "I let it go this time..." and like we
were bothering HIM!

INTERESTING OXYMORONIC GESTURES

MY FRIEND WHISPERS AS LOUD AS HE
SCREAMS, SO WHEN HE TELLS ME A
SECRET... WE STAND MILES APART.
HER BOYFRIEND TOLD HER THAT HER
BEAUTY EXCEEDS THE UGLINESS OF
HER FACE...THEY BROKE UP!
HIS DESIRE TO BE STRONG, WAS WEAK, SO
HE GAVE UP THE USE OF HIS FIVE-POUND
WEIGHTS AND TOOK THE PICTURE OF "THE
ROCK" OFF THE REFRIGERATOR DOOR.
THE NIGHT WAS LIGHTENED BY THE SUN,
AND IN THE MORNING, WE SHALL BASK
IN THE BRIGHTNESS OF THE MOON.

I HATED THAT I LOVED THE DOZEN OF COOKIES
IN FRONT OF ME—HELLO & GOODBYE...

SHE SAID SHE WAS SICK OF BEING HEALTHY,
BUT THE DOCTOR WAS PATIENT WITH
THE FOOLISHNESS OF HER WISDOM.

If God Spoke Like Us!

I was reading the book of Job in The Bible today, and after hearing
the cold, judgmental remarks of his "Friends" during his time of
distress, sickness, and crippling grief, I...in my crazy, vivid, busy,
and often times weird imagination, pictured God leaning over His
throne in heaven, looking down and pointing at them saying...
"I wish yaw'l would shut up and stop tryin' ta speak on
my behalf! How yaw'l gon tell Job how I feel about him?!
Just worry 'bout how I feel about you all! If you were

EDIE BOWMAN

busy about yo own business, you wouldn't have soo much
time on yo hands worrin' 'bout somebody else's!"
*(Sorry for giving The Lord a Down South accent,
but that's how I heard it in my head.*

First You Have to Admit You Have a Problem...

It's so sad that I busted out in great jubilation just
because I learned how to close one thing out on my
computer without disturbing what I was working on,
which, by the way... happens to be this book!
My ability and patience pertaining to technology of any kind, is
laughable to say the least. Because I struggle with these issues, I
understand the frustrations older people have with their cell phones
and other more challenging gadgets. Well...to be embarrassingly
honest, some of them are more advanced than I am.
Lord, PLEASE help a Sista out!

Sunday Evening, April 5ᵗʰ, Sitting on the Couch

I'm watching John Legend and Kane Brown sing together on the
American Country Music special in support for our country during
the Coronavirus crisis, right?...So, I asked my daughter, "If Kane's
singing is a mixture of rap and country and John is R&B, and they
sound this good together... and if Lil Nas X has a Country/Rap
vibe and sang "Old Town Road" with Billy Ray Cyrus...then why
can't I mix Opera/Rap/Soul (something I do ONLY in the house or
around the Elite few)?" She rolled her eyes, slowly turned around,
put her air-pods back in her ears, and continued to wash the dishes!
"Why?!... I said, It's fun!" She continued to ignore me.
Wait...now they're doing a tribute to Kenny Rogers!!! I
remember listening to "The Gambler" and "Lady" when I
was little. I especially liked hearing him sing it with Lionel

Richie. I'm so glad I was introduced to a plethora of music
genres as a child…something I've passed on to my children.
HEY! It's okay to go from an Old Spiritual, to R&B, and then
to Rap, all in the matter of three minutes! But, what's REALLY
FUN is singing any of them in an Operettic style with major
dramatic facial expressions, and a touch of comedy… I can do it!

Redefining "Fun"

I have a headache that would make a migraine
seem like a walk in the park.
I don't remember what I did last night
and with whom I did it with…
I have a few cuts and bruises on my body and
a peculiar odor lingering in the air:
a mixture of vomit, skunk, and urine, Perhaps…
Okay…there are two people that I have never
seen before laying on my couch.
I just received a text to go pick up my friend
from jail in another county…
I don't quite know why I have a tattoo on
my…Whoa!!! Are You serious?!
But Boy Did I Have FUN!

Flowerpots

We're like flowerpots…
Empty until filled with the colors of life.
We need a little Sunlight: nurtured by love and attention.
Rooted in Soil and made to blossom…
when Watered and firmly planted by hands of expectation.

How A Bee Can Shut A Whole House Down!

It started with a text: "Be on the lookout...there's a bee (picture of a bee) in the house. I saw him and got up to get something to kill it, and it disappeared."

My daughter had a slight disappointment in the tone of her text towards her dad for not killing it, "Are you serious, dad?! You didn't kill it?!"

My first response was, "OPEN THE FRONT AND BACK DOOR, HOPEFULLY IT'LL BE DRAWN TO THE LIGHT AND I CAN LET HIM OUT OR KILL IT ON THE DOOR!" (I'm always in attack mode!)

Unfortunately, he was in an important zoom meeting...it was now up to me!

I cautiously went downstairs looking behind curtains, doors, and hiding places like the police do on the NCIS and SWAT shows. My only weapon was a flyswatter. I gently tapped on the messy table to see if he was there, then I tapped on the dining room curtain...no sign of him! I opened the back door, and made sure the living room door was open, hoping he'd land on one of them so that this could end peacefully. After looking around a while downstairs, I decided to go back up the stairs in case he snuck pass me and was hiding up there.

I opened my daughters' door... "Did you get it, mom?!"

"No, I didn't see it anywhere..."

"Close my door!" she yelled.

I made sure all the doors were closed upstairs. The whole house was on lock down, now!

"I see it! I see it!" my husband screamed.

I ran down the stairs with the flyswatter in my hand like it was a gun, and I was coming to rescue him from a murderer!

"Hurry up, give me the flyswatter, Edie!"

I handed him the flyswatter... "Where is it?!" I asked.

"I think I heard it buzzing in the window!"

"Good, that's a good place! Make sure he doesn't get out of the curtain, Charles!"

"Oh!" *Slap! Slap! Slap!* "Whoa! Whoa!" *Slap! Slap!*

"Get em'! Get em'!"

"Did you get em'!"

"I think so, he's on the floor..."

"Are you sure?!"

"Let me hit 'em one more time to make sure!" *Squash!!!*

PHEW!!!! The Deed Was Done!

Really? All because of a bumble bee?... Man!

If it were a bat or something, I guess we would've torn up the whole Entire House!

AND NOW...

<u>Being Human</u>

Have you ever seen something funny or heard someone say or do something funny, and then you remember it at the wrong time and/ or place? I've actually been in heated arguments, or in intense disagreements with people before, and in the midst of it they made a funny facial expression, an awkward sound, or a movement that made me fight back the laughter! My internal dialogue was like, *Don't do it Edie... think about something else! Don't concentrate on their face or how their foot keeps shaking and their fingers are twitching...this is a SERIOUS moment right now! OH, NO...they just changed the tone of their voice, and it's so funny! Ok, think about something sad or something serious...just DO NOT LAUGH!* (Is it just me...I know it's weird...OR...am I just brave enough to share it? Hmm...)

Chapter Twenty
More Things to Ponder...

Let's admit it, some things are hard to talk about, but there comes a time when you have to do it anyway. I've been in many conversations that I was reluctant to be a part of: I knew they'd leave an uncomfortable feeling between me and the other person(s). There are a lot of politically incorrect, touchy, and controversial topics going on in our homes, family get-togethers, places of business, and even our churches that we disagree on. I've decided not to hide my head in the sand when confronted with these conversations anymore, especially if they are dear to, and in line with my Father's heart!

Jesus spoke to the Pharisees, Sadducees, and to any religious or political leader that approached him with heresies, lies, and beliefs that didn't align with the Kingdom of God. Now I'm by no means, Jesus, but I desire to be like him. I figure...if people around me can boldly say and do all sorts of crazy, ungodly things, and have ridiculously horrible ways of thinking and living, and be proud of it—screaming it in the streets and from the rooftops, then why should I sit passively and quietly by and Say nothing...Do nothing... and WRITE nothing?! Sometimes silence is as bad as agreeing with the wrong-doings of those around us. He's God in Every Moment... even in uncomfortable moments like these.

Many years ago, I was afraid to tell my father about salvation because the last time I did, it didn't go so well—he got very angry. I felt like I had done something wrong—I felt like a little child who had disobeyed her father. What I realized later was I was a child who had to obey her Heavenly Father. So, six days before he passed away in the hospital, I spoke to him again, prayed with him, and he received Christ. It was uncomfortable, many people might have thought it was the wrong time, the wrong place, and the wrong thing to do period, but it was necessary! If we ask God, he will tell us what to do and what to say, and even what not to. May all of our conversation and disagreements be spoken in love and not hate. May we leave having heard the other side and may the truth and understanding of God's Word prevail in the end. Afterall…His opinion is all that matters to the Righteous—He is the judge!

Psalms 1:1-2 (NLT)

"Oh, the joys of those who do not follow the advice of the wicked, or stand around with sinners, or join in with the mockers. But they delight in the law of the Lord, meditating on it day and night."

Romans 1:32 (NLT)

"They know God's justice requires that those who do these things deserve to die, yet they do them anyway. Worse yet, they encourage others to do them, too."

REVERSE

Charity walked up to the podium with pride and humility, knowing that God was the one who guided her through every fine detail of this journey of such astronomical advancement in research. The President of the United States stood to the right of her as she took her place, smiling with joy in his heart, for this had touched him greatly, like so many others, just three weeks ago. The FDA were there, The CDC were present, heads of pharmaceutical companies, hospitals, families, and representatives from every nation across the globe. The State's Capitol had never experienced a moment quite like this before. The silence was almost unbearable, as they waited in unfathomable anticipation to hear the words come out of her mouth. How could this woman, whom the greatest doctors in the world had never heard of until recently, actually figure out what we've fought for decades to discover? She adjusted the microphone gently, giving much attention to not making any unnecessary noise in the unnerving silence. Clearing her throat and broadening her shoulders, she desperately panned the crowd looking for her parents. She needed to feel the support that they so persistently had given throughout her life. *"Ahh...there they are."*

It is 10:10am. Saturday, October 10th, 2020. "Good afternoon everyone. Speaking to such a vast crowd is not something that I'm accustomed to, but here we go! I had a dream a little over three years ago, and in that dream, I saw, whom I believe to be, God. Now, I know that many have their own ideologies about the existence of God, or the non-existence of Him...but

I'm not here to debate that today. I'm here, only, to tell you what happened to me during and after that dream, and how the result of that dream has brought me here before you today. Cancer is a word that brings many thoughts, emotions, and experiences with it. I'm sure it has touched each and every one of us in some way, and it has been a passion of mine to one day find the cure for every kind there is, and today…I am indescribably proud, and humbled to say that God has given me the cure in a dream. Somehow it doesn't matter, one iota, if we believe in Him or not when we're faced with the word cancer, does it? So, I fell asleep early one morning after studying and praying one night, I do those two practices together on a regular basis. I had an espresso in one hand, and my medical book in the other, when I began to see billions and billions of blackened cells around me in the midst of a great, awe inspiring light. God placed an enormous syringe in my hand and told me to squeeze droplets of this serum on the cells. As I did this the cells began to change and somehow become a part of the light; they were still there, but they became translucent. I asked Him, what was in the serum, and he said it contains three major minerals and vitamins that must be administered in exact measurement, and at specific times depending upon the individual's unique, biological make up. The first mineral is potassium, the second is…"

It's 10:00am. Saturday, October 10th, 1991.
Crying silently, she closes her eyes and tries to drown out the voices.
Her legs are shaking, her heart's beating quickly, the room is cold and lifeless.
Sweat is rolling from her forehead like her body is trying to tell her something is not okay…

But, louder than her voice, *and the other...* they tell her that it is... okay.

"Is it?" she begins to question, again.

No...

"Just relax, honey."

"Okay..."

"It'll be over soon."

What will?...

"Open up just a little wider," he said.

"Okay," she said with struggling certainty.

(Grabbing the strange instrument from the nurse) "There we go... now just relax and breathe...now, you're going to feel a little tugging and discomfort," he continued.

I can't breathe...

"I feel sick...something isn't right..."

Ow! That hurts...something isn't right...my head...

(Reaching for another medical device) "Just a little bit longer..."

"No, this doesn't feel right, stop!"

My leg...why are they hurting me?

(Caressing her hair and wiping her forehead)" It's fine, dear...we're almost there...just hold on," said the nurse.

I can't hold on anymore...my arm! They're ripping my...

"I...I don't want to do this...I changed my mind, Doctor!"

Why?...what did I do?!

"I'm sorry young lady, but I've already..."

"What?!...you've already what?!..."

"The Fetus...I've already removed parts of her—"

"Doctor!" the nurse said, angrily

(Extremely uncomfortable) "I mean, *It*! I've removed parts of it... which is to say, the Fetus..."

*Fetus?... It's me Mommy! It's ME, **Charity**!!!*

(Sobbing) "Her?!...it's a girl?"

What's happening...I'm trying to hang on, but I can't Breathe...

It's 10:10 am...**Silence.**

Act Like I'm Dead

Such nice things are usually said at funerals...I mean we don't want to be rude and tell the absolute truth about the dead, do we? So, with our words we turn them into angelic beings who walked the earth among us. The crazy thing is, the people in the pews are thinking, "Huh? I never saw that side of him, and I've known him all of my life!" Now don't get me wrong, we all have good and bad in us, but you know what I mean...the accolades can go a little overboard in these settings sometimes. For instance, the man so peacefully laying there could've been a womanizer, had twenty children all in the same city, with ten different women all in the same city, he could've abused them all, dodged child support every chance he got, and hardly ever saw a sober day in his life, but someone will stand up on that day and say something like, "He was such a good man, he loved Everybody he met *(except those women, evidently)*. He'd give you the shirt off of his back *(but wouldn't pay child support? Hmm...)*. He never met a stranger... (*I guess not when half the city is filled with his women, children, and grandchildren*), and he was one of the greatest examples of a strong man I've ever seen *(Really?!)*.

The word "eulogy" means to speak good of someone, and we should be able to find something good to say about anyone regardless of how difficult it might be. Sadly, I've been to way too many funerals in my lifetime, and I've yet to hear the preacher, or the family and friends say more negative than positive words about the deceased. While this is a good thing, as it makes the living feel better, we should be careful not to speak untruths, either. When my time comes, I want my family and friends to say that I was a woman who modeled the love of God, who loved her family, that everyone felt valuable in my presence, and that I used all of my gifts and talents to uplift, inspire, teach, entertain, and enlighten. However, I do not want them to act like I had no flaws. I've said, thought, and have done things that I'm not proud of, and honestly, they've felt the brunt of it the most.

Going to funerals over the years have taught me one thing for sure...Life is Too Short! There used to be a time when most of the people you saw in the obituaries were old. Now a days the young and the old share the same page. I've learned that whatever you dream of doing, do it now, and whatever you desire to say to a person, say it now (*hopefully it's productive*), because we just don't know when our time is up!

There is another observation that I've made that's quite unfortunate when it comes to the dead and the living. I've noticed that we tend to say more loving, kind, and warm-fuzzy words to or about people when they're dead, than when they're alive. Unfortunately, I'm guilty of this also. We have the tendency to hurt those closest to us because we know that they truly love us and choose to put up with us. I'm learning that we have to conscientiously be aware of doing this and correct it. We can often treat our husbands worse than we do our male co-workers, pastors, or bosses. Is it because we know that they have something that we need from them, like acceptance, praise, or recognition? Well, this should not be. Why do we treat strangers nicer than we do our own spouses? Some men will go out of their way to say a kind word, or joke with a cashier at a convenience store, while their wives are at home dying for attention and just a mere sparkle in her husband's eyes when he looks at her. This also cannot be. We parents applaud the achievements of our friends' children, and constantly overlook and criticize the unique blessings in our own homes.

I've decided that I'm going to not allow myself to show more love and respect to those outside my home, than those inside of it. I know that there will be some challenges, especially when we're all so immensely different, but it is possible, and wise. I refuse to speak most of my words of adoration and praise over the dead bodies of my loved ones when I can say and demonstrate them now. Why should I wait until they can't hear them, and experience the actions that accompany my life-giving words? So, this is what I'm going to do, and what I will encourage others to do, and that is… "Act Like I'm Dead!"

If we do this, we will say now, what we would've said if that person were dead. We'll say things like, "Honey, you're a good man, thank you for working hard to take care of our family, I appreciate you."

"Sweetheart, I long to get home to you each night to see your face and to hear about your day."

"Children, we love you, and we know that you will become who God has created you to be regardless of how you're acting right now."

I know this may be a stretch for some, but I'll give it a whirl! Speak it until it becomes reality. Encourage one another to speak words that create an atmosphere for love to grow in, and if it's a little too hard to do at times then, "Act Like They're Dead!"

The Benefits of Seeing the End, First

Today I watched John Wick on TV and I was aggravated when they showed Part 2 before Part 1. But, during the first 20 minutes of Part 2, I realized that I had a clearer understanding after watching it backwards. NOW the ultimate destruction in Part Three TOTALLY makes sense! (*I know I sound really crazy, but I promise you I'm not a lover of death*). Action movies never used to be my type of movies until I met my husband. The main character(s) show extreme frustration and anger, blow up things, shoot up people, torture, decimate whole cities, and will even destroy the whole universe if need be, to get what they want. And even though I'm not an advocate for violence and destruction, once I see all of the chaos that these characters have caused, I can't seem to turn away until I find out WHY they did what they did!

Three of my favorites action movies are the *John Wick, The Bourne Identity,* and *The Equalizer* movies. There is no distance that they will not go to accomplish their mission. Whether it's the brutal death of loved ones at the hand of evil, an unquenchable desire to find out who they are and where they came from, getting revenge for someone else, or the threat of harm coming to them or someone else that pushes them to kill, they are committed to finishing the deal at all costs. These characters are passionately driven and obsessed to be satisfied by getting what they want.

Watching a movie backwards allows you to enter the story of a person's excruciating pain of the heart, and slowly understand why he/she feels what they feel. I've found that this practice works the same way in life. Have you ever seen or met people who are angry, negative, standoffish, sad, overly comedic/silly, aggressive, belligerent, narcissistic, extremely shy, etc., and wondered why they are the way they are? I have...and I'm training myself to look beyond what is in front of me and focus on the WHY. I do realize that this is very difficult when you are with the individual(s) on a regular basis, like at work, church, or in your home because you are so close to them.

One of my favorite things to do is to sit down over a cup of coffee with someone I've never met before and listen to their life's story, or to sit down with someone I've known for a long time and find out something new about them. There have been many times where I've found out things about a person that I'm in relationship with, that changed my whole perspective of them. The light came on and I suddenly understood the reasons behind their actions, attitudes, and thinking patterns. These patterns can be good or toxic. We are complex people with many experiences that have shaped us both positively and negatively and taking out the time to get to know THE WHY in the lives of those you love, and are connected to in some way, can be very beneficial in the art of communication. Understanding is the key to any healthy relationship—it enhances, brings light, and stimulates change for the better.

Imagine a wife being married to her husband for thirty-five years. He likes to walk on the curbed side of the sidewalk when they go for walks. He never verbalizes it, but he gently guides you to his left side as soon as you start your journey. Perhaps the wife never thinks much of the act because it's so natural, comforting, and she's just used to it. She thinks he's being chivalrous and trying to protect her from cars that may lose control and come onto the curb. She thinks he's making sure that he's the one who would take the brunt of the impact instead of you, so that's why he makes sure you're on the inside and he's on the outside *(sounds sweet, right?)*. But, one day you're both feeling a bit talkative and nostalgic, and in the midst of conversation he tells you, "When I was a little boy, my father used to make sidewalks for a living, people said he was the best sidewalk maker around town, but he was exceptionally skilled at curbs; he did them with precision. Every time we walk, I like to be on the outside because I like looking at the curbs in detail... I know it sounds silly, I mean how different can they look, but something inside of me has to do it. He died while making these curbs, and a part of me feels like I'm honoring him as I walk next to them, and as simple as they are...I know they were made with pride and excellence because that was his way."

This suddenly gives his wife a whole new piece of the puzzle in their relationship: she sees her husband a little differently now, she loves him even more, she listens closely, she appreciates him more, she grabs his hand a little more tightly, and their walks...well their walks are much more anticipated, and oh...so meaningful.

"Ready or Not Here I Come..."

I went to the funeral of one of my customers years ago,
and the Minister's message stuck with me. He explained
how when we were little, we'd play Hide -N- Seek, and we
used to say, "Apple, peaches, pumpkin pie, if you're not
ready, holler 'I.'" After the seeker would count to twenty (or
whatever number) he'd say, "Ready or not, here I come!"
That's how it is with our lives; we act as if we have all the time in
the world to receive Christ as our savior, and we even try to hide
from Him (as if we actually could). We carry on as if we'll never
die and have to face His judgement. We continue sinning and
doing whatever we feel like doing when we know it's not right.
We keep telling ourselves that we have time to get it together.
Despite of all of this, God In his amazing love, grace, and mercy,
gives us more time, and many chances to answer his call to
be Found by Him. But don't play the game too long, because
one day he's going to say, "Ready or not here I come...

LIGHT

I thought I was in the light…but then someone greater appeared, and in his light, mine quickly began to fade. I found myself in a dimmer light, until… I met someone whose light was dimmer than mine. His light made my light seem lighter, so I felt fine…until I saw a light that was the brightest light I ever saw, even brighter than the greater light that I saw that dimmed all of our lights. This light was the brightest of all…I thought. But then, one day I saw a light that was beautiful, undeniable, and drew me into itself. It was amazing… this light! I followed it and it gave me such power and freedom to be and do all that my heart desired. I needed this light…it was feeding me and giving me everything I've ever wanted…until it didn't. The light turned into darkness, and now there was no other light to be found…It seemed.

One day I was drawn to this girl in class; she always carried herself differently than the others. She often sat in a very small group of other guys and girls who seemed to carry themselves like she did. They weren't weird or anything: they dressed like others around them, talked like others…pretty much. I'd even see them at campus events sometimes. But there was definitely something different about them…about her.

I saw her crying one day alone by a stairwell in one of the lower-level dorms. For some reason I couldn't walk away, even though I wanted to. "Are you okay?" I asked.

"Oh, hi A.J." she said while wiping her eyes. "I'll be fine, thanks for asking."

I couldn't believe she knew my name.

"Are you sure? You look like you could use a listening ear right now."

"How sweet of you…I guess that's okay."

I sat down beside her on the stairs. "So, what's going on?"

"I just found out that my dad lost his job and I may need to go home to help out. I may not be able to finish out the semester."

"That's a lot…I'm so sorry to hear that, Heather."

"Oh, I'm surprised you know my name."

"So am I…I mean, surprised that you know mine that is…"

"Oh, yeah…I make it a duty of mine to know ever person's name that I…well, never mind that."

"No…every person's name that you what?"

"Every person's name that I pray for."

"Pray for…you pray for me? Why?"

"I know it might sound weird, but he told me to."

"He?... He who?" Oh, I get it, I don't mean to be offensive, but you're one of those Jesus fanatics, huh?"

Softly giggling, I said, "No…no offense taken, and yes, if you mean a person who believes in and follows Christ because he is the only way to heaven, and is the only light in this dark world, then I am one of those 'Jesus fanatics.'"

"Whoa...hold on there! I didn't mean to upset you, I..."

"You didn't, I'm just passionate about what I believe that's all, aren't you?"

"Well...yeah, of course!"

"And what's that?"

"What's what?"

She giggled again, "What do you believe? Silly..."

"Oh, yeah...that, well...I believe that we are here by either accident, or evolution, or Darwinism, or..."

"So, you don't know what the flippity flop you believe, huh?!"

"Hey, no need for foul language young lady!" We both began to laugh uncontrollably. "I...I guess I don't."

"Well that's okay, you will..."

"I will?... And how are you so sure?"

"Well, I don't want to overwhelm you so...how about another time, okay?"

"Nope! I want to know now, besides... I'm not easily overwhelmed, so let's have it."

"Okay...you asked for it. Brace yourself..."

"I'm braced... shoot!"

"So, me and a group of friends meet weekly, and we pray for students who God puts on our hearts. We call their names out before the Lord and ask Him to help them see The Light...His Truth...His salvation. We ask Him to intervene in their lives to bring them to an understanding of who He is."

"Okay, so that does seem a little strange to me and weird, but I'm still not overwhelmed, as you say. And... what does any of this have to do with me?"

"Well, just hold on...so, last week at our meeting, I told the group that I had a dream that I was taking you by the hand and leading you through different rooms on campus. And each room that we would go in got dimmer and dimmer. The crazy thing is that you thought that they were getting more and more bright, it was like you were being deceived, because you had all that you desired."

My hands began to sweat, and I become uncomfortable, but I tried to stay cool.

"Okay...okay" I said, calmly..." (*yeah...fake, calmly*).

"Are you okay? You don't look good..."

"Yeah, I'm fine. Keep going, please"

"Okay, so the last room we entered was the darkest of all, but you saw it as the brightest. Then, I continued to lead you by the hand, and we were on our way to somewhere else."

"Where?!"

"This is the crazy part..."

"What?! Where were we going? Where were you leading me?"

"Well, that's up to you..."

"What do you mean?"

"A.J. would you like to know more about Jesus, the True Light... the One who delivers us from darkness?"

"Yes...Yes, I would."

"Then, take my hand..."

I took her hand, and she led me through the greatest moment of my life, right there on a dark stairwell, I met the Light of the world.

AND NOW...
<u>Being Human</u>

Have you ever walked down the stairs, missed a step, almost fell, or Actually Fell? Have you ever walked down the street and tripped over...NOTHING AT ALL?! You turned around, looked at the ground to see what caused the mishap, and to see who might have seen your mishap, and then realized nothing was there. You were like, "Maybe it was that tiny pebble over there...or maybe the sidewalk was a little uneven." Nope! you just tripped over NOTHIN!

Chapter Twenty-One
Hope in Dark Places

The people who walk in darkness will see a great light.
For those who live in a land of deep darkness, a light will shine.
Isaiah 9:2
(KJV-paraphrase)

Since I can remember, I've always seemed to be drawn to the darkness. I loved the nighttime more than the daytime. I love to take walks at dusk (well, not much anymore...like the older people say, "we're living in the last and evil days!"). I love sunsets more than sunrises, and I'd rather have outings in the evening, rather than in the day. When I was younger, I couldn't wait until the night came so that I could see the streetlights come on, and to sit on the porch (Even though that meant it was time to stop playing!) with family and friends.

Now that I'm older, I realize that it wasn't the darkness that I was drawn too, it was the light that was present IN the darkness that I was subconsciously drawn to. I see now that the light was more evident when darkness was there. The power of the light was making its presence known in the midst of darkness. Lampposts, which are some of my favorite things, show forth the beauty they were created for more prominently in dark places.

When I was about sixteen years old, the Apostle of our church (Sam Sallis), and the pastor of our church at that time (Elvester Keeton), called me up to the front of the church and called me out amongst all of my friends. They both took me by the hand and walked me back and forth in front of the altar. They kept saying "You are a light...and a star...and the Lord will lead you and guide you..." I was nervous because both of these men were used in the gift of prophecy and they were HUGE!!! I felt like I was a baby in the middle of two Angels—soo soo very small. I felt safe, and at the same time, I felt afraid. I didn't know what that word of prophecy meant then, I thought I'd be a singer on a big stage one day, when they said I'd be a star! Now, forty years later, I realize that I'm to be an example to others who are in darkness, to lead them to righteousness—to the light, to the knowledge of God. I know that he will use every gift that he has given me to help people see truth. And I know that He will lead and guide me through all aspects of life, because he's "God IN Every Moment."

Daniel 12:3, written in a time of great anguish says, "Those who are wise will shine as bright as the sky, and those who lead many to righteousness will shine like the stars forever." This passage shows how important it is to have light, and that light is desperately needed in times of pain, despair, and confusion. I am called by God to BE light in every dark place, and to shine in this world, and so are YOU!

Appointed Times...Strategic Music

Have you ever been in a hard, crushing, lonely, painfilled time in your life where you couldn't even pray anymore? You were exhausted by all of the emotions going on inside of you, and friends and family couldn't quite understand? All you could do was lie on the bed and cry: depleted of joy, energy, and strength. I remember feeling this way during many times in my life: when I struggled with making a hard decision, was hurt by a someone, when things didn't turn out the way I thought they should, when I didn't know what to do in a situation that brought hurt to me and others, and when I was grieving the loss of a loved one.

I remember this one particular day... I was so tired of praying about a decision I had to make, that I flopped down in the bed and played a song on my phone over and over again. I would play it in the car, on the porch with my headphones on, Everywhere! The song was *"Pressure"* by **Johnathan McReynolds**. I laid there crying as the song was giving me strength and healing. During a time when the ticket sales of one of my theatre productions was low, I needed to trust God that all would work out well. I played *"Jesus I Believe"* by Big daddy Weave." (Hey! That rhymes!)

When my youngest child couldn't breathe on her own at birth and it looked like she might not make it, *"Your Steps Are Ordered"* by **Fred Hammond**, got me through those two weeks of uncertainty at Rainbow babies, in Cleveland, Ohio. When I was oppressed by a heavy spirit of depression for a while in my life, this one Sunday morning my pastor, Bernard Lawson, led by the Spirt of God, kept singing and playing *"No Weapon"* a song also by Fred Hammond. That song literally set me free while being sung under the anointing of God that day. While standing with my hands lifted in worship, I felt the oppression leave off of me.

When I was a teenager, I used to listen to the group **Commissioned** a lot. Their music brought me through times of hurt and loneliness, especially the song "Ordinary Just Won't Do." I was realizing that only the Lord could satisfy my soul and fill up all the empty places. I also loved the song "Running Back To You." It spoke of God's forgiveness and love towards me, even when I felt that I had done too much...He was standing there ready with open arms. **Amy Grant** was another singer that I enjoyed. She was different—her music was out of my norm of Christian music, and I loved it! It was creative, thought provoking, and told stories that I could feel and imagine. It spoke to a part of my soul like no other music. *"If These Walls Could Speak,"* "Say Once More," "Shadows," and "What About the Love" were some of my favorites... I still have that cassette! When I play those songs today (on my phone...), I'm instantly a teenager again, hanging out in my bedroom, riding the bus, washing the dishes, or in the mirror singing!

These songs were used as instruments of God at specific moments in my life. They were hope in the dark places of my life, given to me by the God in Every Moment—breathing through these vessels of music.

<u>Music:</u> <u>An Unexpected Ally</u>

And still my heart is
Barely Beating, but I can feel it aching:
Constantly fighting the
Dimming light inside.
Existing…just existing…
Faking to survive as
Grief greatly gave way to the
Haunting Hounds of
Inexhaustible fears.
Judging lips like the friends of Job were the
Kiss of death to me:
Loving and loathing at the same time.
Music unwittingly awakened me to
Notable rhythms of Life again.
Opportune sounds incessantly
Pounding loudly inside my chest
Quickly empowering me to dream,
Realizing what could possibly be…
Syncopated
Thoughts were
Unleashing
Volumes of emotions once
Waxed cold from
Xtreme
Yearnings once depraved, now healing me as a
Zephyr's wind…

RAIN

It keeps raining, then stopping, then raining again.
Ahhh... here comes the sun Nope, wait... there it is again—
the rain.
Ahhh the sun again...it feels so good upon my face.
MAN! Here comes the rain, Again!
Such is life...Keep an umbrella handy and keep on walking!

Transformation

Somehow the Night enveloped me, but I chose to keep on
singing, and the Light, somehow... accompanied me there.
Soon it brought with it a chair and established its own little
space—irritating the Night's pride—insisting to play along.
Pressing in harder to silence me, I managed to
Sing louder assuring its enduring presence.

The amber glow was warming me, I welcomed
the gentle embrace of that Light.
The embers began to speckle the dark places—
breaking up its intensity—forming a new existence
for me—encouraging me to Fight.
I kept persisting...and heaviness, somehow...
reluctantly gave way to Joy.

The Poor Rich Man

When the old preacher approached the poor man telling him how to
receive eternal life, he looked towards the sky in a sort of intellectual
wonder, stroked his beard, and said, "That makes no sense to me... a
good education, money, family, and influence is all we need in life.
I haven't been so blessed to attain any of these things, but they're

what truly makes one happy. There's no need to worry about the here-after, this is the only life there is, but you know what… I have an open mind—all is relative anyway, so I will take this into careful consideration and get back with you…ponder it around a bit in my mind."

The rich man, having attained all of the aforementioned things that the poor man believed makes one happy, acknowledged his need for true treasure—listened with his heart and was transformed for eternity.

We Need You Now!!!
Whether We Believe It or Not!

(Monday May 25th, 2020)

I keep trying to think of something nifty, funny, or impressive to say, but again…another life (George Floyd), has been inhumanely taken today right before our eyes. As I watch the protests, the looting, the brokenness, anger, grief, and the racial unrest, I have to take a moment and cry. A couple weeks ago another unarmed black man was shot down while jogging.

Lord, teach us how to listen and understand—just talking is not enough. Teach us to reason together… have peaceful and truthful dialogue, but also pray and take action—actions that bring successful change, soon! We need you now…but how long will we continue to not listen? How long will we refuse to read AND apply your word to our hearts as well as our policies and systems? How long will we ignore the fact that you know what you're doing, and we don't—YOU'RE GOD!

Your word says that the fear of the Lord is the beginning of wisdom and the nation that forgets God will be turned into hell. What we see in our streets today are the exact results of not following you and your principles, and the streets of Minnesota actually looks like hell, as the flames ascend from the burning buildings. Therefore, we MUST look to you—The Sum Total of All Knowledge.

WAKE UP AMERICA!!!

#JESUSINOURHEARTS
#JESUSINOURWORLD

"What's Goin' On?..." Said Marvin Gaye.

I'll tell you...ARE YOU READY?... **It' a spiritual thing:** Evil and wickedness are in the hearts of mankind. Just like in the days of Sodom and Gomorrah: we are doing what is right in our own eyes! We are choosing to reject righteousness, and instead we are choosing to do what feels good to us. We have a Sin problem—a disease of the soul that can only be remedied by Jesus! Without this remedy we will continue to see what we are seeing, we will continue to get the same results that we are getting, and we will keep going in a vicious cycle of destruction and death in our personal lives as well as in our land.

If we have an itch that we cannot soothe, we try to appease it for a short time, but it comes again. We try to scratch our itch of anger, frustration, sexual pleasures, wealth, satisfaction, etc., by any means necessary, but the scratching will NEVER satisfy the itch! We have a choice to either accept God's remedy—His son Jesus The Christ or reject Him and keep on trying to soothe our itch our own way.

Listen to what the Lord warns those who will not listen to His wisdom...

> Wisdom shouts in the streets. She cries out in the public square. She calls to the crowds along the main street, to those gathered in front of the city gate: "How long you simpletons, will you insist on being simpleminded? I called you so often, but you paid no attention. You ignored my advice and rejected the correction I offered. So I laugh when you are in trouble! I will mock you when disaster

overtakes you—Therefore, they must eat the bitter fruit of living their own way, choking on their own schemes. For simpletons turn away from me—to death.

(Proverbs 1:20-22, 24-26, 31, 32 NLT)

If It Ain't Workin' Let's Try It God's Way!

G...R...O...A...N

The earth is crying out, waiting... The ocean, birds, tress, and winds, our bodies, our minds...our very souls are groaning. Can't you hear it?... The groan?... Communicating their agonies differently we all grieve outwardly what's inside. I hear the sounds echoing throughout the land.

Listen to what the winds are saying... brushing gently upon our faces with subtle warning of what's to come. "I do not know how to control my frustrations," it says, "I've lost my ability to flow with ease and calm." Brushing against our faces with anger, they work out their inner turmoil at our expense. Clashing personalities that express themselves in the atmosphere of our lives...in the air of our existence, we lay bare before the winds' whims.

Our bodies scream, "Let me out of here!... Release me!... I want to be free!" But there is no freedom found...at least for now. Death is the only hope. Well... for some death means more death, everlasting. Our minds are left wanting...ever wanting...for peace. They think thoughts too grim to be expressed. Wandering thoughts that overwhelm tends to drive one to be overwhelmed.

The ground feels the feet of those who run to do evil, and it mourns with sounds of agony deep within its crust. The blood of the innocent is engraved within its foundations; the stench causes such rumbles of pain that it cracks above to show us the depths of its heart. The rocks are shaking beneath our soles trying to get put attention, but do we sense it? Do we listen to what happens beneath us? Dare we try?...

The trees seem to have forgotten to change its leaves this year. Summer leaves come in winter, and fall leaves come in summer. The leaves of the trees talk amongst themselves whispering stories of confusion and chaos, "When shall we be who we are...who we really are again?" But were they ever Really who they were meant to be, here? Their trunks suck poisoned nutrients from the cracked black ground and deliver it to its branches only to bring death to the fruit it barely... bares.

The animals are telling their stories in ways without words; that look in their eyes... that longing stare we see as adoration is sorrow. They're Groaning too...becoming increasingly vicious as we pretend to deny the difference in them. Some are more subdued, losing the playfulness and loyalty that used to vigorously course through their veins towards us. The blood to their hearts is now mixed with fear and rage: a cocktail of disaster. So, Beware! The darkness has entered in.

The aches and pains of our souls emanate through our bodies and force us to do that which we thought we never would. Like *The Phantom of The Opera*, we become obsessed with our passions until they hurt what we once loved. Longing for relationships to fulfill, our souls are left with an unfathomable type of anguish...you can smell the decay coming through our pores.

Babies come here with a GROAN...passing from light to a hopeless diming...from knowing to shadows of truth...from life to impending death...and from glory to droplets of happiness. They bring such joy to our lives until they began to feel IT... until they began to change before our very eyes, demonstrating what we know too well but are feckless to change. Until HE comes and we are changed...**We GRRROOOAN...Groans** of wild anticipation that fill the earth with yearnings for what someday shall be...

Romans 8:19-23

Thirsty...

The Thirsty ones are walking around with beautifully made-up faces, dirty faces, nice clothes, borrowed clothes, expensive cars and no cars... with crusty mouths: dry, cracked and darkened by existence... They live in houses broken down by oppressing emptiness and unfulfilled longings that should be rightfully theirs, and their mouths are crusty, dry, cracked and darkened...

Traveling on a wide road full of dainties guaranteed to satisfy, they continue the routine in search for that destination—paper town. In and out of relationships, cheating, deceiving, killing, abusing and stealing are only side-effects to what they're missing.

The Carriers... those equipped to pour—to rescue and bring relief to their thirstiness, take calamitous comfort in working with them, hanging with them, talking the same talk as them...feasting and laughing in their faces, and trying hard not to offend or appear too different from them. They sip coffee with them in coffee shops and chat about trendy topics, personal issues, and politics, then walk away possessing bottles of water in their Nike bags, briefcases, book bags, purses and fanny packs...

Refreshing, cleansing, hydrating, life sustaining water is at their disposal, yet never reaching the mouths of those who need it—dry, cracked mouths…how gravely polarizing? Water which makes one thirst no more is withheld by the very hands ordained to pour it into empty vessels of clay—those crusty, dry, cracked, darkened, Beautiful jars of clay are thirsty…so please, Pour…

The Quarantine Blues…

(Monday, April 20, 2020)

I'm sitting here across from my husband at the dining room table in awe of how he's remotely teaching math to his students. He's happily talking about cube roots and radicals WITH A SMILE ON HIS FACE?! (Huh?... Who does that?!) At the same time, he's expressed to me his desire to move about his classroom again. Directly to his right is me…I'm gleefully studying a book of artists: admiring their use of color, the dimensions of the paintings, brushstrokes and styles while daydreaming of the time when I can get out of here and enjoy the theatre and museums again.

Wait! Just In…

Ohio's Governor, Mike Dewine has ordered that schools are closed for the rest of the year.

Aww…the look on my hubby's face--he had hoped to see his students again. And, my heart goes out to all of the seniors missing out on what is supposed to be their greatest year; the year they've all been waiting for. I'm so proud of all the hard work that our teachers and administration are putting in to celebrate our seniors. Creativity is being pushed to the limits to make sure that they get the most out of this memorable time in their lives.

High school Seniors, right now it may seem daunting, but when you look back on this one day, you will have quite the story to tell your children and grandchildren.

Stand strong, things will get better. What you've waited for will definitely look different, but when you look back on the sacrifices of love that many are showing on your behalf, I hope you feel honored.

LAMENTATION

(April 21, 2020)

I wanted to laugh today—to allow the craziness within
me to explode and have its way—to change the stale
atmosphere...but I just heard that WE (because we should
all be touched) lost another young man to violence today,
and the atmosphere inside of me has changed now... so It's
time to cry...to mourn, to weep, to pray, to rent our clothes
and put on sackcloth and ashes... to scream...**LAMENT**.
A Mother has lost her child, Again...
A Father has lost his son. Children have lost their Daddy.
A family is incomplete...Empty.
LAMENT...as we struggle to understand...
as we ponder what to do—to bring change...
to hope...to heal...
LAMENT.

It's Just Not Meant to Be...

Someone I love was asked on Facebook if they "still" grieve their
loved ones who have passed away. Her reply was simple, "Yes! Until
the very last breath I take. We miss them because we love them! I
wish more people would understand that..."

The pain of losing someone never goes away—it's not meant
to. The strength of the pain can diminish over time, but we can still
experience that emptiness when we think of them. Every Easter
morning, I think of my Pops driving us to church, dressed in his
Sunday's best, and I feel it. Every time I hear "My Girl" playing on
a movie or on the radio, or hear a man singing with a soft, soulful
tenor voice, I think about Daddy, and I feel it. Every time I hear that
another black young lady/man was taken away by violence, I think
about them, and I feel it again. In Jr. High school a very popular man

died by suicide…and today, when I hear of someone dying that way, I feel the gnawing confusion in my soul, and I think of him.

Through the years I've heard many people say things to a grieving person that made them feel bad for grieving a long time over a loved one. I've learned, that in most cases, they meant no harm. We have to be careful not to judge another's experience in comparison with our own. There are times when grief can turn into depression, and we need help in those cases, but the amount of time that a person grieves does not determine how much they loved the departed. It's possible to have known an individual for a year and to have loved them just as much as a person who knew them for twenty years. It all depends on the depth of the relationship. Grief is normal, and it cannot have a timespan attached to it, so please don't place one on other people; they are not you. We are individuals: we are unique in our experiences, and complex in our design.

God never intended for anyone to die when he originally created us. Death will NEVER be normal. It does not resonate in our minds and hearts—it was never meant to be… and our souls will forever grieve that truth. The sting of death will always ache within us when we think about our loved ones who have passed away. It is not natural…we think it is because that's all we've ever known, but it's unnatural. God never wanted us to die, but to be with Him eternally. So, I hate it, I loathe it, it hurts…SIN brought DEATH upon us, and unfortunately, it will continue to take from us. But, for those who have a relationship with Him, death is now the one thing that translates us into the presence of our Creator. We can see our loved ones again—those who also believed. That's how we overcome death, by receiving Life through Jesus Christ.

A Juxtaposition I thought I'd Never See

Today is **Thursday, September 24th 2020**
Within nine days at least four people have
been shot in our community.

The ages ranged from six years old to forty-six years old. Two have died, and two are fighting for their lives. GOD HELP US! Then, I turned on the news and saw that in Moscow, Idaho at least three people were arrested for peacefully singing hymns at an outside church service without a mask, and a mother getting tased and removed from her son's game for, initially, not wearing a mask. Really?... while Rioters and Looters march unrestrained in our streets daily, without wearing them?!

Prayer and holding Church Services to help uplift our communities ARE essential—Rioting, Looting, and destroying communities are NOT!
GOD HELP US!!!

Friday, September 25th, 2020
LORD HELP US!!! Three more people (women) were shot today in our community...
On Saturday, September 26th, 2020 there will be a day of prayer and repentance led by Johnathan Cahn and a Prayer March led by Franklin Graham, from the Lincoln Memorial to the Capitol Building in Washington, DC.
"...The LORD was moved by PRAYER for the land..." – 2 Samuel 24:25 (NASB)
GOD WILL HELP US...IF WE PRAY...IF WE REPENT...IF WE CHANGE, AND ACT.

AND NOW...

<u>Being Human</u>

Have you ever been talking with someone, and during the conversation they kept saying, "To make a long story short... to make a long story short...to make a long story short..." and then, forty-five minutes later, you were like "Man! Since when did the word "Short" become Sooo Looong?!

Chapter Twenty-Two
Concerning Relationships...

It doesn't matter what type of relationship it is—God is concerned about it. He's concerned about what concerns you, so whether it's between you and your children, a boyfriend, girlfriend, spouse, or co-worker...he wants it to work out for your good. Sometimes what is for our good is not what we want. We want to hang on to what is not good for us, sometimes.

I remember the summer when I was leaving Jr. High school and entering High school, a boy came over to my house to ask if he could date me. I knew how my mother felt about dating before eighteen years old, I also knew what I had to do. I slowly walked down the steep stairs that led to the front door where I could see him standing on the porch. He and a friend had ridden over on their bikes. He told me I was different...special, and that he'd treat me like I should be treated knowing that I was a Christian girl. Well, it might have started off that way, but my mother new where it could end up! It broke my heart to tell this boy that I couldn't date him, I thought I was going to die!!! I hung my head down and sheepishly told him..."I'm sorry but my mom won't allow me to date yet... she said that I have to tell you no." He looked confused, because that didn't mean much to the average teenager—they'd just sneak and do it anyway. I didn't want to disappoint my parents or my God by not honoring what they told me to do. As I watched them ride down the street that day, I felt sick—I was soo angry with my mom!

"It was just dating" I thought to myself that day. "He's a nice guy...he will treat me different." Ahh...how naïve I was. I am thankful to have had parents that knew better than to let me date, and who didn't back down off of what they believed was right for me. Many people thought my parents were too strict but, looking back now...I'm soo very grateful. My life could've been very different today had I not listened.

It's Your Way or The Highway

The further we get away from your plan—your way of having
relationships, we will continue to be out of your will. You said
to wait to have sex until we are married. You said to marry
ONLY those who believe as we do—as a Christian, a true
believer...one who will practice your word and not just hear it!
It's time to forgive those who hurt us, to esteem others higher
than ourselves, to stop fighting, and reason together...to pray
together and stop warring with our brothers and sisters in
Christ—Unify! Children listen to your parents. Parents, let's
not provoke our children to wrath, let's show forth a marriage
that pleases God and encourages our children. Families... come
back to God! Friends...be loyal and speak the truth in love.
I will walk uprightly before you, in word and in
deed, and love you with all of my heart.
It's time to listen...to do things your way...to please you, Oh God.

"S E E N"

She looked at his outward appearance and decided to pass
him by...he ended up being the love of someone else's life.
She looked at his outward appearance and decided to
marry him...he ended up being her worst nightmare.
He focused on her heart and found a priceless jewel within her...
He looked at her heart but was blinded by her
outward appearance...his heart was broken.

Cycles

Sin is like Thriller/Dramas, such as *Sleeping with
the Enemy, Enough,* and *The Perfect Guy.*
It starts off presenting you with romantic façades, fun, and

excitement that feels too good to be true, but the pursued are convinced to believe, despite their unbelief. It promises to fulfill magical dreams of fulfillment and illusions of ecstasy, but in the end delivers nothing but emptiness and destruction. It flirts with us... drawing us in and taking advantage of our insecurities and secret desires, then uses them against us to trap us—keeping us in bondage. It keeps us hanging on to the hope that it will continue to deliver what we think we need.

Sin will overtake us, overwhelm us, and ultimately take us under, We Must Wake Up!!!

It hates when we wake up. It hates when the light comes on—when we finally SEE its deceptive plan. For many of us, we wait too late, and the Enemy of our souls wins: it has completed its goal to Woo and Destroy.

Sin only satisfies for a moment, whether that "Moment" lasts for a day or for years...it will eventually lead to Death, unless you kill it first. Don't play around with it.

Wake up! Stop Sleeping with the Enemy... It's Enough! It is not The Perfect Guy.

Dissonance!

My spirit relentlessly screams, "No!"
But my body consistently goes through the motions, as if not to hear.
Like clashing chords on a piano, they struggle to harmonize.
BOTH CONTINUE TO DISAGREE... ASKING EACH OTHER WHY.
Why?... why do I keep doing what I know I shouldn't?...
I'm losing this fight within.
I MUST RETURN TO GOD...I MUST...
Before my body wins.

Just What I Needed

The other day my youngest child was driving her new car to Columbus, Ohio. This was her first lengthy trip driving alone. I had multiple concerns in my heart and mind concerning this trip. I prayed over her, anointed her AND the car, and told her my motherly precautions (you can imagine…it was like 1,000 things). But, as I turned towards the house and away from her backing out of the driveway, I still felt that uneasiness in my gut! As I walked up the stairs, I said something out of my mouth that I never said before—I knew it was inspired by God…I said, "Lord, give me the releasing Anointing…" I instantly felt His presence over me—His calming peace and grace. He enabled me at that moment, to believe what I prayed, trust him with her, and to let her go. This moment reminds me of Hannah in the bible who prayed fervently for years for a child and was blessed by God with a son, Samuel. She was so thankful to him for answering her prayer that she dedicated him back to the Lord as a child and sent him to the temple under the tutelage of the priest Eli. I'm not embarrassed to say that this is a constant letting go, because I'm human—I'm still affected by what I see, feel, and know concerning them. But you've given me the grace/anointing/power to keep offering my children up to you who loves them most! Thank you for the Releasing Anointing

EDIE BOWMAN

Sister Friends

We laugh and cry together and share things that are dear.
We're there for each other for the important moments.
We may get mad sometimes, but we talk it out and grow.
We bounce things off of each other when we're not sure.
We're not afraid of outshining the other—knowing
God has a plan for us individually.
We all shine in our own way!
We pray for each other because life can be hard.
We go out to dinner and a show, have coffee and get-
togethers, because life should be enjoyed.
We forgive each other because life is way too short.
We Are Friends—We are Sisters

"Mutha Wit"

(A term that older women use to describe a mother with a lot of untaught, innate wisdom)

It's hard to watch you crash into a brick wall
when I can tell you how to avoid it.
It causes me pain to be silent when I have
to for you to finally get it!
I lose sleep every time I know you're
somewhere I wish you were not.
My heart is heavy knowing that you chose that relationship
based on the beginning when I already saw the end.
I long to see you be the person I know that you
can be while you're far from him/her
You keep me on my knees in prayer hoping
that you will not run out of time...
Lord Please, in your great mercy...give my child time.

UNMASK

On Facebook she has hundreds of "Friends."
On Twitter Followers can't wait to hear what she has to say.
On Instagram she's smiling while on family vacation.
On Snap-Chat she's always laughing—
posting lots of videos with friends.

At school she doesn't know who her "real" friends are...
At work she feels invisible...
Her boyfriend doesn't respect her...
At home with her family, she never measures up...
And in a crowd of people, she feels alone...
"It's Time to Be Real
Unmask...and find your identity in Me."
--God

An Ode to the God-Fearin' Woman

(While she loves her God and her family, she is aware that there is still a lot of personality traits she has to work on...)

She may go to bed at night with a satin bonnet or a do-rag on, but that's okay cuz her hair will be "On Fleek" (that means it's going to look amazing) in the morning.

She has trained her children to eat everything that their father has prepared (cuz he cooks too!) for them whether they like it or not cuz she doesn't have time to be catering to everybody's food choices. This ain't no restaurant...don't git it twisted!

She realizes that she can't do it all herself so she delegates chores to her family to help her out, and if her children get sassy with her and ask, "Why do we have to do all these chores, Mom?" she looks them in the eyes and firmly says something like this... "Do you butt sit on the toilet, do you wash your hands in the sink, do you eat off these plates, do you get food on the table and spill things on the floor?...alright then! We all in this together, that's what a family does."

She makes sure that her children don't git on daddy's nerves and that she doesn't tell him all the crazy things they did all day that got on her nerves as soon as he comes in the house after a hard day's work. She allows him to sit down for a few minutes and unwind. She makes sure that he has something in his belly, and then...right at the dinner table, let it rip!

She makes sure that she does not get played by her offspring if they're pretending to be sick to get out of going to school, cuz having them out of the house for a few hours a day is crucial for her mental health! She checks their temperature, and if they're not bleeding, they're out the door!

Her good name and deeds are known in the city and her husband is respected and honored even more because of it. She gives her husband his props while lifting him up in prayer. She endeavors to understand him and encourages him to do the same.

Her husband trusts her when she's on her grind in the city wherever she goes. He praises her for her trustworthiness. He has her heart, and she longs to get back home to him, for she has his.

Her husband teases her about her snoring but secretly admires it knowing that it comes from the hard work she does all day long to keep him and their children well taken care of.

Her lap is gives him peace of mind as he unloads the cares of the day. She rubs his head with patience and understanding. She listens with care and tenderness.

Her husband is happy when he's short a few hundred dollars—or a thousand or so… to take care of a need, and just when he starts to scratch his head in worry, she goes into her secret bosom stash and closes the deal.

Her husband loves to be in her company, especially at the end of the day when she's exhausted and has used up most of her words: now she talks less, just wants to be held, and get her feet massaged. But after that, she's ready to talk again.

Her children love her and thinks she's dope. She calls their names out in prayer and shows what a woman of God looks like.

Her God favors her in the midst of all her struggles for he is always faithful towards her,not looking at what she is now, but what she shall be.

A Funny Marriage Song for Those Strugglin' Moments

(Set to the melody of Amazing Grace)

Verse 1: Amazing Grace how sweet the
sound that saved a wretch like me…
this wife you gave has most certainly made me long for eternity…

Verse 2: Through many dangers, toils and
snares, we have already come…

Lord, if this man keeps workin' my nerves,
then I shall bring him home...

Verse 3: When we've been there ten thousand
years, bright shining as the Sun...
We've no less days to sing God's praise, for now we're Finally One!

I know it Aint Easy, But...

I refuse to go that way again—that's what I said...
And I thought I meant it, until he showed
up wanting to just be "friends."
I'll do better next time...I'm stronger now...
But I was lonely and became weakened by his smile.
I asked the Lord to strengthen me...and He did.
I prayed, went to church, and even changed my friends,
But the fear of being alone came...
Before I knew it, I was entangled again!
The other day I had a meeting with myself
And I said...
My children are watching me, so I'm stopping this vicious game...
I have to do it for them, or they'll do the same thang!
My daughters will think it's okay to find
their worth between the sheets
And my sons won't think it wrong to
have sex with anyone he meets.
It's time for ME to change...

A Love Like This...

You and I will last forever...If all other relationships fail.
My mother and father may forsake me,
but you will always be there.

If those I thought would never leave, choose to walk away
I know one thing for sure, you will always stay.
Who would leave a love like this?

AND NOW...

<u>Being Human</u>

Remember a couple years ago or so, it was trending to agree with someone who was talking to you by saying "Right, right, right, right, right," (Yes, five times! No more, no less!) really fast while nodding your head vigorously in agreement?... Wasn't that annoying?! Sometimes it felt like they were saying it so many times, and so fast, just to make you stop talking! Sometimes, when I'm in a picking mood...I do it just to get on my husband's nerves when he's talking to me (poor Chuck...he hates it, Lol). I could be wrong but, I'm just sayin...It was an annoying trend.

Chapter Twenty—Three
Just A Few More Things...

"And, I am certain that God, who began the good work
within you, will continue his work until it is finally
finished on the day when Christ Jesus returns."
Philippians 1:6 (NLT)

VAPORS

Since our lives are just vapors—here one moment, gone the next...
Write that book, sing that song, start that business, better that
relationship, right that wrong, try something new! But what's
most important is to remember that while life is short, eternity
is forever. The juxtaposition of our time here on earth and
eternity is so extreme, it's like comparing a second to one
hundred thousand years—its ridiculously incomparable!
Lord, help us to make each decision with eternity in mind—
weighing out the consequences...Will what I do and/or say in this
moment affect my future, and better yet, where I spend eternity?
Don't live for the second.
Live for Eternity.

THE PROCESS...

CHANGE ME SO THAT I MAY HELP
SOMEONE ELSE TO CHANGE
DELIVER ME FROM EVERYTHING THAT IS NOT LIKE YOU
AND I WILL BE FREE TO TEACH OTHERS HOW TO BE
HEAL ME OF WHAT HAS BROKEN ME
THEN I WILL BE ABLE TO HEAL...
RESTORE ME SO THAT I CAN RESTORE
THE BROKEN
AND AFTER I'VE GONE THROUGH THE PROCESS
MAY I REMEMBER HOW IT FELT
SO THAT I'LL STAY HUMBLE

EDIE BOWMAN

Peace Within Thy Word

When I start to get worried, confused, or stuck
trying to figure things out in this little brain of
mine, I remember something David said…
"LORD, my heart is not proud; my eyes are not haughty.
I don't concern myself with matters too great or too
awesome for me to grasp." Psalm 131:1 (NLT)
AND…
When I feel like I don't quite measure up to my own
standards or the ones of others, I remember…
Nothing can separate me from the love of God: neither death nor
life, neither angels nor demons, neither our fears for today nor
our worries about tomorrow—not even the powers of hell can
separate me from God's Love!" paraphrased Romans 8:38 (NLT)

"Keep on Keepin' on, Baby…"

(As the older church women would say)

2020 will soon end and 2021 is almost here…
YOU have been my resting place,
my hiding place, and my peace.
YOU have kept me through it all
and grounded my feet.
YOU stabilized me and protected me
showing me your mercy.
YOU have settled my heart in times of uncertainty
covered me in trouble
and loved me at all times.
YOU'VE been good to me…
Gracious, forgiving, and kind.
And when I get weary
and want to give up this race
YOUR love causes me not to fall
But to Keep on Keepin' on, Baby…

You are a VIP

You may never sit at the table with the President of the United States, and you may never dine at the table with your favorite entertainer or shake the hand of your favorite sports team player...but you have a place in the heart of The King of Kings and the Lord of Lord's. He loves you and wants you...He has prepared a place for you in heaven to live with him forever. He only asks for you to believe in him, trust him, and follow him. You are a Very Important Person to him. He created you, died on the cross for you, and will forgive you. He loves you with a pure love—a love you've never experienced on this earth. He will do for you what no one else can ever do—give you eternal life! So, ask him to come and live within your heart today.
You are a V.I.P.!

A New Thing...

New things can be exciting, refreshing, and
stimulating; They generate life.
New things can also be scary.
Scary doesn't mean that it should not be done...
New things can be very uncomfortable—unstable: you
can feel like a toddler taking his/her first steps.
First steps lead to walking, and one day
running...but not without stumbling.
New things are necessary to life: most things that
remain the same—stagnant, begin to die.
A New Thing can mean different ways of
thinking about something old.
Old doesn't mean forgotten...but to be looked at
through new lenses—with new ideas and vision.
A New Thing should be bathed in prayer: you
will need the wisdom of God to do it well.

EDIE BOWMAN

A New Thing can be hard... do it anyway.
A New Thing will take patience and help: prepare,
proceed with caution, and seek wise counsel.
A New Thing can make you feel vulnerable...
Good. It produces a need to Trust others.
Behold, I AM Doing A New Thing in You...
Isaiah 43:19 (NLT)

At the Risk of Sounding like an Easter Speech or Mr. Rogers, Listen...

God made you different...special! There IS no one else like you!
As long as who you are, and what you do, is accordance
with the principles of God—the Giver of your life...
Go For It!!!
He is with you—He loves you and created
you to represent Him in this world—
to bring light into the darkness-to bring Him Glory and Honor!
He wants you to have confidence and Joy in the
gifts and talents that he gave you—
Use them ALL for the betterment of yourself and others.
Allow the courage of being yourself, inspire those around
you to be bold enough to be themselves as well.
God made YOU Unique!

A Note from The Author...

If I have, through this memoir, caused someone to think a
little deeper, love a little stronger, find encourage to go after
your dreams, inspired you to draw closer to God, or begin the
journey of getting to know him...develop better relationships,
be more creative, be vulnerable in expressing your feelings
and emotions, reach out and make a friend, have hope, feel

heard and understood, and perhaps, to feel seen for the first time…I am blessed and privileged to have reached my goal.

In the end it's all about learning how to develop and maintain healthy relationships with God our creator, ourselves, and others, while embracing our own unique ways of being who He has created us to be, in this world… and ultimately, in Heaven.

FOR EVERYTHING MATTERS TO GOD… Especially YOU!

AND NOW…
(Because I couldn't help it…)

<u>**Being Human**</u>

Have you ever (during Covid) pulled your mask down off of your face to hear somebody better when they were talking to you? I have…as if I could REALLY hear them better. Sometimes, ya just gotta laugh at yourself!

Printed in the United States
by Baker & Taylor Publisher Services